SHREDDING THE SOCIAL CONTRACT

The Privatization of Medicare

John Geyman, MD

Common Courage Press   Monroe, Maine

Library of Congress Cataloging-in-Publication Data is available from publisher on request.
ISBN 1-56751-376-x paper
ISBN 1-56751-377-8 hardcover

ISBN 13 9781567513769
ISBN 13 9781567513776

Common Courage Press
121 Red Barn Road
Monroe, ME 04951

207-525-0900
fax: 207-525-3068

www.commoncouragepress.com
info@commoncouragepress.com

First Printing
Printed in Canada

DEDICATION

For the tens of millions of older and disabled Americans in this generation and those to follow, may a reformed and sustainable Medicare be there for you.

CONTENTS

ACKNOWLEDGMENTS

Having explored the corporate transformation of U.S. health care and the increasing fragility of a safety net in my last two books, the seed for this book was planted when I saw the excellent monographs put together by Dr. Tom Bodenheimer and the Senior Action Network in Northern California on the impacts of Medicare privatization on beneficiaries in California. I decided then that the entire Medicare program called for an in-depth examination of its history, structure, and future prospects as the trend toward increased privatization continues. This project took further urgency in the aftermath of the passage of the Medicare Prescription Drug, Improvement, and Modernization Act of 2003 (MMA), the most significant change in the program since it was established in 1965.

I am indebted to these colleagues who reviewed selected chapters and made helpful suggestions: Dr. Rick Deyo, Professor of Medicine and Co-Director of the Center for Cost and Outcome Research at the University of Washington; Timothy Jost, J.D., Robert L. Willett Family Professor at Washington and Lee University School of Law, and Theodore Marmor, Professor of Public Policy & Management at Yale University.

As this project progressed, I found reports from these sources especially useful: the Kaiser Family Foundation, the Commonwealth Fund, the Century Foundation, the National Academy of Social Insurance, the Medicare Rights Center, Public Citizen, the Medicare Payment Advisory Commission (MEDPAC), the General Accounting Office (GAO) and the Centers for Medicare—Medicaid Services (CMS). I am indebted to the agencies, journals and publishers who granted permission to reprint or adapt material originally published by them, as cited throughout the book.

Thanks are due to Virginia Gessner, my administrative assistant for 28 years, who meticulously typed the entire book from handwritten copy to finished manuscript, and to Bruce Conway at Lightwatcher, Friday Harbor, Washington, for his expertise in preparing all of the graphics.

Finally, I thank Greg Bates, Publisher at Common Courage Press, for recognizing the importance of this work to the public interest, for his many helpful editorial suggestions and for his skill in converting manuscript to finished book. As always, I am grateful to Gene, my wife and partner for 49 years, for her patience and support through my immersion with this project.

PREFACE

Medicare was enacted in 1965 when it became widely recognized that private markets were failing to meet the medical needs of the elderly and disabled in America. As such, a social contract was established between the federal government and this more vulnerable population for help with their health care. Despite some gaps and areas of limited coverage, the Medicare program has provided a predictable and reliable safety net for the nation's elderly and disabled, and brought them into the mainstream of health care.

Today, that 40-year social contract is under siege and threatened beyond any time in its history. Although effective and with strong public support, Medicare has become the target among conservatives and many moderate Democrats for dismantlement as an entitlement program. Medicare politics have reverted to those seen in the 1950s and early 1960s, when the major political parties waged battle across no man's land between their ideologic trenches.[1] Shortly after the 1994 elections, when Republicans gained control of both houses of Congress, Newt Gingrich, then Speaker of the House, proclaimed "If we solve Medicare, I think we will govern for a generation."[2] By "solving" the problem, he meant dismantling Medicare as a social insurance program, transforming it to a privatized program, calling for more personal responsibility by its beneficiaries, and reducing the role and responsibility of government.

As a result of recurrent corporate compromises over the last 40 years, which have already partially privatized Medicare, an enormous for-profit industry has enveloped the program, siphoning off large sums of money from patient care to bureaucratic waste and corporate profits. Despite the claims of stakeholders in the private marketplace, the track record of private Medicare plans has been one of less efficiency, less choice, increased costs, higher overhead, and less reliability compared to traditional Medicare. Access, continuity, affordability, and quality of care are all being eroded. The future sustainability and viability of the program are open to question unless corporate profiteering and waste of privatization can be reined in. Indeed, if present trends continue without major structural reform of Medicare, all the elements of a perfect storm are on the horizon—many millions of elderly and disabled Americans who are unable to afford or gain access to an under funded and shredded safety net program. The human costs of such an outcome would be incalculable, and at odds with established traditions of American society.

This book has four main objectives: (1) to give historical perspective to Medicare as a social contract, including highlights of efforts over the last 30 years to privatize the program; (2) to examine the claims and track record of private market-based involvement with Medicare; (3) to discuss some contentious policy questions concerning the Medicare program today; and (4) to describe current politics concerning the future of Medicare, particularly as to whether it will continue to serve the public interest. Up-to-date and creditable sources will be brought together in four parts of the book. Part One provides historical background; Part Two examines the claims of privatized Medicare versus actual experience; Part Three discusses five contentious policy issues; and Part Four considers the future of Medicare as a highly charged political issue, and offers recommendations for reforming this essential program. Over 30 patient vignettes are included to illustrate the many problems encountered by Medicare beneficiaries in privatized Medicare plans. These are real people and situations drawn from the literature, press reports, and the files of consumer advocacy groups.

My perspective is that of a family physician with 13 years experience in rural practice, 25 years in academic family medicine (including 14 years as a department chairman), and editor of national family practice journals for 30 years. My study of health policy and the health care system has led to 3 books—*Health Care in America: Can Our Ailing System Be Healed?* (Butterworth-Heinemann, 2002), *The Corporate Transformation of Health Care: Can the Public Interest Still Be Served?* (Springer Publishing Company, 2004), and *Falling Through the Safety Net: Americans Without Health Insurance* (Common Courage Press, 2005). Over the course of my research for these books, I have come to the conclusion that incremental market-based "reforms" of the health care system work against the patient and the public interest. In this book I will again take a societal perspective, and as David Halberstam has said of his own excellent work over the years, attempt to "find true on the compass."[3]

The intended audience for this book includes physicians and other health professionals; policy makers and legislators; business and labor groups; citizens' reform groups and others involved in planning, financing, delivery or evaluation of health care services for the elderly and disabled. The book should also be of interest to many consumers and lay readers concerned about the future directions and stability of the Medicare program. A glossary is added at the end of the book, together with useful resources about Medicare.

An intense and continuing political struggle is underway through the 2004 election campaigns and beyond over the future of Medicare. At issue is whether its social contract with the elderly and disabled will be honored or whether the program will be dismantled as a responsibility of government and converted to a welfare program. Despite the failure of privatized Medicare plans over the last 20 years, they are again being proposed as "reforms" to "improve and modernize Medicare." Increased public, professional and legislative awareness of the problems of market-based "reforms" will be needed to inform the ongoing national debate over Medicare. As will be pointed out in the last section of the book, the problems of Medicare can be fixed if we have the political will to confront private stakeholders which put their interests above the public interest. It is hoped that this book will be helpful to that end.

John P. Geyman

PART I

HISTORICAL BACKGROUND

CHAPTER 1

PRIVATIZATION, CORPORATE POWER, AND THE PUBLIC INTEREST: SOME HISTORICAL PERSPECTIVE

"A Nation without a history is like an individual without a memory"

Arthur Schlesinger, Jr., 2001 [1]

As Medicare in the United States marks its 40th birthday in 2005, it continues to be the object of controversy and intense political struggle between its supporters and critics. News headlines blare with up-to-the-minute twists and turns about Medicare "reform." Today's political battles, which seem to us to be so fresh and new, can only be understood in the context of historical cycles of privatization, corporate power, and deregulation in this country.

SOME HISTORICAL BENCHMARKS

Tension and conflict between privatization of markets, best illustrated by corporate interests, and the common good of society have permeated U.S. history since Abraham Lincoln's time. There have been recurrent battles pitting citizens' groups, labor and other groups against corporate interests during periods of widespread corruption and scandal. Government and the courts have been influential in determining the outcome of this conflict at any given time.

Post-Civil War Corporate Excesses and the Gilded Age

During the Civil War years, the nation was divided by war and anti-draft riots as industrial interests profiteered from military defense contracts and expanded their power. In the wake of Lincoln's assassination, depression and a weakened government, corporate titans took center stage and created a government of their own. The presidential election of 1876 was marked by corruption and secret negotiations among corporate giants, leading President Rutherford Hayes, as the ultimate winner, to remark, "This is a government of the people, by the people, and for the people no longer. It is a government of corporations, by corporations, and for corporations."[2] The rulers of the time, including Andrew Carnegie, Jay Gould, J. Pierpont Morgan and John D. Rockefeller, bought legislation to their liking, in such areas as banking, labor, railroad and public lands, through a weakened and corrupted legislative process. In his classic book on that period, *The Robber Barons*, Matthew Josephson noted that "The halls of legislation were transformed into a mart where the price of votes was haggled over and laws, made to order, were bought and sold."[3]

In what became known as the Gilded Age of the 1880s and 1890s, a conservative court system favored corporate interests, regularly interpreting the public interest as maximum production, regardless of the product or who would be harmed.[4] During that period, industrial safeguards fell by the wayside as 700,000 American workers were killed in industrial accidents— about 100 a day—between 1888 and 1908.[5] A landmark case before the U.S. Supreme Court in 1886—Santa Clara County v. Southern Pacific Railroad—gave rise to the concept that corporations are to be accorded the rights of persons. This remarkable concept carries down to this day despite the facts that corporations are not even mentioned in the U.S. Constitution and the Supreme Court never made an official ruling to this effect. This language was inserted by a court reporter in an introduction (head notes) to the case and have no legal standing on their own. In effect, the Constitution was rewritten at the bidding of the railroad barons. As a result, corporations have been granted rights of free speech (to lobby their interests), protection from searches, Fifth Amendment protections, and coverage by due process and anti-discrimination laws.[6]

Progressive Period and Trust-Busting

Although he came from a background of privilege and was initially a Republican, President Theodore Roosevelt found uncontrolled corporate power a threat to the Republic. In an address to Congress in 1907, he had this to say.[7]

> *"The fortunes amassed through corporate organizations are now so large, and vest such power in those that wield them as to make it a matter of necessity to give to the sovereign—that is, to the Government, which represents the people as a whole—some effective power of supervision over their corporate use. In order to ensure a healthy social*

and industrial life, every big corporation should be held responsible by, and be accountable to, some sovereign strong enough to control its conduct."

Teddy Roosevelt's proposal for campaign finance reform legislation was struck down by the Supreme Court as a violation of First Amendment free speech rights of corporate persons. He persisted in his efforts to break up the trusts, in such industries as oil, railroads, steel, and tobacco through aggressive enforcement of the Sherman Anti-Trust Act. When corporations later tried to outlaw unions on the basis of the Sherman Act, the U.S. Congress passed the Clayton Anti-Trust Act of 1914, which banned court injunctions against striking workers. The Federal Trade Commission (FTC) was established soon thereafter.[8]

The Roaring Twenties and Renewed Corporate Dominance

In what was to become periodic shifts from regulatory to deregulatory cycles, corporate monopolies again flourished during the 1920s. The "free market" system was touted for its role in national prosperity, corporate excesses ran rampant, as social and income disparities widened, and the nation's financial system became highly leveraged.[9]

The Depression and New Deal

Market exuberance came crashing down in October 1929 as fortunes evaporated overnight and the Depression set in. A strong grassroots political backlash to the depression involved much of the population—farmers, laborers, women, the elderly, blacks and others. Assuming the Presidency in 1933, Franklin D. Roosevelt (FDR) set about to rescue the country through a broad agenda of social and regulatory reforms, which soon became known as the New Deal. At his urging, Congress passed the National Industrial Recovery Act (NIRA) in an effort to increase governmental regulatory powers over the free market. However, a conservative Supreme Court voided the NIRA soon thereafter, and also ruled that states could not set minimum wage standards. FDR reacted vigorously by packing the Supreme Court with more liberal Justices and strong enforcement of the Sherman Act. Business and financial markets were more strongly regulated, public works programs were initiated, and workers' rights legislation was passed.[10]

World War II and Economic Recovery

World War II brought an immediate and widely accepted strong central role of government in gearing up the wartime economy. Controls were placed on consumption, national resources were re-allocated, and industrial production was coordinated. At the same time, a highly progressive tax structure was established and a social safety net was strengthened. As the country united behind the war effort, the nation enjoyed full employment at good wages and many millions of working families joined an expanding middle class. A new social contract was drawn between government, business and labor which was to persist well into the 1970s. The U.S. became the leading economic power in the world while Congress passed legislation broadening the role of government in regulating business, strengthening product and worker safety, and promoting worker safety.[11]

The Second Gilded Age

With the election of President Ronald Reagan in 1980, a new period began of deregulation and corporate-friendly policies as the country reasserted free market principles in pursuit of the dominant role in a global economy. Taxes on the rich were reduced, corporations were given more freedom to merge and downsize their workforces, and protections of labor and the environment were weakened.[12] Appointments to the Supreme Court were once again more conservative and a second Gilded Age was launched. The CEOs of large multinational corporations became the robber barons of the 20th Century as income gaps within the society grew to unparalleled levels. Corporate CEO compensation grew from 40 times that of median incomes of U.S. workers in 1978 to 500 times as much by 2000, while the average family in the middle quintile of income saw its income barely increase over that period from $31,700 to $33,200.[13] The number of American billionaires soared from 1 in 1978 to 120 in 1994 as greed and corporate fraud ruled the day.[14] This number has climbed to 313 today, led by Bill Gates and Paul Allen, co-founders of Microsoft, and family members of Wal-Mart.[15] Unfortunately, as we see in Figure 1-1, corporate crime pays all too well.

While this brief overview accurately summarizes some important historical highlights over these years, what progressive advances that did occur could not have happened without ongoing popular struggle and strong

Figure 1.1

Crime Pays

CEOs Who Cook The Books Earn More

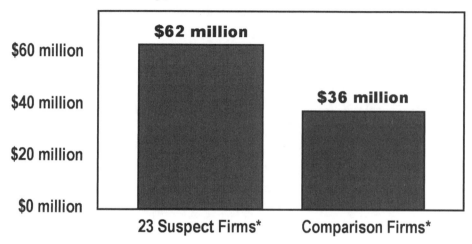

Source: United for a Fair Economy 8/26/02
* Firms under SEC Investigation vs. other firms in Business Week pay survey

Reprinted with permission from Physicians for a National Health
Program (PNHP), Slide set. Chicago, 2003.

public pressure, as pointed out by Howard Zinn's *A People's History in the United States*[16] and other works.

ENRON: TIP OF AN ICEBERG

The mere mention of Enron has come to symbolize all the worse of investor-owned corporations in this country. As a well-established pipeline company dating back to the late 1920s, its aggressive, highly leveraged policies in the 1990s led to its boom and then bust in a cloud of corruption and fraud. Its many egregious and illegal practices have been recounted in well-documented detail in a recent book by Robert Bryce, *Pipe Dreams: Greed, Egos, and the Death of Enron*. The case is established that its demise was a predictable result of a failure of leadership morally, ethically, and financially. The company was transformed from an operations company to a deal company, while top management led the way to wildly excessive executive compensation, over-indebtedness, and devious accounting practices. Their stock soared with false claims of revenues and hidden debts, then crashed when its bubble burst without enough real cash to sustain itself.[17]

Later post-mortems revealed a tangle of deceptive and illegal practices, including different accounting for stockholders and the IRS, tax evasion of $2 billion, exorbitant executive compensation and fraud, and conflicts of interest with banks, legal and accounting firms.[18-20] In pursuit of its tax avoidance strategy, Enron created 881 offshore subsidiaries, 692 of them in the Cayman Islands.[21] In the aftermath of the collapse of America's largest energy trader, close connections were found with the current Administration, which may have led to a delayed response to the crisis by the Securities Exchange Commission (SEC). Over the years 1990 to 2002, the Center for Responsive Politics reported that Enron contributed large amounts of money to 71 of 100 senators, including 19 of the 23 members of the Senate's energy committee, tasked to investigate the company's collapse.[22] Even as Enron was sliding into bankruptcy, Enron was an active lobbyist and participant in planning the new Administration's energy policy after the election of 2000.[23]

The California energy crisis of 2001 provides an instructive case to illuminate the damage that can quickly be done to the public interest by the freewheeling greed of investor-owned corporations. Enron, El Paso, and Dynegy were three energy traders to rush into the California energy market. By various price manipulations, they saw their share value skyrocket as electricity rates soared in some parts of the state from $30 per megawatt hour to $1,500 per megawatt hour. One of the state's largest public utilities, Pacific Gas & Electric, was forced into bankruptcy, and the state was seriously affected by rolling blackouts. By the time the Federal Energy Regulatory Commission finally approved limited price caps, the state was left with a multi-billion dollar debt and the energy traders' stock prices were in free-fall.[24,25]

It would be one thing if the Enron story was just an exception, but there are many other similar examples throughout corporate America during this current deregulatory era. WorldCom, Tyco International, Health South, and Imclone are just some of the firms infected by similar scandals, but each example brings to light previously hidden conflicts of interest in other industries as well. Arthur Anderson and other accounting firms have been implicated in these investigations, as have investment banks and Wall Street analysts. The extent of ongoing corporate cronyism is suggested by the recent finding that 420 chief executives of 2,000 major public corporations have conflicts of interest with their boards' compensation committees, often including relatives.[26]

CORPORATIZATION VS DEMOCRACY

Despite the political rhetoric of our times, carried nearly to the point of patriotic fervor, that holds that free trade and markets in a global economy are an effective way to advance democracy, they are fundamentally antidemocratic. David Korten, an economist with wide international experience and author of *When Corporations Rule the World,* calls attention to this important difference—in a political democracy, each person has one vote, while in the market, each dollar is a vote. Markets are biased in favor of the affluent and discriminate against the less so. As markets become more free and global, it therefore follows that governance increasingly passed from national governments to global corporations.[27] William Greider, National Affairs Correspondent for *The Nation* and author of *Who Will Tell the People: The Betrayal of American Democracy*, points out the irony of this historic paradox:

> *"At the very moment when western democracies and capitalism have triumphed over the communist alternative, their own systems of self-government are being gradually unraveled by the market system."*
> [28]

The U.S. is fully committed to the global market, and governance has largely shifted to corporate interests. Corporate governance takes place through a mix of strategic alliances, contracting networks, and interlocking board directorships linking almost all Fortune 500 corporations with each other.[29] It also occurs through coordinated advocacy efforts of the Business Roundtable, which includes the heads of 42 of the 50 largest U.S. industrial corporations, 9 of the 11 largest U.S. utilities, 7 of the 8 largest U.S. commercial banks, 7 of the 8 largest U.S. transportation companies, 7 of the 20 largest U.S. insurance companies, and 5 of the 7 largest U.S. retailers. The Roundtable campaigned strongly for NAFTA, and actively pursues the bottom-line interests of its members quite aside from the usual legislative process. Their interests are further served by the granting of "fast track" authority by Congress to the President for trade negotiations like GATT. Once a trade agreement is reached, Congress can only vote once to approve or reject the entire package, without any opportunity to amend or reject particular sections.[30]

For-profit public relations firms and business-sponsored policy institutes provide another vehicle for corporate advocacy and image-building campaigns. In what Greider has termed "democracy for hire," these firms produce opinion polls, op-ed pieces, press releases, and policy-oriented papers aimed at the public as well as legislators.[31] In the U.S., there are now some 170,000 public relations employees serving the interests of paying clients compared to only about 40,000 news reporters. More than one-third of the news content in a typical U.S. newspaper is based on public relations press releases, story memos and suggestions.[32] Meanwhile, ownership of much of the media by our largest corporations further serves the interests of corporate America under the umbrella of managed news. The 100 largest U.S. corporations pay for about 75% of commercial television time as well as 50% of public television time. Since each one-half minute of prime-time network time sells for between $200,000 and $300,000, only the largest corporations can afford such advertising.[33]

GLOBALIZATION AS THE NEW WILD CARD

Free trade and globalization have become the mantra of U.S. economic policy over the last two decades. An alphabet soup of new international institutions has been created in recent years to implement these concepts—the World Trade Organization (WTO) (established in 1995), the General Agreement on Tariffs and Trade (GATT), the General Agreement on Trade in Services (GATS), the Agreement on Trade Related Investment Measures (TRIMs), the Agreement on Trade Related Aspects of Intellectual Property (TRIPs) and the North American Free Trade Agreement (NAFTA). Together with the World Bank and the International Monetary Fund (IMF), these institutions and agreements provide the structure for a new global economic order which operates largely beyond the reach or accountability to national governments. The U.S. played a leading role in shaping this structure, and our large corporations strongly influenced that process. The corporation has thereby emerged as the dominant player on the world's economic stage, eclipsing all but the largest nation-state-in size, scope and power.[34]

Corporate interests see globalization as an opportunity to pursue a common market and capital source while avoiding many market barriers or constraints from national governments. WTO governance is largely a process of closed-door negotiations, which in many instances can supersede laws or regulations of any given country. Unfortunately, however, there are serious downsides to this New World order. Corporations can readily pit countries against each other in "a race to the bottom" to realize maximal profits from whatever country offers the lowest wages, most lax pollution standards, and lowest taxes. As Lori Wallach and Michelle Sforza observe in their book *Whose Trade Organization? Corporate Globalization and the Erosion of Democracy*:[35]

> *"Enactment of these so-called free trade deals virtually guarantees that democratic efforts to ensure corporations pay their fair share of taxes, provide their employees a decent standard of living or limit their pollution of the air, water and land will be met with the refrain: "You can't burden us like that. If you do, we won't be able to compete. We'll have to close down and move to a country that offers us a more hospitable climate." This sort of intimidation is extremely powerful. Communities already devastated by plant closures and a declining manufacturing base are desperate not to lose more jobs. They know all too well that exit threats of this kind are often carried out."*

Here are just some of the negative impacts experienced by the US and other participating countries at the expense of largely unfettered corporate exploitation of global markets:

- In our pursuit of free trade at all costs, U.S. companies are free to send both their manufacturing and service jobs overseas and then reimport their own products and services with almost unlimited access to U.S. markets[36]

- Under NAFTA, 3 million U.S. jobs have been eliminated as a result of trade deals since 1994, including 1.7 million jobs in manufacturing[37]

- The free-trade zone on the Mexican side of the border with the United States has attracted many U.S. corporations (including General Electric, General Motors, Ford, RCA, Westinghouse and

Honeywell) to over 2,000 factories employing Mexican workers at hourly wages about one-tenth the average U.S. manufacturing wage, without either benefits or the right to unionize[38]

- As the world's largest corporation, General Electric has led the way since the early 1990s to India's outsourcing boom, including establishing the first international call center there[39]

- Transcriptions of U.S. medical records outsourced overseas have no privacy protections under our privacy statutes[40]

- Major American companies employ millions of adolescent children in Mexico, often at salaries of less than $1 a day without benefits (e.g., General Electric)[41]

- IBM's workforce is composed of 40% foreign employees, while Chrysler buys cars from Mitsubishi and sells them as its own[42]

- The income gap between the rich and poor within participating countries continues to increase; by 1997 the richest 20% took 86% of world income, while the poorest 20% accounted for only 1%[43]

- In the U.S., the trade deficit has soared from $98 billion in 1994 to $450 billion today, the highest level in our history[44]

Korten describes this new world economic system as a "global suicide economy," adding this perspective:[45]

> "The global economic system is rewarding corporations and their executives with generous profits and benefits packages for contracting out their production to sweatshops paying substandard wages, for clear-cutting primal forests, for introducing labor-saving technologies that displace tens of thousands of employees, for dumping toxic wastes, and for shaping political agendas to advance corporate interests over human interests. The system shields those who take such actions from the costs of their decisions, which are borne by the system's weaker members—the displaced workers who no longer have jobs, the replacement workers who are paid too little to feed their families, the forest dwellers whose homes have been destroyed, the poor who live next to the toxic dumps, and the unorganized taxpayers who pick up the bills. The consequences of delinking benefits from their costs is that the system is telling the world's most powerful decision makers that their

decisions are creating new benefits, when in fact they are simply shifting more the earth's available wealth to themselves at the expense of people and the planet."

Today, under ongoing secret WTO negotiations under the General Agreement on Trade in Services (GATS), leaked documents reveal that privatization is being promoted under WTO rules (which supersede local, state and federal laws of WTO countries) across a wide range of industries; including banking, energy, construction, telecommunications, tourism, and even "essential public services" such as education, health care, mail delivery, and bulk water.[46] Michael Dolan, Western Director of Public Citizens Global Trade Watch, has this to say about GATS:[47]

> *"The whole point of the GATS is to privatize public services, dump essential service regulations and then pour cement over that mess to make it permanent—we saw how that worked in California with energy."*

BACKLASH TO CORPORATE EXCESSES

Soaring corporate profits during the Second Gilded Age of the 1980s and 1990s resulted from a seven-fold increase in sales by the world's 500 largest corporations. During that time, however, employment in those companies shrank by about one third. While free market advocates claim the economic advantages to U.S. shareholders, about 40% of U.S. owned individual shares are held by the top 1%, in no way comparable to the more democratic capitalism of the 1950s. Public opinion is now voicing serious concerns about the increasing corporate power over too many aspects of American life as reflected by about 80% of respondents to a *Business Week*/Harris poll in 2000.[48] There is also growing public awareness that the country is facing a loss of national sovereignty as a result of the structure and policies of the WTO and various supranational trade agreements, together with increasing concern about a "democratic deficit." As a political and economic commentator for over 30 years, Kevin Phillips observes in his recent book *Wealth and Democracy: A Political History of the American Rich*:[49]

> *"Corporate power retreated during the Progressive and New Deal eras, as we have seen, and then again between the mid-1960s and late 1970s. The early twenty-first century should see another struggle*

because corporate aggrandizement in the 1980s and 1990s went beyond that of the Gilded Age—the parallels of political corruption and concentrated wealth—to frame issues of abandoning American workers, communities, and loyalties."

There is some evidence that the pendulum <u>may</u> be starting to change towards more corporate accountability. *Time* magazine's Persons of the Year for 2002 were three whistle-blowers—Sherron Watkins of Enron, Cynthia Cooper of WorldCom and Cowleen Rowley of the FBI. *Time* also named Eliot Spitzer, New York's attorney general, as "crusader of the year," though the $1.8 billion recaptured from corporate fraud is but a small fraction of the many billions taken from the public.[50] A federal judge in Houston ruled that virtually all banks, law firms and investment houses that participated in Enron's off-the-books partnerships are liable to suit by investors.[51] There is growing opposition around the world to the WTO's globalization trade policies and its largely secret trade negotiations.[52] There is also increasingly widespread public resentment to NAFTA and the more recent proposal to extend similar trade agreements to Central America (CAFTA).[53] Alan Murray, Washington bureau chief for CNBC, editorialized in the *Wall Street Journal* in late 2002 with this overview:[54]

> *"The era of market fundamentalism is over. Marketization, deregulation and privatization, and the opportunities for market manipulation offered by inadequate regulation...all central elements in the rise and fall of Enron... are now discredited in the United States. And in developing countries, where their effects have been most devastating, they are the object of widespread public opprobrium."*

Recognizing their vulnerability to public opinion in the wake of numerous corporate scandals, a new national organization was formed during the 1990s, Business for Social Responsibility. Although a growing number of large corporations are joining this group, there is a sizable gap between the rhetoric of social responsibility to workers, communities and society and the actual practices of large corporations. Many of these corporations, such as Reebok and General Motors, preach the social gospel while downsizing and paying workers in developing countries less than two dollars a day.[55] Robert Kuttner, Co-Editor of *The American Prospect*, draws this conclusion:[56]

> *"No matter how hard the enthusiasts of the new corporation try to*

infer social values from the logic of competition itself, markets remain fundamentally amoral; values need to be found elsewhere—and then imposed on corporations lest they overrun everything else we hold dear... A recent spate of books pointing to cleaner air and water... conveniently ignored the fact that environmental progress was entirely the result of citizen consciousness translated into public regulation, and not at all the result of newly enlightened oil company executives realizing that, as one ad put it, 'we have to live here too.'"

Despite the welcome first signs of a pendulum swing toward more corporate accountability, the wide reach of corporate influences and governance remains intact. The WTO and its mechanisms are alive and well, and threaten to negate an effective political response to corporate practices not in the public interest. One recent example is the reaction of a commissioner of the European Union to the Sarbanes bill, legislation recently passed by Congress seeking to prevent conflicts of interest between corporations and their auditors. Under GATS, WTO countries are not allowed to create or enforce any domestic regulations that might leave foreign competitors at a competitive disadvantage, so the U.S. has been informed that the Sarbanes bill will be challenged as a trade barrier.[57]

WHAT CAN WE LEARN FROM HISTORY?

President Harry S. Truman once said "The only thing new in the world is the history you don't know."[58] Fortunately, the First Gilded Age and other periods of corporate dominance are instructive if we can only recall and apply their lessons. These are some of the lessons from history that help to put our times in perspective.

1.   After a boom, you can count on a scandal

Periods of corruption and scandal have been a recurrent theme throughout U.S. history in the aftermath of economic booms.[59]

2.   Increasing income gaps and social disparities accompany economic booms, and sow the seeds for public rebellion

The historians Will and Ariel Durant have observed that wealth, as a product of markets as well as politics, inevitably is partially redistributed, either peaceably or violently, when it becomes too concentrated in the hands of a few.[60] Given the behavior of large transnational corporations in recent years within the global economy and the WTO, the "race to the bottom" represents a special concern this time, with the 6 billion people in poorer nations competing for much of the same work as has been done by 1 billion people in countries of the developed world.[61]

3.   *In the United States, periods of capitalist booms have shared common characteristics*

Kevin Phillips has profiled the convergent themes of "Capitalist Heyday" periods since the First Gilded Age in the late 1800s. Table 1-1 lists these common characteristics. It is striking how much all of these apply to our current times.[62]

4.   *The U.S. corporation, as a "legal person" since the Supreme Court's non-rule of 1886, poses an ongoing obstacle to reform*

We have now seen how the head note language in a Supreme Court document in 1886 gave the corporation the opportunity to claim constitutional rights and protections, unlike any other organizations in the country, such as unions or churches. Corporations have been granted special freedoms to pursue their interests, and also have advantages over mortal citizens. They can live forever, can live in many places at the same time (including overseas), can change at will or even sell themselves to foreign owners.[63] Ironically, as Paul Hawken has observed, "corporations achieve precisely what the Bill of Rights was intended to prevent: domination of public thought and discourse.[64] Further, when corporations are prosecuted for crimes, they then claim that they are "artificial legal entities, not personally accountable for their misdeeds."[65,66]

5.   *There are many ways by which the corporations can co-opt whatever regulatory system is in place*

That corporate influence goes with affluence is a given at any time. Corporations play a dominant role in governmental policy through lobbying, campaign contributions, and a revolving door of leadership between industry and government. What may be less obvious is the extent to which industry can protect itself from competition by designing the regulatory process itself. One recent example is the lobbying effort by Monsanto and other corporate chemical giants against proposed legislation intended to eliminate

Table 1.1

The Twelve Shared Characteristics of the "Capitalist Heyday" Periods—the Gilded Age, the Roaring Twenties, and the Great Bull Market of the 1980s and 1990s

1. Conservative politics and ideology, with mostly Republican presidents but even Democratic presidents in these eras—Grover Cleveland, Bill Clinton—tend to be economically conservative.
2. Skepticism of government—from laissez-faire to program cuts and deregulation—and emphasis on markets and the private sector.
3. Exaltation of business, entrepreneurialism, and the achievements of free enterprise.
4. Replacement of public interest politics by private interest politics, with high levels of corruption.
5. Aspects of survival-of-the-fittest thinking—from social Darwinism to welfare reform and globalization.
6. Labor union weakness and/or membership decline.
7. Major economic and corporate restructuring—repeating merger waves and the rise of trusts, holding companies, leveraged buy-outs, spin-offs et al.
8. Obstruction, reduction or elimination of taxes, especially on corporations, personal incomes, or inheritance.
9. Pursuit of disinflation-supportive of creditors—in response to prior inflation (from the Civil War, World War I, and the Vietnam era).
10. A two-tier economy with stronger prosperity along the coasts and in the Great Lakes area, and greatest weakness in the commodity-producing interior.
11. Concentration of wealth, economic polarization, and rising levels of inequality.
12. Bull markets and rising, increasingly precarious levels of speculation, leverage, and debt.

From WEALTH AND DEMOCRACY by Kevin Phillips, copyright 2002 by Kevin Phillips. Used by permission of Broadway Books, A Division of Random House, Inc.

regulations concerning genetically engineered plants. A journalist covering the story reported that

> *"contrary to conventional wisdom, Monsanto and other industry giants love EPA regulation. It adds another stamp of approval to their*

products, and it squeezes out smaller companies that can't afford the time and money the regulatory process demands. The big firms will spend whatever it takes to topple the competition, and Monsanto's lobbying is so masterful that once regulation is in place, manipulating the process is a breeze."[67]

WHERE ARE WE NOW?

As the world's only superpower in the early years of the new millennium, the U.S. has also become the leading economic power. Global markets are already well entrenched under a new system of supranational governance. The U.S. has played a leading role in the development of this new global economic order, and now owns 60 of the world's 100 largest public companies. Table 1-2 lists the 10 largest public companies, eight of which are American, ranked by market value in 2002.[68] Through mergers and consolidation, monopolies of global markets have become common. The top five corporations now control more than 50% of the world's market in the automotive, airline, aerospace, electrical, electronics and steel industries.[69]

The WTO and IMF, through their boards of representatives from member states, represent a new shadow government, neither democratic nor accountable to the public. As chairman of the U.S. Senate Commerce Committee in 2001, Senator Fritz Hollings (D-South Carolina) observed that "the WTO puts our social contract in jeopardy; its one-size-fits all capitalism threatens to destroy America's standard of living."[70] From a historical perspective, Kevin Phillips draws this conclusion:[71]

> *"As was true a century ago, current day Americans have watched theories of marketplace morality and survival of the economically fittest displace notions of commonwealth, public good and economic justice. Just as the Gilded Age had Social Darwinism, our Second Gilded Age has globalization and its inexorable, values-free markets."*

In the U.S. our system of corporate welfare remains well entrenched. Each year, taxpayers subsidize corporations through a wide range of government-sanctioned favors, including tax breaks and direct government subsidies to pay for research, training costs and advertising. From the mid-1950s to the mid-1990s, corporate taxes as a share of the nation's tax revenues dropped from 28% to 11.8%, while the corporate share of property taxes fell from 45% to 16%.[72, 73] A report of the General Accounting Office

Table 1.2

The World's 10 Largest Public Companies

Ranked by value as of August 29, 2003, as determined by Wall Street Journal Market Data Group
(In millions of U.S. Dollars at Dec. 31, 2002, exchange rates)

2003	2002	COMPANY (Country)	Market Value
1	1	General Electric (U.S.)	$294,206
2	2	Microsoft (U.S.)	283,576
3	3	Wal-Mart Stores (U.S.)	259,501
4	4	Exxon Mobile (U.S.)	251,813
5	5	Pfizer (U.S.)	236,203
6	8	Citigroup (U.S.)	222,849
7	21	Intel (U.S.)	187,003
8	9	American International Group (U.S.)	155,382
9	10	Royal Dutch/Shipping (Netherlands/U.K.)	154,194
10	7	BP (U.K.)	151,431

Source: The global giants: amid market pain, U.S. companies hold greater sway.
Wall Street Journal October 14, 2002:R10.

in 1995 concluded that a majority of corporations, both foreign and U.S. controlled, were paying *no* U.S. income tax.[74]

Corporate insiders rotate back and forth between government and corporate management, thereby perpetuating corporate dominance over government and its regulatory agencies. A classic example of the extent to which Social Darwinism has permeated government today are the suggestions in 2001 by Paul O'Neill, then Secretary of the Treasury and previously a top executive at two large multinational corporations, that corporations should be tax-exempt, like churches, and that Social Security, Medicare and Medicaid should be eliminated since "able-bodied adults should save enough on a regular basis so that they can provide for their own retirement, and for that matter, health and medical needs."[75]

Whereas globalization has served corporate interests well, it has not been kind to the populations of America and other countries in the world. In the U.S., for example, the Index of Social Health, developed and monitored by Fordham University's Institute for Innovation in Social Policy, shows increasing divergence over the last 40 years between the GDP and markers of social health, which include such measures as child poverty, youth homicide, and health care coverage. (Figure 1-2)[76]

Figure 1.2

Index of Social Health of the United States. 1970 - 2001

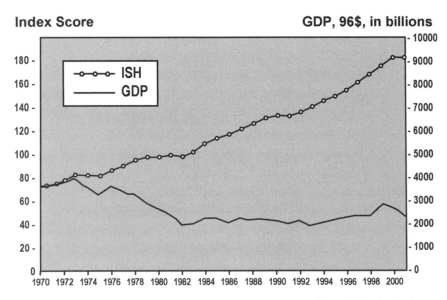

Source: Reprinted with permission from Opdycke, S. et al *The Index of Health: Monitoring the Social Well-Being of the Nation* (Institute for Innovation in Social Policy, Tarrytown, NY 2003), 12.

SO THERE YOU HAVE IT

More than one-half of the 100 largest "economies" in the world today are corporations, not countries.[77] This chapter, however, highlights the inevitable tension and conflict between unfettered free market forces, accentuated under privatization and globalization, and democracy as well as the welfare and standards of living of participating people, their communities and nations. These problems are not new, as this historical overview clearly shows. The question remains how much we can learn from history, and to what extent it will once again repeat itself. The great debate of the 21st century will be about how the new rules for a global market can be rewritten in the public interest. The current model of "corporate managed trade" serves corporate self-interest at the expense of entire populations.

In the next chapter, we will turn our attention to how a 40-year social contract with the nation's elderly and disabled is threatened by current efforts to further privatize Medicare. That threat will be more understandable, more predictable, and less surprising within the context of this historical perspective.

CHAPTER 2

MEDICARE AS A SOCIAL CONTRACT

As one of the 'elderly' as a widow, living on social security, I felt I must write to you. I have three daughters, who my husband and I were able to give a college education to by working endless hours in a small store—and by saving pennies bit by bit. We also saved to be independent when we grew older. One of our daughters has four children, one daughter has gone back to work to be able to send her college age children to school, and one daughter is alone, and is working to support herself and her son. My husband and I carry hospital insurance—but he had a heart attack which forced him to give up work and which kept him in the hospital for 6 weeks—with the need for round-the-clock nursing care at $75 a day, and physicians' bill and medicines that cost over $2 a day. Our savings dwindled. Then came a disabling stroke, which again meant long hospitalization and nursing care and medicines and payments for rehabilitation service. With good medical care we were able to prolong my husband's life, so he could take pleasure with his family, but my husband is now gone, and the $8,700 of our savings. My children, who have so many needs of their own—must help me meet the necessities of everyday living. Every bit of my life's work seems wasted, if I have to ask help of my children and if I become ill now—must I ask them to assume an even greater burden? I would have been so willing to pay for necessary medical coverage through a social security prepayment plan. Every parent wishes to pay his own way. Every parent wants to be able to be giving—not taking—we want to be independent, even if we are ill and old. We need the coverage that the Medicare bill provides.

—Mrs. M. Rawitch, Fairfield, Connecticut. Letter to the National Council
of Senior Citizens, submitted to the House Committee on Ways &
Means, 1964.[1]

This vignette is but one of millions describing the vulnerability of the nation's elderly concerning their economic and health security 40 years ago. After a protracted political battle between opposing interests in the late 1950s and early 1960s, Medicare was enacted in 1965 as the country's first program of publicly-financed social health insurance. With strong bipartisan support, a social "contract" was established at that time between the federal government and senior citizens 65 years of age and older, then 10% of the population.

This contract has lasted to this day, despite many tests along the way.

Today, powerful opposing forces are again involved in an intense debate over the future of Medicare. Conservatives and some moderates are promoting privatization of the program with reduction of Original Medicare, a more limited role of the government, and more personal responsibility among senior citizens for their own care. Liberals and progressives argue for continued improvement of Medicare as a universal, publicly-financed social insurance program. The debate has again become polarized and distorted by conflicting ideologic views and disinformation.

This chapter addresses four questions: (1) what were the circumstances leading to the passage of Medicare in 1965; (2) what major changes to Medicare have occurred as it has evolved over time; (3) what are the scope and limits of Medicare's social contract; and (4) what political battles are now underway over the future of Medicare?

HOW AND WHY MEDICARE CAME INTO BEING

After three failed attempts in the U.S. to establish a program for universal coverage through national health insurance (1912-1917, 1932-1938 and 1945-1950), the issue of health insurance coverage for the elderly took center stage on the domestic agenda during the presidential election campaigns of 1960 and 1964. There was growing and widespread public concern over the increasing inability of the nation's elderly to afford rising costs of health care. Hospital costs were climbing faster than any other consumer items. Only about one-half of people 65 years and older had any form of health insurance at that time, and many of those policies were both expensive and skimpy on coverage. Those with hospital coverage found only one-quarter of their expenses covered.[2] More than two-thirds of people over 65 with chronic conditions limiting major activities were uninsured. A spokesman for Blue Cross, then entirely not for-profit, summarized the problem in this way: "Insuring everyone over 65 is a losing business that must be subsidized."[3]

By 1965, the country already had 30 years of favorable experience with Social Security, enacted in 1935, under which benefits were accorded to those who paid into the system through their social security taxes. As a Commissioner of Social Security, Robert Ball observed that this gave American workers the feeling that they have earned their benefits.[4] In his

1970 book *The Politics of Medicare,* Theodore Marmor, Professor of Political Science and Public Health at Yale University, made a convincing case that Medicare evolved as a middle-class program.[5] As Lawrence Friedman, Stanford law professor noted, "benefits tend to be a matter of right; eligibilities are earned; benefits are restitutionary; the means-test is avoided."[6] This is in direct contrast to a charity program which may provide benefits on the basis of need only if the recipient is eligible by means testing.

Medicare was designed as a social insurance program with universal coverage of all seniors 65 and over in one large risk pool. It is "social" through its role in protecting seniors who would not otherwise be able to afford health insurance in the private market. Medicare provides a set of benefits defined by law for all eligible individuals without regard to health conditions or income level. Its benefits are considered an earned right since beneficiaries have paid into the program through mandatory contributions from individuals and/or employers.[7]

Strong political forces confronted each other for and against the Medicare law of 1965. Proponents included organized labor, the American Association of Retired Workers, the American Geriatrics Society, the National Farmers Union, and the National Association of Social Workers. Opponents included the American Medical Association (AMA), the American Hospital Association (AHA), the National Association of Manufacturers, the Life Insurance Association of America, the National Association of Blue Shield Plans, and the Chamber of Commerce.[8] The AMA fought fiercely against Medicare, labeling it "socialized medicine" and a dangerous first step toward national health insurance. It proposed Eldercare, a state administered program which would subsidize the elderly poor to buy private health insurance. However, there was broad recognition that the private health insurance market had already failed the elderly, and that publicly-financed health insurance would be required.[9] The AMA's proposal received little support in Congress, and the AMA was marginalized as the Medicare bill went forward.[10] Meanwhile, the AHA and Blue Cross joined forces to support the bill, especially when it appeared that it would pass and after they were assured that Blue Cross would process all claims for hospital services.[11] Many employers also jumped on the bandwagon in support of Medicare, seeing the bill as a way to limit their responsibility for their retirees' health care.[12] The final votes for Medicare in Congress showed overwhelming bipartisan support—307 to 116 in the House and 70 to 24 in the Senate.[13]

Because of the intensity of opposition to Medicare's enactment by the medical, hospital and insurance industries, the federal government, in an effort of political reconciliation, avoided regulatory authority over the practice of medicine and the hospital industry. Permissive reimbursement arrangements were carried forward as well as generous reimbursement levels, as were customary in the private sector. Blue Cross, as the lead private intermediary under contract to Medicare to deal with providers, was in a privileged position to set rules and procedures favorable to providers.[14] Fiscal intermediaries were empowered to determine whether claims were a covered benefit, medically necessary, and charges reasonable. Most Medicare coverage decisions were therefore to be made at the local level.[15] Since then, there have been wide variations in Medicare coverage decisions, as well as reimbursement levels, from one part of the country to another. According to the Medicare Payment Advisory Commission (MedPAC), there are now about 9,000 different local medical review policies.[16] Of course, these kinds of arrangements were inflationary to Medicare costs, and later observers of Medicare politics have described the implementation of Medicare as a "corporate compromise" among employers, physicians and hospitals.[17]

Despite the early opposition of the medical, hospital, and insurance industries, the passage of Medicare became a bonanza for these industries. Medicare rules on costs were vague, with little oversight.[18] In 1966, the first year of operation of Medicare, physicians raised their fees by 7.8% (more than twice the increase of the consumer price index for that year) while the average daily service charge in U.S. hospitals rose by 21.9%.[19] Most services of physicians and hospitals were well reimbursed through a large industry of contract intermediaries during the 1970s and 1980s. By 1990, the annual cost of Medicare had grown to $100 billion, ten times the budget projected in 1965 for Medicare in 1990.[20]

EVOLUTION OF MEDICARE SINCE 1965

Medicare was never intended to cover all of the health care costs of the elderly. In the 1960s the cost of hospital care was the most urgent of these costs, so that Original Medicare was especially targeted to these services, together with associated physician services. Table 2.1 lists the benefits of the Medicare Program in 1965, while Table 2.2 summarizes financing and provider payment arrangements.[21]

Table 2.1

Medicare Program Benefits and Eligibility, 1965

Part A, hospitalization insurance

60 days of inpatient hospital services during any spell of illness, after $40 deductible (deductible scheduled to rise over time to reflect increases in average cost of hospital day)

30 days of hospitalization coverage subject to daily coinsurance set at 25% of the deductible

Posthospital extended care (nursing home) services up to 100 days

Posthospital home health visits up to 100 days

Outpatient hospital diagnostic services, with 20% coinsurance

Lifetime maximum of 190 days of inpatient hospital psychiatric services

Part B, supplementary medical insurance

Payment for 80% of "reasonable charges" for physicians' services for office visits, surgery, and consultation, after $50 deductible; 20% coinsurance required

Home health services up to a 100 days a year; 20% coinsurance required.

Outpatient psychiatric and mental health treatment (with 50% copayment required)

X-ray tests and diagnostic laboratory tests

Ambulance service

Eligibility

Eligibility for hospitalization insurance initially open to all persons age 65 and above; after 1968, eligibility restricted to individuals 65 and older who were entitled to Social Security benefits; part B was a voluntary program, open to anyone eligible for Medicare part A who paid the required premium

Note: "Spell of illness" was defined as beginning the first day of hospitalization and ending with the close of the first period of 60 consecutive days during which the patient was not hospitalized or enrolled in an extended care facility.

Reprinted with permission from Oberlander J. *The Political Life of Medicare*. Chicago: University of Chicago Press, 2003:32.

Table 2.2

Medicare Financing and Provider Payment Arrangements 1965

Financing

Medicare part A funded through an earmarked payroll tax on workers and their employers; the payroll tax was initially set at .35% on an earnings base of $7,800 and was scheduled to rise in five increments to .80% in 1987

Medicare part B funded through equal contributions from general revenues and monthly premiums (initially 3$) paid by beneficiaries; the premium was to increase over time so that the sum of beneficiary contributions would be maintained at a level of 50% of the total costs of part B

Provider payments

Hospitals reimbursed retrospectively for their "reasonable costs"

Physicians reimbursed retrospectively for "reasonable charges"

Program administration

Claims processing and bill auditing contracted out by the Bureau of Health Insurance of the Social Security Administration to private fiscal intermediaries and carriers (mostly Blue Cross and Blue Shield plans)

Reprinted with permission from Oberlander J. *The Political Life of Medicare*. Chicago: University of Chicago Press, 2003:33.

From the beginning, there have been large gaps in coverage for Medicare beneficiaries, particularly for prescription drugs, home care, and long-term care. After a failed legislative attempt in 1967 to extend coverage to the disabled, they were included in 1972, when patients with end-stage renal disease were also included.[22,23] Other than a few other benefits, such as podiatry, there has been very little expansion of benefits under Medicare since its inception. Despite the claims of its proponents, and as will be discussed in some detail later, coverage of prescription drugs, as provided in the Medicare Prescription Drug, Improvement, and Modernization Act of 2003, is unlikely to be of much benefit to most Medicare beneficiaries.

Since the costs of drugs, long-term care and other services not covered by Medicare have grown well above cost-of-living levels, a large market for supplementary private health insurance has become firmly established in this country. Many variants of supplemental Medicare insurance (Medigap) policies have been developed to cover gaps in coverage and to provide some degree of cost sharing. By 1984, three of four Medicare beneficiaries carried some form of supplemental insurance, typically covering the deductible and coinsurance payments for hospitalization and 20% copayment for physician services.[24]

Although Medicare and private supplemental Medicare insurance have helped to bring elderly Americans into the mainstream of U.S. health care, there have been profiteering and other abuses along the way. Because of concerns over insurance industry practices in selling duplicative coverage, limited benefits and related marketing abuses, Congress passed the Baucus amendments in 1980 in an effort to regulate the Medigap market. These amendments established standards for voluntary state certification of Medigap policies, including requirements for minimal benefits packages.[25] Since comparison shopping between Medigap policies continued to be difficult, further federal legislation was passed in 1990 which mandated that any Medigap policy fit one of ten categories of benefit packages.[26]

The costs of long-term care have been a persistent problem for elderly people requiring such care. If poor or lower-income, they may become eligible for coverage of nursing home care under Medicaid, which has mandated state coverage of skilled nursing home care since it was enacted in 1965.[27] Otherwise, there are many barriers to the purchase of private long-term care insurance, including unaffordable costs, inadequate coverage, and the difficulty of selling such policies to younger, healthier people.[28]

By the 1980s, U.S. health care spending was accelerating at record rates, including costs of the Medicare program, and the federal government shifted to a more regulatory mode. Since hospital and physician reimbursement account for such a large part of overall Medicare spending, cost containment efforts have targeted these two areas. The first target was to restrain the growth of hospital costs by enactment in 1983 of the prospective payment system for hospital reimbursement. This cost containment effort led to the use of diagnosis-related groups (DRGs) as the basis for payments to hospitals for care for Medicare beneficiaries. By 1990, the hospital payment-to-cost ratio, (which measures the extent to which insurers pay for the costs of hospitalization) declined to 0.89 (89% of costs), as compared to 1.27 (127%) of costs for hospitalizations for private patients.[29]

Medicare payments for physician services, which increased at a rate three times that for hospital payments during the 1980s, became the next target for regulation. Congress imposed a fee freeze on Medicare physician payments from 1984 to 1986, but physician payments still rose by almost 12% each of those years due to increased volume of billings.[30,31] In 1989, a resource-based relative value scale (RBRVS) was instituted by Congress for reimbursement of physician services under Medicare, thereby replacing the "reasonable charge" system with a predetermined fee schedule. This approach cut the average annual growth in Medicare expenditures for physician services from about 10% to 5% a year. Since that time, Medicare reimbursement for physician services has been substantially below reimbursement rates in the private sector, often leading physicians to withdraw from caring for Medicare beneficiaries. As we shall see in later chapters, this has had an adverse effect on access and continuity of care for Medicare beneficiaries.

Medicare coverage is less than that in other industrialized Western countries, paying for less than one-half of all health care expenditures incurred by its beneficiaries.[32] Nonetheless, Medicare spending has been increasing steadily over the last 30 years. Although Medicare has been more successful than the private sector in reining in some of these cost increases,[33] its continued growth as an ever-larger part of the federal budget has brought into question its long-term viability unless changes are made.

Today, Medicare is a very large program. As the largest public purchaser and payer of U.S. health care services, it is the major source of coverage for one in seven Americans—41 million people, including 6 million non-elderly people with disabilities. Medicare's reach is enormous. A 1999 HCFA report listed involvement with over 6,000 hospitals, 830,000 physicians, 167,000 clinical laboratories, 3,500 end-stage renal disease facilities, 3,500 rural health clinics, 2,600 ambulatory surgical centers, 2,500 outpatient physical therapy facilities, 2,300 hospices, 700 portable x-ray units, and 600 outpatient rehabilitation facilities.[34] Its total expenditures in 2005 were about $325 billion, and its costs are expected to increase by 30% from 2005 to 2007 as the new prescription drug benefit is implemented.[35] Medicare accounts for about one-fifth of total personal national health expenditures and one-third of hospital and home health services.[36,37]

HOW SOLID IS MEDICARE'S SOCIAL CONTRACT

As a social insurance program enacted 40 years ago in response to the failure of private markets to serve the elderly, Medicare has extended a social contract to its beneficiaries rather than individual contracts. This "contract" is based on the premise, well documented over the years, that the private insurance market typically fails to serve whole population groups (such as all people 65 years of age and older) by insuring healthier people instead of sicker people who place insurers at higher financial risk (i.e., "cherry picking" the market). The rationale for such a social contract is also based upon the essential role of government to assure affordable access to benefits as well as recognition that voluntarism and charity care cannot effectively meet the needs of those who don't have health insurance.[38,39] The National Academy of Social Insurance convened a Study Panel on Medicare's Larger Social Role in 1997, chaired by Dr. Rosemary Stevens, well-known health care historian and policy expert. In its 1999 report, these seven characteristics were identified which describe Medicare as a social insurance program.[40]

- compulsory participation (Medicare Part A for hospitalization is mandatory; Part B, as supplementary health insurance is voluntary, but tied to Part A)

- government sponsorship (with administration through a combination of public agencies and private contractors)

- contributory finance (Medicare Part A financing through a flat-rate contribution by employers and employees, Part B through general revenue and beneficiary premiums)

- eligibility derived from prior contributions (based on previous and current individual contributions, with spouses of eligible beneficiaries also covered)

- benefits prescribed by law (with a uniform set of benefits)

- benefits not directly related to contributions (thus enabling lower-income people to obtain the same benefits as higher—income people)

- separate accounting and explicit long-range financing plan (Part A Hospital Insurance fund supported by payroll taxes; Part B

Supplementary Medical Insurance Trust Fund draws largely from federal tax revenues)

The universality of Medicare as a social contract, with coverage available to everyone 65 years of age and older, was severely tested in 1988 with the enactment by Congress of the Medicare Catastrophic Care Act. This legislation expanded Medicare's coverage of hospitalization to an unlimited number of days, eliminated coinsurance requirements for hospitalization, and provided other new benefits.[41] However, that bill was to be financed entirely by Medicare beneficiaries. As a result, a widespread backlash soon developed among the elderly on two counts—first, that these benefits were to be financed by their age group alone; and second, that more affluent elderly would pay additional premiums based on their incomes. This meant that 40% of Medicare beneficiaries would pay over 80% of the cost of catastrophic coverage. The reaction to this bill by the nation's elderly was so heated that Congress was forced to repeal the legislation in 1989, much to the surprise and chagrin of many legislators and the American Association of Retired Persons (AARP), which had supported the bill.[42]

The ability of Medicare to meet its original goals and social contract is now threatened on two counts—budget projections confirm the long-term non-sustainability of the program without major reform and cost containment, while out-of-pocket health care spending by Medicare beneficiaries already far exceeds levels when Medicare was enacted in 1965 and continues to increase. In its 2004 annual report to Congress, the Medicare Board of Trustees projected that the Hospital Insurance Trust Fund will be insolvent in 2019, that Medicare will grow from its present 2.6% of GDP to 7.7% in 2035, and will exceed the costs of Social Security by 2024.[43] Spending on Social Security, now about 7% of the economy, is projected to climb to 12% by 2030.[44] Some have called for increasing eligibility ages for Social Security and Medicare, and trimming benefits for both programs.[45]

Medicare beneficiaries are now paying, on average, about 22% of annual household income on premiums and out-of-pocket health care costs, compared to 15% when Medicare was enacted in 1965.[46,47] Medicare pays for only about one-half of these costs.[48] One might think that retirees are protected from these costs by health insurance through their former employers. Unfortunately, this is not the case, if it ever was. The employer-based health insurance system is unraveling, and many employers are cutting back, or even eliminating coverage for employees and retirees. About 40 percent of U.S. companies with more than 5,000 employees now offer retirees no health benefits whatsoever.[49] This trend has led Paul Starr, author of the classic 1982 book *The Social Transformation of American Medicine* and Co-Editor of *The American Prospect*, to this recent comment—"The old corporate America that took responsibility for workers' pensions and health care is dying, and the nation's political leadership has hardly taken notice of the implications."[50]

Eight of 10 retirees depend on Social Security as their primary source of income. In 2005, Social Security benefits for 47 million Americans will rise by 2.7%, but about one-half of this increase will be taken up by a 17.4% increase in Medicare premiums.[51] A recent projection by the Office of Management and Budget (OMB) shows that Medicare premiums, deductibles, and copayments in 2015 will consume 44% of a typical 65-year-old's Social Security benefit (50% for an 85 year-old).[52]

These trends and dire fiscal projections, combined with current and projected large federal budget deficits, raise the specter of conflict across generations in addition to perennial disagreement by class and income over potential reform alternatives. In a 2003 report of the National Academy of Social Insurance, it is recognized that the social contract of Medicare is subject to reassessment "against the reality of changing societal circumstances and competing needs." And further:[53]

> *"Because Medicare, like Social Security, is primarily financed by current taxpayers, it confers to those taxpayers the general expectation that they, too, will reap the benefits of the program when they become eligible in years hence. The program was enacted with the expectation of long-term endurance and people have developed a sense of having earned its benefits as a result of many years of paying into the system. Despite these symbolic features of Medicare, there is no explicit contract among generations defining Medicare's precise character or roles. Its sustainability over time depends on its continued political resilience. Medicare typically enjoys broad popular support, but ongoing political endorsement requires that current and future (potential) beneficiaries continue to identify with the program."*

POLITICS AND THE FUTURE OF MEDICARE

The long-term fiscal problem of Medicare is indeed a time bomb, especially because of changing demographics in the U.S. and relentless cost increases throughout the health care system. People 65 years of age and older are the fastest growing part of the population. Their numbers will more than double over the next 40 years, as shown in Figure 2.1. In fact, 20% of the U.S. population will be 65 years of age or older by 2036, double that proportion in 1972.[54] Within that age group, the numbers of people over age 85 will also grow rapidly, as shown by Figure 2.2. These marked changes are due to the impact of the "age wave," which will start in 2011 when the first of the baby boom generation (born after World War II from 1946 to 1964) reach age 65.[55] This sea change in demographics, together with increasing life expectancy and the growing prevalence of chronic disease, will seriously stress a health care system which is already under severe pressure from runaway costs.

Figure 2.1

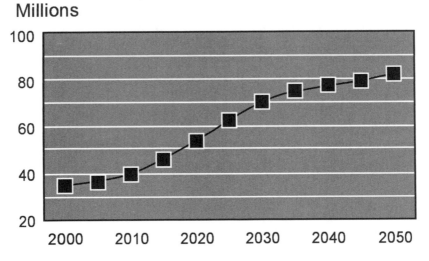

Population age 65 and Older, 2000 to 2050

Source:U.S. Census Bureau, Stastical Abstract, 2000.

Reprinted with permission from Institute of the Future. *Health & Health Care 2010: The Forecast, The Challenge.* San Francisco: Jossey-Bass, January 2003: 151.

Figure 2.2

The Coming Surge in the Population of Age 65 Years and Older

Number (in Millions)

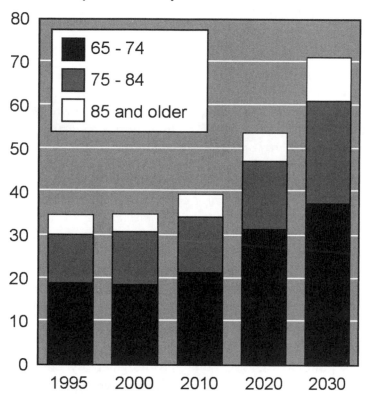

Reprinted with permission from Institute of the Future. *Health & Health Care 2010: The Forecast, The Challenge.* San Francisco: Jossey-Bass, January 2003:18

The surging costs of Medicare only mirror the rest of the health care system. The costs of health care are difficult to restrain, since they are driven by many factors, including increasing intensity of health care services, the impact of new technologies, aggressive marketing by suppliers and providers of care, a sizable amount of inappropriate and unnecessary care, high cost of administration and profits in a swollen private sector, and others.

Although long-term budget projections vary considerably and depend on what assumptions are made, the potential future fiscal crisis of Medicare is staggering in degree. The Congressional Budget Office has projected that federal spending on Medicare will grow by more than five-fold by 2050 to consume over 15% of GDP, surpassing Social Security by many trillions of dollars. This situation is even worse since the federal budget is in deficit at least until 2010 and the government is already borrowing more than $200 billion a year from Social Security and Medicare to cover its operating deficits.[56] This looming fiscal crisis has fueled a renewed and intense debate over the future of Medicare. As observed by Jonathan Oberlander in his recent book *The Political Life of Medicare*:[57]

> *"Medicare's future, then remains uncertain. What is certain is the transformation of program politics that has taken place. During Medicare's first thirty years, the program was governed by the politics of program management, which focused on rationalizing Medicare. Policymaking centered on technical issues of the most efficient means to pay for Medicare services. Political disputes were contained in a bipartisan consensus in which both parties accepted Medicare's existing structure and the need to control costs. The politics of management, however, has now receded, and with it so has the era of consensus in Medicare. Medicare politics is now transparently a battle of ideas about the role of markets and government in public policy. This is, in many respects, the same debate held in the 1950s and 1960s before Medicare's enactment, replete with the same sharp partisan cleavages, high-visibility politics that reach into national elections, a broad scope of conflict, and an engaged public. The new politics of Medicare is an echo of the past."*

Today's political rhetoric being promulgated by conservatives and the current Administration would have us believe that Social Security is facing an imminent fiscal crisis requiring prompt structural reform to assure its long-term viability. As with Medicare, privatization through personal accounts is being promoted which in both cases would shift considerable financial responsibility and risk from the government to the individual under the guise of increased personal choice and responsibility in an "ownership society." Meanwhile, conservative legislators and this Administration push for making recent tax cuts permanent, thereby building a case (in their view) to make further cuts in domestic programs. Many believe that the threat of a fiscal crisis in Social Security is overblown for political reasons, and that the program can be effectively managed without channeling large sums of money to Wall Street through privatized accounts. Largely missing from the public debate so far are other ways to manage the country's enormous deficit while maintaining essential programs in the public interest. Instead of revisiting funding priorities and ways to eliminate inefficiencies and waste in public programs, stakeholders and supporters of the market-based system continue to promote the illusion of greater efficiency and value in the private sector compared to "government-run" programs. Later chapters in this book will examine this premise in more detail and find that claim to be a myth.

The basic question today is whether Medicare will remain an earned entitlement program within a 40-year-old social contract with the elderly and disabled or be privatized with abrogation of that contract as the government reduces its obligation to the program. As in the 1960s, the national debate is again polarized, with a fog of disinformation dividing opposing views. A fundamental issue is the extent to which the private sector is to be involved in Medicare of the future, both in delivery of services and administration of the program. Liberals and progressives, together with nearly all of the nations elderly and disabled, strongly support continuance of the social contract established by Original Medicare. The current Administration, with support by conservatives, many moderates, and powerful economic interests within an enormous medical-industrial complex, promote a larger role of the private sector with market-based approaches to the "Medicare problem," despite a 20-year track record of their failure to contain health care costs.

There is a great irony and deception in the persistent drive by conservative interests and stakeholders in the supposedly competitive health care marketplace to further privatize the Medicare program. Private Medicare plans, as will become clear in later chapters, select out healthier enrollees and still operate with administrative overhead costs five to nine times larger than Original Medicare.[58,59] "Government-run" traditional Medicare serves as a reliable health care safety net for our most vulnerable citizens while maintaining higher levels of public satisfaction than private plans.[58,59] Thus the private sector, while claiming to be more efficient, is actually both less so and more expensive, a fundamental contradiction neither recognized nor acknowledged by private market advocates. It is difficult not to conclude that privatization of Medicare serves private interests at the expense of the most vulnerable in our society.

The Medicare issue goes to the core of the political battle over tax policy and the federal budget. As an example, the Center for Budget and Policy Priorities recently estimated that, if most of the 2001 and 2003 tax cuts are made permanent, the revenue lost to the federal government over the next 75 years would be about the same as the combined shortfalls of the Social Security and Medicare trust funds over that period.[60]

There can be no doubt that the Medicare program needs some major course changes if it is to be fiscally viable and effective over the long-term as an essential part of the nation's safety net for health care of the elderly and disabled. In its 1999 report *Medicare and the American Social Contract*, the National Academy of Social Insurance has emphasized the need to test all reform proposals against these values and public policy concerns:[61]

- **Financial Security**: The degree to which Medicare (under the current program or as a reformed program) provides financial security to the elderly and disabled (and their families across generations) as they incur costs for medical care.

- **Equity**: The degree to which Medicare is able to serve all populations fairly, including beneficiaries and future beneficiaries, regardless of age, health, gender, race, income, place of residence and personal preferences.

- **Efficiency**: The ability of Medicare to promote the use of appropriate and effective medical care for the beneficiary population, i.e., care that is technically efficient and minimizes the use of ineffective or unnecessary services, is consistent with the preferences of patients, and recognizes the real costs of services. Efficiency also includes the degree to which administration of the program is timely and responsive to the needs of consumers and providers, and the application of financing methods that are not unnecessarily burdensome.

- **Affordability over time**: The degree to which the costs of Medicare can be borne without diverting public revenues needed for other important public priorities.

- **Political accountability**: The degree to which the information needed to determine whether the program is achieving its goals is available, and mechanisms are in place to identify problems and institute corrective actions in a timely manner that is fair to all beneficiaries, to providers, and to taxpayers.

- **Political sustainability**: The degree to which the Medicare program enjoys the support of the American population, regardless of the state of the economy, political climate, or social atmosphere.

- **Maximizing individual liberty**: The extent to which Medicare policies, including incentives structured to promote efficiency, allow individual beneficiaries to exercise their own judgment and individual preferences in making choices about their health care."

These traits and values have to a large extent defined the social contract established with elderly and disabled Americans over the years. As to ways in which Medicare can be sustained and strengthened in future years, that is what the rest of this book is about. Since further privatization of Medicare is one of the main policy alternatives, we will review its history in the next chapter and then examine its track record in Part Two of this book.

CHAPTER 3

MEDICARE, PRIVATE MARKETS AND THE CORPORATE COMPROMISE

"If we cannot learn from history, we are doomed to repeat it."

George Santayana

The origins of Medicare and its evolution have been shaped in large part by the concept of "corporate compromise." Powerful private economic interests have accepted government-financed programs playing a larger role in return for acquiring new markets in their own self-interest. As will be apparent throughout this book, it also explains why costs of the Medicare program cannot be effectively contained and why the present public-private "partnership" is not sustainable in the long run.

This chapter addresses two questions: (1) what is the corporate compromise as illustrated by the politics leading to Medicare's two major pieces of legislation in 1965 and 2003; and (2) what are the major highlights of efforts to privatize Medicare over the intervening years?

THE CORPORATE COMPROMISE OF 1965

In the ongoing debate in the late 1950s and early 1960s over universal health insurance, as on previous occasions in earlier years, the medical, hospital and insurance industries strongly opposed any form of publicly-financed health insurance. Seeing government-sponsored insurance as a threat to the private system, they promoted government subsidies to private insurers as a better way to meet the health care needs of the uninsured. While the AMA remained vehemently opposed to Medicare as a government-financed entitlement program for the elderly, the hospital and insurance industries began to see that promising new markets could become available to them, especially if they could shape the way such a new program was to be implemented.

The political gridlock over Medicare was broken in 1964 when Wilbur Mills, as chairman of the House Ways and Means Committee, pulled three different proposals together, to become known as the "three-layer cake," including Medicare Part A (universal hospitalization coverage for the elderly), Medicare Part B (voluntary, supplemental physician coverage for the elderly), and Medicaid (an expansion of the Kerr-Mills federal-state program for indigent health care). By accommodating the concerns of the opponents, the combined bill gained passage the next year with strong bipartisan support. The private insurance industry was strengthened since coverage of the elderly and the poor relieved it of its worst health risks, allowing it to concentrate on insuring younger people at less risk and therefore more lucrative to insure. Hospitals could look forward to many years of generous reimbursement of their costs of care for a previously disadvantaged population. How the government was to pay physicians for their services to Medicare beneficiaries was hotly contested. The AMA lobbied hard for a liberal reimbursement system, voicing serious concerns of a national fee schedule as a "worrisome shift toward socialized medicine." The powerful AMA lobby prevailed as a "usual, customary and reasonable" reimbursement policy (UCR) was adopted. This liberal system was a compromise between a rigid fee schedule and "blank check" reimbursement. It preserved some physician autonomy and was flexible enough to allow wide variations in reimbursement for similar services from one part of the country to another. As we will see in later chapters, geographic variations in reimbursement have led to major problems for Medicare in terms of adverse impacts on access, costs, and quality of care. As a result of the passage of Medicare in 1965, physicians became well compensated for taking care of many lower-income elderly patients for whom they had previously rendered services on a charity basis.[1,2]

The Medicare program was modeled after the employer-based private insurance market in terms of benefits, administration, and fee-for-service reimbursement of physicians and other health care providers. When Medicare was established, employers and employees paid into the system as shown in Table 2.2 (page). Physicians and other providers were reimbursed by visit, procedure or other service provided. Medicare was initially administered by the Social Security Administration, later by the Health Care Financing Administration (HCFA), and in more recent years by the Centers for Medicare and Medicaid Services (CMS). From the beginning, however, the federal government has contracted out to private providers and intermediaries day-to-day administration of the program, including claims processing, provider reimbursement, and auditing.

Critics at the time of enactment of Medicare observed that the federal government was surrendering direct control over the program and predicted (correctly) that costs of the program were bound to become highly inflationary.[3] With its history as a non-profit insurance company, Blue Cross promoted itself as a "voluntary way" to safeguard the public interest, and was seen by the government as well qualified to serve as the main private intermediary for Part A of Medicare (hospitalization), with Blue Shield taking the lead for Part B (physician services).[4] The federal government agreed to rules that were very favorable to hospitals and providers. Medicare began to compensate hospitals based on their costs, as Blue Cross was already doing for-private hospital care. Physicians were reimbursed under the usual, customary and reasonable fee system (UCRS), which locked in wide geographic variations in fees across the country as a base for later raises.

As a result of the corporate compromise of 1965, Medicare was created as an open-ended entitlement program. Medicare beneficiaries were given open access to providers, who in turn could decide what services were to be rendered with very few cost controls built into the system. Because it was open-ended, the private sector gained both discretion and the opportunity to maximize its own reimbursement. This degree of latitude led one cynic to comment that "the result will be not so much the subsidizing of needy people as the subsidizing of an industry."[5]

CONTINUED EFFORTS TO PRIVATIZE MEDICARE

With enactment of Medicare began a long drive, continuous to this day by private economic interests to cash in at the public trough of the program. Ironically, in many cases they profited from playing both sides of the street. Thus, some insurers played a large and profitable role as fiscal intermediaries for Medicare even as they promoted advantages of the private health insurance market. The Health Insurance Association of America (HIAA) believed that it became "increasingly important after 1965 for the insurance carriers to develop an effective public relations story that will demonstrate to the non-indigent segment of the population why they are better off with private insurance than under a government program."[6]

This public relations effort by private insurers has become the basis for attacking the Medicare program. The underlying concept for privatization of Medicare has for many years been the premise (unproven by actual experience) that the private, competitive marketplace for health care offers more efficiency, cost savings, value, and choice than any government program. This concept has been promoted with such persistence in our society as to become a meme (a self-replicating idea or slogan which by constant repetition makes its way into common language and culture regardless of its merits).[7] Despite abundant evidence to the contrary, the frequently asserted claim by market advocates that privatization is a solution instead of a problem has become uncritically accepted much more widely than warranted by experience. For many, the debate is thereby narrowed to how, not whether, to privatize.

Social Security Amendments of 1972

With these amendments, Congress authorized Medicare to develop cost and risk-sharing contracts with federally qualified health maintenance organizations (HMOs). Payment rates were negotiated between these HMOs and Medicare on the basis of capitation. Set amounts would be paid to the HMO each month or year for the full care of a designated number of beneficiaries. Rates of payment for this new idea of managed care were set based upon costs and fee-for-service rates then existing in counties where beneficiaries lived, with wide variations from one area to another. Contractual payments were determined in advance, thereby placing participating HMOs at some financial risk. If an HMO's costs were less than these payments, it would be required to share its savings on a 50-50 basis with Medicare and was limited to a profit of 10% of Medicare's payments. HMOs were subject to retrospective cost adjustments and were fully responsible for any losses incurred. By 1980, however, only one HMO had contracted with Medicare on this kind of risk basis, as the private market found this level of risk unattractive.[8,9]

Tax Equity and Fiscal Responsibility Act of 1982 (TEFRA)

In an effort to encourage more enrollment in Medicare HMOs, Congress passed TEFRA in 1982, which liberalized payment arrangements for participating HMOs. Since it was still assumed that managed care would save money, payment rates were set at 95% of HMOs' adjusted average per capita cost (AAPCC), (Medicare's estimate of what Medicare would spend for fee-for-service care in beneficiaries' county of residence). HMOs were no longer required to share profits with Medicare, and could waive co-insurance and deductibles and offer additional benefits not covered by Original Medicare.[10]

Despite recurrent complaints by many for-profit Medicare HMOs that their payments were too low, reimbursement arrangements under TEFRA allowed many Medicare HMOs to generate sizable profits. They did so by marketing their plans to healthier beneficiaries and cherry-picking the market through favorable risk selection.[11] Medicare HMOs' costs were therefore often lower than those insured in the traditional fee-for-service program. Mechanisms to calculate adjustments of reimbursement for different risks were too crude to measure the extent of favorable risk selection. A 1997 report by the Prospective Payment Assessment Commission (ProPAC) estimated that risk adjusters accounted for only about 1% of variation.[12] In addition, many Medicare HMOs restricted care to their beneficiaries, as illustrated by one study which showed that beneficiaries who were disenrolled from Medicare HMOs incurred 160% higher costs of care in the traditional Medicare program over the next 6 months.[13] In short, by insuring healthier Medicare beneficiaries and rejecting those who were sick, and later disenrolling many sick beneficiaries requiring expensive care, Medicare HMOs could keep their costs well below what the government was paying and reap large profits.

By the end of the 1980s, it was becoming clear to some auditors that Medicare HMOs were costing the government and its taxpayers more than Original Medicare instead of less. In large part this was because Original Medicare was left to pay for the most costly patients while continuing to pay HMOs generously for the less costly care of healthier beneficiaries. A 1989 report by Mathematica Policy Research, under contract to HCFA, found that Medicare was paying 15 to 33% more for the care of beneficiaries in Medicare HMOs than in the fee-for-service program.[14] Nevertheless, the managed care industry continued to lobby for higher reimbursement, and many Medicare risk plans withdrew from the market during the late 1980s, citing inadequate reimbursement. In 1989, Congress considered but did not pass a proposal to raise the AAPCC from 95% to 100%.[15]

Although only 6% of Medicare's beneficiaries were enrolled in Medicare HMOs by 1994, Medicare managed care received a boost with the 1994 elections, when Republicans took control of both the House and the Senate for the first time since 1954. As part of the Contract with America, Republicans intended to transform Medicare from an entitlement program to one managed by the private sector, with a lesser burden on the government. House Speaker Newt Gingrich proclaimed, "If we solve Medicare, I think we will govern for a generation."[16] The insurance industry saw new opportunities in an expanded private market. Bill Gradison, as head of HIAA observed: "the thrust we see in Congress on Medicare and Medicaid is toward privatization. That creates enormous opportunity to offer our services to literally tens of millions of people who are not in the insurance market today."[17]

The Balanced Budget Act of 1995

The new Republican majority in Congress brought this bill forward in an effort to transform Medicare toward a market-based program, shifting the program from one of defined benefits to one of defined contributions. Instead of having their benefits defined by law, Medicare beneficiaries would receive a defined contribution from the government toward the costs of their care, with each beneficiary responsible to pay for any shortfall. Payments were to be reduced to Medicare providers, and it was hoped that 25% of Medicare beneficiaries would be enrolled in private plans by 2002. President Clinton vetoed the bill in defense of Original Medicare because of concerns that Medicare beneficiaries would pay more for less benefits. Despite the veto, however, the bill became a template for legislation passed two years later.[18]

A $30 million media campaign was carried out by the conservative Heritage Foundation between 1995 and 1997 to promote market-based solutions to the "Medicare problem," touting the Federal Employees Health Benefits Program (FEHBP) as a model. (We will consider the drawbacks of FEHBP in Chapter 15). This campaign was intended to "convince Americans that Medicare provides inferior medicine and poor financial security," and that "Medicare cannot be sustained for long."[19] During those years, the National Bipartisan Commission on the Future of Medicare met, but could not reach enough consensus to issue a report. Nevertheless, its two co-chairs, Senators Bill Frist (R-Tenn.) and John Breaux (D-La) did produce a legislative proposal calling for a "competitive" premium system for Medicare whereby beneficiaries could receive a defined contribution from the government to help them purchase a health plan of their choice (premium support).[20] The premise of the legislation, and of privatization generally, is that consumers can purchase better quality care for less if they are allowed to buy it from competing insurance companies instead of a government program. Yet, as we will see throughout this book, this assumption is not correct.

The Balanced Budget Act of 1997 (BBA)

This legislation put in place many of the provisions of the 1995 BBA attempt, including establishing a new part of the Medicare law—Part C— with the creation of an array of private options under Medicare + Choice (M+C). Three new types of private plans were authorized under the BBA— provider-sponsored organizations (PSOs), organizations of hospitals and/ or physician groups which contract to provide covered services and bear substantial financial risk; preferred provider organizations (PPOs), loose-knit organizations in which insurers contract with a limited number of physicians and hospitals who agree to discounted reimbursements and utilization review; and private-fee-for-service plans (PFFSs), plans which neither restrict beneficiaries' choices nor place providers at any financial risk. A demonstration project was also set in motion to test medical savings accounts, private accounts held by individuals for tax-deductible medical expenses. A complex new reimbursement formula provided for annual capitation rates, whereby one payment would be made by private Medicare plans to providers each year for all of each beneficiary's care over the year. These rates were to be set at the highest of these three amounts for each county—a blend of local and national rates, a minimal "floor" rate, or the minimal increase authorized by law.[21] It was projected that one-third of Medicare beneficiaries would be enrolled in one of the private options by 2005.[22]

Medicare HMO enrollment doubled between 1994 and 1998 as many seniors switched to private plans touted as better deals, peaking in 1998 at 17% of all Medicare enrollees. After that, it was all downhill for Medicare HMOs, as many withdrew from the market as their hopes for a continuing market bonanza faded. Although they blamed BBA97, which had reduced annual payment increases to 2%, a more important reason was their inability to contain their costs, especially of rapidly rising hospital rates and drug prices.[23,24] Nationwide, almost 2.4 million Medicare beneficiaries were dropped by Medicare HMOs, mostly investor-owned and for-profit, between 1999 and 2003.[25]

The Balanced Budget Refinement Act of 1999 (BBRA)

Faced with a mass exodus of Medicare HMOs from the market, Congress attempted to reverse the tide by passing the BBRA in 1999. This Act provided new incentives to M + C plans, including slowing the introduction of risk adjusters, calculations which would be used to adjust reimbursement downward to private plans enrolling healthier beneficiaries needing less care than sicker beneficiaries. Delayed use of risk adjusters would allow private plans to increase their profits longer by enrolling healthier seniors (favorable risk selection). Under BBRA 1999 bonus payments were also offered to new plans, and PPOs were relieved of the cost and burden of establishing quality assurance programs. Competitive pricing demonstrations were also delayed, putting off the time when private Medicare plans would have to demonstrate lower costs in a supposedly competitive marketplace. Competitive pricing demonstrations have never been popular with private Medicare plans, and have so far been a failure, as will be discussed in Chapter 11. However, despite passage of BBRA intended to entice Medicare HMOs to stay in the market and offer care, 53 plans reduced their service areas for 2001, and the managed care industry and its allies increased their lobbying pressure on Congress for even more payment concessions.[26]

The Medicare, Medicaid, and SCHIP Benefits Improvement and Protection Act of 2000 (BIPA)

According to the rationale that services and insurance are cheaper when provided by the private sector, the government should have been saving money. Yet in 2000, the General Accounting Office found that Medicare spent about 21% more on M + C enrollees than it would have on Original Medicare.[27] Despite this escalation—which was a clear indication that privatization wasn't working—Congress passed the BIPA in the same year aimed at making it even easier for the private sector to make money, by providing further increases in M + C payments while reducing their regulatory requirements. As with the BBRA, however, this bill was largely unsuccessful in attracting greater enrollment in M + C plans. Only 18% of the new federal money was spent on enhanced benefits. Over 500,000 beneficiaries were affected by withdrawals or reductions of M + C service areas in 2002, and there were only 6,500 new enrollees in that year.[28] Before exiting the market, many M + C plans had raised premiums sufficiently to achieve large profits.[29] Profits had been gained, yet only at higher cost than Original Medicare, and only by restricting services and engendering such dissatisfaction among Medicare beneficiaries to such a level that not enough people would choose it.

THE CORPORATE COMPROMISE OF 2003

In response to rapidly increasing costs of prescription drugs and frustration over the failure of Congress to add a drug benefit to Medicare over the previous six years, the Medicare Prescription Drug, Improvement, and Modernization Act of 2003 (MMA) was finally passed by a narrow margin in November 2003. The political process, both before and after its passage, reflects the same degree of polarization and compromise as in the 1965 legislation.

As the largest and most important change to Medicare over the last 40 years, the bill was fought from the right as an expensive entitlement and from the left, as too small a benefit responding more to special interests than to Medicare beneficiaries. Conservatives and some moderates pushed for a restrictive benefit, higher deductibles and privatization of the Medicare program, while liberals and progressives favored a prescription drug benefit for all seniors under traditional Medicare. The AARP threw its support behind the bill in its late stages, playing a pivotal role in its ultimate passage. As will become clear below, the AARP's interests in this bill conflicted with the interest of its members it supposedly advocates for. Again, as in 1965, corporate stakeholders in the present system sought to expand their markets at public expense, while continuing to argue the superiority of the private system. The drug industry fought to preserve its pricing prerogatives against any system of price controls, claiming that, if its prices were not sustained, the industry would lose the ability to fund expensive research and development for new drugs. This claim has been made by the drug industry on many occasions since the 1960s, and there is an extensive literature showing that drug companies grossly exaggerate their research and development (R and D) costs.[30-32] For example, the drug industry spent four times as much on marketing as on research in the 1960s,[33] while a 1998 study found that U.S. drug industry R and D accounted for only about one-third of marketing and administrative costs.[34] In addition, many "new" drugs are not really new, just slight modifications of existing drugs, and public NIH funds support much of U.S. drug research.[35]

Lobbyists descended upon Washington, D.C. in droves in an effort to shape the legislation to their special interests. The drug industry hired 675 different lobbyists in 2002, almost seven for every U.S. Senator and more than one for every member of Congress. These lobbyists included 26 former members of Congress, with 51% of the entire group having revolving door connections between K Street and the federal government. The drug industry spent almost $650 million on political influence since 1997, including lobbying, hiring academics, and producing and airing issue ads.[36] Some special interest groups were disguised under titles suggesting the public interest, such as Citizens for Better Medicare, a front group funded by the drug industry to oppose price controls accompanying a prescription drug benefit under Medicare.[37] The two largest health insurance trade groups—the American Association of Health Plans (AAHP) and the Health Insurance Association of America (HIAA) agreed to merge in September 2003, having spent over $9 million in 2002, and more in 2003 lobbying for increased payments and a larger role for private Medicare health plans.[38] As the Medicare legislation made its way through Congress in 2003, other health care industry lobbyists joined the process, lobbying an array of other special interests, ranging from improved reimbursement of radium implants for prostate cancer and faster coverage decisions by Medicare for medical devices to Medicare coverage for chiropractic services.[39] Between 2000 and 2003 when the bill was passed, the health care industry had spent more than $15,000 a day and $1,896 per hour on lobbying its interests in the legislation.[40]

As it emerged from Congress in 2003, the final Medicare bill of 678 pages ended up as a Christmas tree with many provisions unrelated to a prescription drug benefit, including increases in reimbursements to hospitals and physicians, and a demonstration project for further privatization of Medicare. The bill was fiercely debated down to the final vote. Democrats saw the bill as a give-away to the drug and insurance industries with only a meager prescription drug benefit. Many Republicans felt that the bill did not go far enough in privatizing Medicare, with some also seeing the bill as inflationary. At the end of the usual voting period in the House, the bill was losing 209 to 194 at 3:16AM. House leaders extended the vote by almost three hours, an unprecedented procedure, while Republican leaders brought intense pressure on the remaining voters to gain narrow passage of the bill by a vote of 220 to 215.[41,42] Voting was largely along party lines, but some Democrats crossed over to vote for the bill, including some legislators from rural states.[43] According to the Center for Responsive Politics, the 220 House members who voted in favor of the Medicare bill received more than twice as much campaign money, on average ($27,616) as those who voted against it ($11,308).[44]

The 2003 Medicare bill (MMA) is complex. Some of its rules are not entirely clear, so it is still uncertain how it will sort out. What is already clear, however, is that the main problem—the soaring costs and increased unaffordability of prescription drugs—was not addressed. The government is even expressly prohibited from using its bargaining clout to negotiate lower drug prices. Without any price controls on prescription drugs, the legislation is a boon to the health care industry, especially the drug and insurance industries. Almost all industrialized Western countries directly regulate the prices of prescription drugs, thereby gaining price reductions of 35 to 55% compared to the United States.[45] Most seniors will probably end up paying more for their drugs. According to an analysis by the Consumers Union, only 22% of projected drug costs over the next 10 years will be covered by the new drug benefit,[46] and there is evidence that drug companies have already increased their prices enough to erode most of the savings that seniors might have realized from discount cards.[47] The prices of the most commonly used name-brand drugs used by seniors rose 22% between 2001 and 2004.[48] Table 3.1 summarizes the major highlights of the 2003 Medicare bill,[49,50] while Figure 3.1 shows how the costs of prescription drugs will be shared between Medicare and its beneficiaries, including the now famous "donut hole" of coverage.[51]

In the aftermath of enactment of the 2003 Medicare bill, the political debate remains as intense as before its passage. Although the Bush Administration and many Republicans claimed victory as the 2004 election cycle went forward, many conservatives feel that the program does not go far enough in privatizing Medicare and that it will be too expensive. This is especially true after it came to light that the chief Medicare actuary, Richard Foster, projected its costs over 10 years at $534 billion, well beyond the $395 billion figure given to legislators before their votes, and that he was ordered by Thomas Scully, then head of CMS, not to share his budget projection with Congress.[52] Some Republican legislators who voted for the bill would not

Table 3.1.

Highlights of the Medicare Prescription Drug, Improvement and Modernization Act of 2003

Feature	Description
Drug Discount Card	Medicare beneficiaries eligible in May 2004 to buy a prescription drug card, which is expected to lower costs by about 15%
Drug Benefits	Starting in 2006, Medicare recipients can enroll in new benefit for prescription drugs. They pay average monthly premiums of $35, and a $250 annual deductible. The government pays 75% of costs, up to $2,250 gap in coverage ('donut') between $2,250 and $5,100 annual drug costs. Government pays 95% of costs after out-of-pocket annual expenses reach $5,100.
Retiree Coverage	Corporations offering qualified drug coverage will receive 28% tax exempt payments for drug costs between $250 and $5,000.
Low-Income Beneficiaries	In 2004 and 2005, low-income beneficiaries will receive an annual subsidy of $600 to reduce drug costs further. Starting in 2006, the premium deductible and coverage gap will be waived for beneficiaries with incomes up to $12,123 a year; in order to qualify for this subsidy, individuals can have no more than $6,000 in assets.
Administering the Drug Benefit	Private companies, including pharmacy benefit managers and PPOs, will administer the drug benefit, and will receive about $12 billion in subsidies.
Competition With Traditional Medicare	Starting in 2010, traditional government-run Medicare will compete directly with private plans in up to six metropolitan areas where at least 25 percent of Medicare beneficiaries are in private plans. If traditional Medicare's cost is more than private health plans, its beneficiaries will have to pay higher premiums.
Drug Imports From Canada	The ban on importing prescription drugs is continued unless the Department of Health and Human Services certifies their safety, which the department has refused to do for many years.
Health-Related Tax Savings Accounts	People with high-deductible health insurance policies—$1,000 a year for individuals, $2,000 for couples—will be allowed to shelter income from taxes.
Means Testing	Beginning in 2007, higher-income seniors earning more than $80,000 per year will be required to pay higher Medicare Part B premiums for physician services
Physician Payments	Planned cuts in physician payments in 2004 and 2005 will be canceled and instead a 1.5% increase is planned for each year, 5% annual cuts are planned for 2006 and beyond.
Rural Health	About $25 billion is earmarked to increase payments to rural hospitals and physicians, among others.
Home Health Care	Payments to home health agencies will be cut, but copayments from patients will not be required.

Source: Reprinted with permission from Geyman JP, *The Corporate Transformation of Health Care: Can the Public Interest Still be Served?* New York: Springer Publishing Company, pp 96-7, 2004.

Figure 3.1

Standard Medicare Drug Benefit, 2006

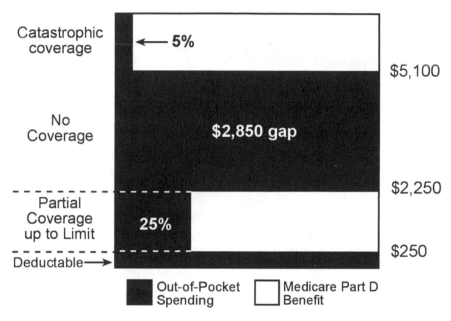

Note: In 2006, the standard drug benefit will have a deductable of $250. For drug expenditures above $250, beneficiaries face a coinsurance rate of 25 percent, until reaching a coverage limit of $2,250. If the program and the beneficiaries have combined drug spending over $2,250, the beneficiary is solely responsible for the next $2, 850 in drug spending, until reaching the catastrophic limit of $5,100. At $5,100 in total drug spending, beneficiaries will have spent $3, 600 out of pocket: $250 for the deductable, $500 for the 25 percent coinsurance on $2,000, and $2,850 for the "gap."

Source: Reprinted with permission from MEDPAC Report to the Congress. New Approaches in Medicare: Medicare Payment Advisory Commission. Washington. D.C. June 2004: p 210.

have done so at that budget level. Amidst the ensuing controversy over the gag order and threats to Foster's job, a legal analysis by the Congressional Research Service found that Bush administration officials appear to have violated federal law by muzzling Medicare's chief actuary, a government actuary for over 30 years.[53] The General Accounting Office went further in recommending that Scully's salary not be paid during the period in 2003 when he prevented Foster from communicating legislative cost estimates for the Medicare bill to members of Congress.[54]

Meanwhile, liberals, progressives and many moderates, together with consumer advocacy groups and others, have labeled the 2003 Medicare bill as a sell-off to corporate interests of little benefit to most seniors. Democrats vowed renewed efforts to protect the universality of Medicare benefits in the traditional program as well as making prescription drugs more affordable. Critics of the bill expressed anger over another budget projection not known at the time of the bill's passage—private health plans will receive subsidies of $46 billion over the next 10 years, more than three times the figure initially released to Congress.[55] Election year politics also clouded the ongoing debate. The Bush Administration was criticized for a misleading taxpayer financed advertising campaign over the claimed benefits of the prescription drug benefit, leading the GAO to find the advertising "flawed, but not illegal."[56] The AARP, caught in the middle of crossfire over a bill it had supported, had to defend itself as an advocacy organization for seniors against charges of conflict of interest. The conflict of interest was clear: about 60% of AARP's revenue, about double that from members' dues, comes from sales of Medigap insurance policies, its membership list, and related activities.[57] Table 3.2 reveals how the money flowed during the political evolution of the 2003 Medicare bill, though the initial $400 billion 10-year projection is already known to be falsely low.[58] In fact, the latest 10-year projection for the cost of Medicare's prescription drug benefit for 2006 to 2015 sets that figure at $724 billion.[59]

CORPORATE PROFITS TRUMP PATIENT CARE

As we have seen, private Medicare plans, even after cherry picking healthier enrollees, still cost more and provide less reliable benefits than Original Medicare. The mantra of privatization is efficiency—greater service at less cost. Yet with their built-in costs of marketing and lobbying, together with their profit mission, it is no surprise that they cannot compete with a not-for-profit government program without marketing and lobbying costs.

There is a fundamental irony and disconnect in the conservative agenda as relates to Medicare. Conservative legislators and the current Administration cry out against Medicare as an inflationary entitlement program which we cannot afford, yet fashion legislation which dramatically increases its costs and imposes scant cost containment provisions. They are advocates not of fiscal responsibility but of handing over nearly blank checks to the private healthcare marketplace. The Medicare Rights Center, a strong and effective consumer advocacy organization for seniors, recently

Figure 3.2

The Medicare Index

$400 billion	Estimated cost of the Medicare drug bill over 10 years
$139 billion	Estimated increase in drug industry profits
$14.2 billion	Additional government payments to the insurance industry to participate in Medicare
100	Members of the United States Senate
435	Members of the House of Representatives
675	Washington lobbyists who work for the drug industry
$21.7 million	Political contributions from the drug industry to Republicans in 2002 (74% of total)
$7.6 million	Political contributions from the drug industry to Democrats in 2002 (26% of total)
$2,400	Average elderly Americans drug costs in 2002
45%	Portion of his drug costs covered by the new Medicare drug benefit
45%	Average markup on United States drug prices relative to Canadian drug prices
3.1%	Average profit margin of Fortune 500 firms in 2002
17%	Average profit margin of the top 10 drug companies in 2002
2.6%	Increase in elderly Americans Social Security checks in 2002
6%	Average price increases in the 50 prescription drugs elderly Americans used most in 2002
50%	Retirees with health insurance before Medicare was signed into law
96%	Retirees with health insurance today
2%	Medicare administrative costs
15%	Average administrative costs of H.M.O.'s
$529 million	Compensation package, including stock options, for the chief executive of one Medicare H.M.O. in 2002
2.4 million	Number of elderly Americans dropped by an HMO in 2002
$25.9 million	Political contributions from the insurance industry to the Republicans in 2002 (69% of total)
$11.7 million	Political contributions from the insurance industry to the Democrats in 2002 (31% of total)
3	Number of months after President Bush signed the Medicare bill that it took the H.M.O.'s to receive more government payments to participate in the program.
25	Number of months after President Bush signed the Medicare bill it will take for elderly Americans to receive drug benefit

Source: Adapted from Brown S, Doyle S. Op-Chart The Medicare Index, New York Times, January 28, 2004: A25

had this to say about the 2003 Medicare legislation:[60]

> *(The drug)* *"benefit is a lost opportunity of historic proportions, which will deliver less help than it could and will damage the successful structure of Medicare. Next January, too many people with Medicare will still miss out on the medicine they need, and many older Americans and those with disabilities will continue to face the awful choice between paying for needed medicine and buying food, shelter and other basic needs. The drug benefit was designed with too much attention to the demands of the drug and insurance industries, and too little attention to the public interest."*

The corporate compromise of 2003 was very much like that of 1965 concerning Medicare inasmuch as Congress is still unwilling to hold private markets accountable to cost containment and the public interest. An intense battle still rages, without resolution yet on the horizon, over the roles of the marketplace and government in U.S. health care, as well as in many other areas of the nation's economy. Over the long-term, the Medicare program is not sustainable in its present form, given the current level of private exploitation of the Medicare market and the impending eligibility of the baby boomer generation. The next six chapters will examine more closely the track record of privatized Medicare over the last 25 years in an effort to better understand the need and urgency for public-private arrangements for the Medicare program to be renegotiated.

PART II

PRIVATIZED MEDICARE: CLAIMS vs. REALITY

CHAPTER 4

DO PRIVATE MEDICARE PLANS PROVIDE GREATER ACCESS AND CHOICE?

"Access to health care is a moral obligation of a good society."

Edmund D. Pellegrino, M.D.[1]

P rivate health plans have been vigorously promoted to Medicare beneficiaries since the 1980s with the promise that increased choice would bring improved benefits and value compared to the traditional Medicare program. We now have enough experience with these programs to assess these claims. This chapter asks two questions: (1) what is the overall track record of Medicare + Choice (M + C) in terms of access and choice; and (2) what are some typical patients' stories concerning how their access and choice of care are affected by M + C plans?

ACCESS AND CHOICE WITH M + C

Access and choice with M + C plans have been seriously compromised to the point that many observers have labeled them Medicare <u>minus</u> choice. M + C has been unstable in the marketplace, seeking out profitable markets, avoiding unprofitable ones, and leaving markets when financial returns are disappointing. About one-third of Medicare beneficiaries (2.4 million seniors) enrolled in M + C plans were dropped when many of these plans abandoned the market between 1999 and 2002.[2] Many of the withdrawing M + C plans had raised premiums enough to turn large profits before leaving their markets.[3] Even after a $1 billion increase in Medicare reimbursement to M + C plans in 2001, only a few of these programs re-entered the market.[4] Four in ten seniors had no choice of any M + C plan in 2003.[5]

M + C plans have been concentrated in large metropolitan areas in more highly-reimbursed markets, particularly in New York, Pennsylvania, Florida and California. More than one-third of the U.S. population, however, lives in smaller markets with limited choice of health plans.[6] Medicare beneficiaries who live in 19 states have no M + C plan available in their states.[7] Table

4.1 shows how little choice of M + C is available to seniors living in non-metropolitan areas not adjacent to metropolitan statistical areas (MSA's), and that even these small numbers declined between 1999 and 2001.[8]

Table 4.1

M+C Plans Available To Beneficiaries, By County Of Residence, 1999-2001

		Metropolitan		Nonmetropolitan	
	All counties	Center city	Other	MSA adjacent	Other
Any M+C plan offered					
1999	71.6%	99.0%	71.4%	37.7%	10.4%
2000	68.5	97.1	67.4	32.4	7.8
2001	63.9	96.5	59.4	22.4	6.6
M+C plan with drug benefit					
1999	61.5	92.1	56.9	24.4	5.5
2000	54.7	89.7	44.5	16.3	2.3
2001	46.9	78.3	39.0	8.6	1.4
M+C basic plan with an annual drug benefit of over $1,000 per year					
1999	35.8	58.3	26.8	10.6	1.5
2000	35.8	63.3	23.2	6.3	0.0
2001	22.0	42.2	13.5	2.5	1.0
Zero-premium basic plan					
1999	61.4	92.7	56.2	25.4	3.0
2000	52.7	90.0	39.0	14.5	1.9
2001	40.2	70.7	29.9	6.5	0.3

Source: Mathematica Policy Research analysis of basic contracts using Medicare Compare data.
Notes: M+C is Medicare+Choice. MSA is metropolitan statistical area. 2001 data are for March.

Reprinted with permission from Gold M. Medicare + Choice: An interim report card. *Health Affairs (Millwood)* 20(4), 131, 2001.

The Medicare + Choice program, mostly Medicare HMOs to this point, was comprehensively evaluated in 2001 by Dr. Marsha Gold, a senior fellow at Mathematica Policy Research in Washington, D.C. Her overall grade for M + C was a "D", if not an "F" concerning access, choice, and value. She has summarized the track record of M + C as follows:[9]

> *"While the aim of Medicare + Choice (M+C) was to expand choice, the choices available to Medicare beneficiaries have diminished since its inception: Existing plans have withdrawn from M + C, few new plans have entered the program from among the newly authorized plan types, greater choice has not developed in areas that lacked choice, and the inequities in benefits and offerings between higher-and lower-paid areas of the country have widened rather than narrowed."*

HOW M + C LIMITS ACCESS AND CHOICE

Here are five common ways in which M + C plans place their business interests at higher priority then serving the needs of their beneficiaries.

Favorable Risk Selection

M + C plans avoid sicker enrollees in two main ways—on the front end by marketing their plans especially to healthier seniors, and on the back end by disenrolling those requiring too much care. A single question "In general, compared to other people your age, would you say your health is: excellent, very good, good, fair or poor?" can screen out a five-fold difference in future health costs between the excellent and poor categories.[10] Asking Medicare beneficiaries screening questions about their health status before enrollment violates federal regulations. Yet a 1995 study found that nearly one-half of Medicare beneficiaries were asked about their health status before enrollment.[11] Two-thirds of seniors have multiple chronic conditions, while 20% have five or more chronic diseases, so it is quite easy through questioning to avoid enrolling sicker people.[12] Advertising by M + C plans has also been found biased toward healthier seniors, with important details buried in difficult-to-read small print. Many marketing seminars have been held on second floors of buildings without elevators not accessible by wheelchair, a blatant but effective means of screening.[13] A 2001 report by the Commonwealth Fund found that Medicare HMOs had only about one-half the numbers of enrollees with both physical and cognitive problems compared with the traditional

Medicare program, as shown in Figure 4.1[14,15]

Some M + C plans have been unapologetic about disenrolling Medicare enrollees unfavorable to their bottom line, then boasting of their enhanced profit margins. Two examples of this practice are the California HMOs, Health Net[16] and PacifiCare.[17] At the national level, the Department of Health and Human Services' (DHHS) Inspector General has found that M + C plans often disenroll sicker enrollees in order to avoid the expense of hospital care. Between 1991 and 1996, Medicare paid $224 million to hospitals for inpatient care of beneficiaries within three months of their disenrollment, more than ten times what Medicare would have otherwise paid to their HMOs through capitation payments.[18]

Figure 4.1

Percentage of Beneficiaries with Health Conditions, by Type of Condition and HMO Status, 1997

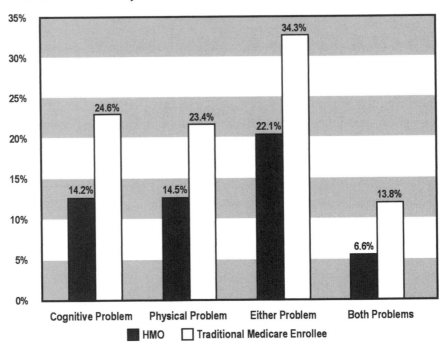

Source: Moon M & Storeygard M. One Third-at Risk: The Special Circumstances of Medicare Beneficiaries with Health Problems. New York: *The Commonwealth Fund*, September 2001, 12. Reprinted with permission from The Commonwealth Fund.

Bait and Switch

For-profit Medicare HMOs have often followed a predictable pattern of attracting new enrollees with attractive benefits (e.g., prescription drug benefit) and no premiums, gaining market share, then adding on increasing premiums, co-payments and deductibles while reducing benefits. This pattern of bait and switch is illustrated by the experience of Mr. B, which unfortunately is an all too common story.[19]

> **_Mr. B_**. *I have had diabetes for 60 years. In the early 1990s, I was insured by Medicare plus a MediGap plan, which treated me well. Because the diabetes clogged up the arteries in my legs, I needed two leg amputations. The insurance paid for everything, including two artificial limbs worth $6,000 apiece. But MediGap became too expensive. A few years ago its premium jumped from $100 to $150 each month, so I dropped MediGap and joined the Medicare HMO that had just come into our California Central Valley county. The HMO seemed great; there was no premium, and the medications were paid for. After the first couple of years, the HMO got worse. Now, the premium is $70 a month and I have to drive 30 miles to another city to get diabetes supplies because the HMO stopped contracting with my nearby supplier. The HMO doesn't pay for the cholesterol pills any more and they cost over $50 a month. The HMO doesn't even pay for my insulin. Since I've had my leg prostheses for years, I'm supposed to get new ones, but I'd have to pay a $950 co-pay for each one, so I can't do it. Now the HMO is leaving the county, saying that it isn't making any money, but I don't really care because it isn't doing much for me anyway. HMOs started out good, but then they got greedy.*

As premiums and cost sharing for M + C plans increased and benefits declined, seniors enrolled in these plans doubled their out-of-pocket spending for health care between 1999 and 2003.[20] Health care costs were already a heavy burden for the elderly and disabled in 2000, when average annual out-of-pocket expenses for the elderly were $3,124 and $3,870 for the (middle-age) disabled; that spending amounted to 21% and 27% of their respective average incomes.[21] Since about 22% of elderly households have annual incomes below $10,000 and almost 60% have incomes below $20,000 a year, seniors have great difficulty in coping with their increasing health care costs. Figure 4.2 shows elderly households' health care spending as a percentage of their income in 2003. As Patricia Neuman, Director of the Kaiser Family Foundation's Medicare Policy Project, testified before Congress in 2003, seniors are in "triple jeopardy" as their health care costs go up:[22]

> *"Those with low incomes are more likely to be without any form of supplemental insurance that covers Medicare's cost-sharing requirements; since those with low incomes also tend to be in poorer health and need more medical services, Medicare's cost-sharing requirements will account for a greater portion of their limited income if they use the necessary additional services; and if they do not use the additional services they need, their health is likely to suffer as a result."*

Figure 4.2

Elderly Households' Health Spending as a Percentage of Income

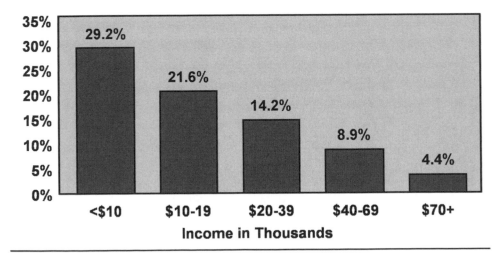

Reprinted with permission from King M & Schlesinger M (eds). *Final Report of the Study Panel on Medicare and Markets—The Role of Private Health Plans in Medicare: Lessons from the Past, Looking to the Future*, p 63. Washington, D.C. National Academy of Social Insurance, September 2003.

Trends in retiree health coverage add to the already serious problems U.S. seniors have in affording health care. Between 1988 and 2003, the proportion of U.S. employers with more than 200 employees providing such coverage dropped from 66 percent to 38 percent.[23] In addition, most retiree health plans have required sharp increases in cost sharing in recent years, with about two in five retirees now responsible for all of their coverage. The Employee Benefits Research Institute, a non-profit research group in Washington, D.C., now estimates that retirees will need to have saved up to $700,000 to pay for their health care expenses in retirement. Given present trends, Watson Wyatt Worldwide, a benefits consulting firm in Washington, D.C., projects that employers will cover less than 10% of their retiree health care costs by 2031.[24]

Lock-in Rules

The Balanced Budget Act of 1997 called for a lock-in requirement starting in 2002 whereby enrollees in private Medicare plans can make but one change a year in their plans, and that only between January and June. An enrollee cannot change in between July and December, regardless of individual circumstances. Here is one story illustrating the lock-in rules, which clearly work more to the interests of private Medicare plans than to the needs of their enrollees.[25]

> _**Mr. D** is a 65-year-old man from Massapequa, NY, who is enrolled in a Medicare HMO. After being diagnosed with throat cancer in November 2001, Mr. D was told that he needed another biopsy to confirm the diagnosis and then he would need treatment. He asked his primary care physician to refer him to doctors at a particular hospital that specializes in cancer but was informed that this hospital recently left his HMO's network. Because Mr. D cannot afford to pay for the cancer treatments himself, he was advised to disenroll from the HMO and purchase a Medigap policy for secondary coverage so he can get treatment at the hospital of his choice._

Fortunately for Mr. D, he was able to enroll in Original Medicare and get treatment from the hospital of his choice. If it were after June 2002, the lock-in requirement would prevent Mr. D from leaving his HMO to get cancer treatment at the hospital specializing in cancer care. The Medicare Rights Center has found that 80% of private Medicare HMOs provide incorrect information on these rules limiting enrollees' ability to change plans, and that most enrollees have little knowledge of their restricted choices.

Not only may many M + C enrollees find themselves trapped into an M + C plan when they want to disenroll during the second half of a calendar year, but they may also find that they cannot qualify or afford supplemental health insurance if they do go back to Original Medicare. Very few insurers guarantee issue to Medigap applicants, and most Medigap policies are underwritten with higher rates based on age and health status. Only 8 states require community rating, whereby all beneficiaries in a market area pay the same premium regardless of age or health status.[26]

Restrict Choice of Physicians and Hospitals

The traditional Medicare program provides beneficiaries with full choice of physicians and hospitals. Not so with M + C plans as this story shows:[27]

Mr. D. I have malignant melanoma. It can only be cured by cutting it out surgically and just in case it hasn't been completely removed from the body, it is treated with a series of interferon shots. But the oncologist on my Medicare HMO's list of doctors delayed by at least 3 months removing the tumor and nearby lymph nodes (which contained many tumor cells) and starting the interferon shots. So I left the HMO and am getting the interferon through the VA Hospital and a good oncologist whom the HMO wouldn't let me see.

That's only a small part of the story. My wife died on March 30, 2002 of breast cancer. She might be alive today if the oncologist her HMO contracted with hadn't delayed ordering an MRI that would have shown that the tumor had come back. The doctors were treating her for a problem in her hand when in fact the vertebrae in her neck were consumed by cancer. By the time the doctors found the recurrent tumor, too much time had been lost. Nothing could be done.

And there's more. For my melanoma, the HMO required me to see the same oncologist who had taken poor care of my wife. I went once but the doctor didn't take my melanoma seriously enough and I wouldn't go back. I appealed to see a good oncologist who was not on the list of HMO doctors in my medical group, and the HMO denied me saying that my illness was not "time sensitive." If living with cancer isn't "time sensitive," I don't know what is. I sent my pathology reports to another oncologist who misread the report, telling me it was normal when it actually showed cancer in a lymph node. He initially told me I was fine and didn't need any treatment. He was wrong. I know who the good doctors are and who are the bad ones. The HMO didn't give me the choice to pick the good ones.

The track record of M + C programs has been one of flux and volatility. Even if M + C enrollees find a physician of their choice on the plan provider list, they cannot assume stability of that choice. M + C plans have experienced an average annual turnover of 14% in primary care physicians, and turnover has exceeded 25% per year in the most volatile four states.[28]

New enrollees to M + C plans have often been given misleading or inaccurate information about their choice of physicians and hospitals, as the following patient vignette shows:[29]

__Ms. T__, who had Original Medicare, called an HMO in her area when she learned it offered expanded coverage for hospital care. When a representative from the HMO visited Ms. T's home, she specifically asked if her current primary care physician (PCP) was part of the HMO's network, as she had an upcoming operation and hospital services that were already scheduled. The HMO representative assured Ms. T that her PCP was in the network and that her upcoming hospital tests would be covered by the plan. Ms. T enrolled in the HMO but was later denied coverage for the hospital services she received. After being threatened by the hospital and its collection agencies for the unpaid bills, she contacted the MRC-HIICAP Hotline for help. An MRC counselor discovered that her PCP had never been a provider with the HMO and informed CMS of the deliberate misinformation given to Ms. T by the HMO representative. CMS granted Ms. T retroactive disenrollment from the HMO and her overdue bills for nearly

$1,000 were paid by Original Medicare.

Withdraw from the Market

As we saw earlier, about one-third of enrollees were abandoned across the country between 1999 and 2002 when their M + C plans left their counties (CMS, 2002). For-profit plans owned by large national corporations have been found to be two-and-a-half times more likely to exit a market than not for-profit HMOs.[30] Here is one patient's story, who had little recourse even with assistance by the Medicare Rights Center.[31]

> *__Ms. C__ has Alzheimer's and diabetes. Until June of this year she was covered by a Medicare HMO. Due to her weakening mental state, she neglected to pay her HMO premium for the months of March, April and May, which resulted in termination of her HMO in June. After receiving the termination notice, Ms. C called MRC, which contacted the HMO to see if it would reinstate her if she paid it the premiums she owed. The HMO representative said it would not reinstate her because it was planning to leave the county at the end of the year. MRC then contacted HCFA to see if would be able to re-enroll Ms. C back into the HMO. Unfortunately, HCFA said it would not be able to re-enroll her because the HMO had officially announced it was leaving Ms. C's county. Now Ms. C's only option is to sign up with a Medigap plan, which will impose a pre-existing condition waiting period of six months on her. This is unfortunate, as she has recently started dialysis, which is resulting in extremely high medical bills.*

When patients are dropped by M + C plans leaving their county, if they do nothing they will be automatically enrolled (or re-enrolled) in Original Medicare on the following January 1. In the meantime, they may explore whether they can qualify and afford retiree coverage from a former job or a Medigap policy, and whether another M + C plan is still available to them in their county. Lower-income disenrollees may qualify for Medicaid coverage during the coverage gap before enrollment in Original Medicare.

Most Medicare beneficiaries face a daunting task in making informed choices as they try to re-establish their health care coverage. One study of over 1,600 Medicare beneficiaries found that only 11% had enough knowledge to make an informed choice.[32] A 2001 study found that only one-quarter of new enrollees or switchers between plans knew what they needed to know to make the change.[33] Among disabled beneficiaries, three of four have problems with reading and one in three have cognitive limitations.[34] A recent report by the Agency for Healthcare Research and Quality (AHRQ) concluded that low reading and comprehension skills are linked to higher rates of hospitalization and emergency services as well as less use of preventive services.[35]

MEDICARE BENEFICIARIES HAVE CAST THEIR BALLOTS

Not only is choice of providers and plans often restricted with M + C, but ongoing volatility in the marketplace forces enrollees into a pattern of repeated reassessments of their choices as costs and coverage change. Many seniors and disabled people find their next choices confusing and difficult to understand. Although Original Medicare covers only about one-half of their health care costs, Medicare beneficiaries have left M + C plans in droves to return to the more solid rock of traditional Medicare. They have voted with their feet, as the drop in enrollment in M + C plans from its peak of 17% in 1998 to today's 11% clearly shows.

CHAPTER 5

CONTINUITY OF CARE:
HERE TODAY, GONE TOMORROW

With all the volatility and instability of M + C plans as seen in the last chapter, it is now of interest to briefly examine what the impact has been on continuity of care for the more than two million Medicare beneficiaries disenrolled from these plans. This chapter addresses two questions: (1) how disenrollment affect the lives and health care of Medicare beneficiaries dropped by M + C plans; and (2) what are the impacts of disruption in continuity of care on their future health care?

DISCONTINUITY OF CARE AMONG M + C PLANS

Discontinuity of care in M + C plans has been so common as to almost be the rule across the country. Texas, Florida, California and New York lead the list for disenrollments.[1] As we saw in the last chapter, M + C plans have gravitated to more profitable markets in large metropolitan areas, so that many rural states have no such plan.[2]

While the main reason given by M + C plans for their departure from markets is underpayments from the federal government, there are other reasons involved. There is incontrovertible evidence that M + C plans have been overpaid, particularly in view of their typical pattern of enrolling healthier people than in Original Medicare. According to the U.S. General Accounting Office, M + C plans were overpaid by more than $5 billion in 1998, even without factoring in their favorable risk enrollment.[3] Federal payments to M + C plans between 1998 and 2000 were more than 13% higher than would have been incurred by the Original Medicare program.[4] A 2002 report by the Kaiser Family Foundation found that for-profit M + C plans owned by large national corporations were two-and-one-half times more likely to exit the market than their non-for-profit counterparts. Another reason for Medicare HMO withdrawals identified by both the GAO and Kaiser studies, is their inability to recruit a sufficient number of providers, especially in smaller markets.[5] That many M + C plans cannot compete in the marketplace and still meet their profit goals is shown by the decline in plans contracting with the Federal Employees Health Benefits Program

(FEHBP) from 476 to 277 between 1996 and 2000.[6]

Here are typical patient stories as experienced by two patients who were dropped by M + C plans in different parts of the country.

- ***Mrs. P*** *enrolled in Vytra on December 1, 1998, which pulled out of her county only one month later. She then enrolled in CIGNA, but was not satisfied with her ability to access care in the plan and could not afford the monthly premiums. As a result, she disenrolled from CIGNA on January 31, 1998 and enrolled in United Health Care on the next day, which pulled out of her county on December 31, 1999. She next enrolled in HIP, which later announced that it is pulling out of her county at the end of the year. MRC staff gave Mrs. P information and advice about her options, including Medicare supplemental insurance (Medigap)[7]*

- ***Ms. S***. *I have very severe respiratory problems. I had measles and pneumonia when I was 7 years old and at age 34 had part of one lung removed due to complications of the pneumonia. In addition, I have asthma and several years ago I had multiple blood clots (pulmonary emboli) in my lungs, a potentially fatal illness. I've been blessed by excellent doctors and as a result, I am still working at the age of 75 even with my lung difficulties. I joined a Medicare HMO several years ago in a San Francisco Bay Area county; then I moved to a nearby county but continued to receive care from the doctors who had saved my life. Last year, my HMO pulled out of that county and I wasn't allowed to see my doctors any more. They call it Medicare + Choice but my only choice was to leave my doctors. I found another good physician in the county where I lived, but soon after I started with her she closed her practice, saying that the HMO was too difficult to deal with. So my medical care has been totally disrupted twice within a year.*

  It is hard enough to stay healthy when everything is going fine with your doctors, but it's a lot harder when the private HMOs get in the way. It was really hard to leave those doctors when the HMO left town. If you have a chronic illness as I do, one needs stable and caring doctors to care for you, doctors who know you and understand what you've been through.[8]

Physician turnover in M + C plans has been a major problem. A national 2002 study by the Commonwealth Fund found an average annual turnover rate of 14% across the country, with three states over 30% (Figure 5.1).

Figure 5.1

Primary Care Provider Turnover Rate by State, 1999

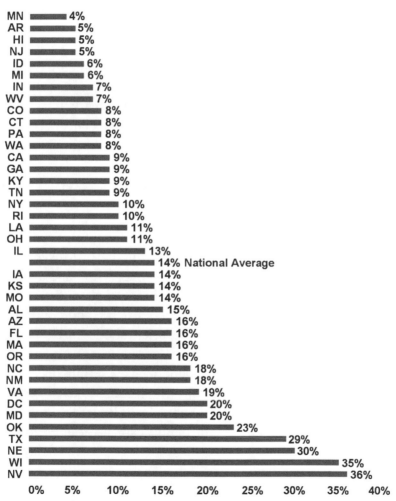

Primary Care Providers Who Did Not Stay in the Plan at Least One Year

Reprinted with permission from King M & Schlesinger M (eds). *Final Report of the Study Panel on Medicare and Markets—The Role of Private Health Plans in Medicare: Lessons from the Past, Looking to the Future*, p 37. Washington, D.C., National Academy of Social Insurance, September 2003.

Some local markets were much higher than that, such as in St. Petersburg, Florida, with rates as high as 61%.[9] Typical reasons given by physicians for leaving a Medicare HMO have included low reimbursement, denial of claims, delayed payments, and financial instability in large physician organizations.[10]

A 2004 study found that people who switch among HMOs have only about a 50% chance of being able to continue with their same physician.[11] Patients disenrolled from M + C HMOs in some areas may be able to retain continuity with their physicians through PPO or fee-for-service plans, but if so, can expect to find that option more costly. Most patients who are disenrolled from one M + C plan seek refuge back in Original Medicare, but even here, they may find that their physicians of choice will no longer accept new Medicare patients. A 2002 report by the Community Tracking Study, involving a nine-year study of health care markets in 12 major metropolitan areas, found that the proportion of physicians accepting new Medicare patients had dropped from 72% in 1997 to 68% in 2001.[12]

IMPACTS ON PATIENTS OF DISCONTINUITY OF CARE

When patients are forced out of an M + C plan, their first reaction is usually confusion. A 2002 study showed that one-half of disenrollees did not realize that Original Medicare would still cover them, and another one-quarter thought that they would lose health insurance altogether. Confusion then gives way to anxiety about losing access to care and continuity with their physicians and their financial insecurity about costs they cannot pay.[13]

About three in four of Medicare beneficiaries terminated from M + C plans have annual incomes of $20,000 or less and have worse health status than the average Medicare HMO enrollee.[14] Regardless of their next steps, their out-of-pocket spending for health care invariably goes up. As personal cost-cutting becomes a larger factor, many patients delay care and cut corners on their own medications, whether by not filling prescriptions or skipping doses.[15]

The impacts of forced disruption in primary care when M + C plans disenroll their Medicare beneficiaries has received little direct study, but we can infer from other studies that the impacts are negative. In a rare randomized trial of the effects of continuity, male veterans over 55 years of age were found to have fewer emergency hospitalizations, shorter hospitalizations, and higher satisfaction than a discontinuity group.[16] A four-year study of patients changing health plans within a large IPO managed care organization in a 10-county area around Rochester, New York, found that the first year after the change was associated with higher expenditures (especially for testing), less preventive care, and higher risk of avoidable hospitalization.[17] Still another study of forced change in insurance coverage found that quality of care was adversely affected as coordination and continuity of care was disrupted, with interpersonal communication and physician knowledge about the patients also reduced.[18]

Many Medicare beneficiaries dropped from M + C plans have little interest in risking further insecurity by joining any such plan, even if available within their county. Here is the experience of one Medicare patient, despite her favorable risk status for any HMO.

- **_Mrs. P_** *is a retired literary agent in good general health who has been on Medicare for over 15 years. Her husband died in 1976, and she continued to live on Manhattan's Upper East Side. She was then enrolled in the Oxford HMO. Because of the high cost of living there, she moved back to Great Neck, a suburb on Long Island where she and her husband had raised their family in earlier years. Soon after that, however, Oxford withdrew from that county, and she was forced to find a new physician. She joined another Medicare HMO, but it too left the county six months later. As she now says: "Apparently we don't fit into the profit picture for these companies—right now I just don't want anything to do with those plans—to me, the only one who's come out with flying colors in all this is Medicare. I don't want anything to destroy that."* [19]

AN OLD PROBLEM STILL NOT FIXED

Congress established the Medicare program in 1965 because the private marketplace was failing the most vulnerable citizens in the country. As we see from the above, that situation is still with us today. Public Citizen has this to say on the matter.[20]

"Instability is fine if we are creating a system to make deodorant or hairspray available to consumers. But when we are designing a health care system for the most vulnerable in our society, seniors and people with disabilities, that is a different matter. Here, continuity must be assured."

CHAPTER 6

COST CONTAINMENT and EFFICIENCY:
MYTHS vs REALITY

As long as Washington remains wedded to the illusion that market-based medicine will cure health care's woes, tens of billions of dollars a year will continue to vanish in waste, inefficiency, fraud, and in profits to companies that make money by denying care.

Donald L. Bartlett & James B. Steele, Authors of *Critical Condition: How Health Care in America Became Big Business—and Bad Medicine*, 2004[1]

From their inception more than 20 years ago, private Medicare plans have claimed their ability to contain costs and be more efficient than Original Medicare. This claim is framed within the larger premise, still unproven, that the competitive private health care marketplace is more efficient and provides greater value than government-financed health care. This chapter asks three questions: (1) what is the track record of M + C plans over the last two decades in terms of cost containment; (2) does competition really exist in the private health care marketplace; and (3) how does the efficiency of M + C plans stack up against Original Medicare?

PRIVATE MEDICARE HEALTH PLANS
DO NOT SAVE MONEY, THEY COST MORE

Although the proponents of private Medicare plans still argue their case for greater efficiency, value, and cost savings, their 20-year record is just the opposite. On its face, the case for cost savings seems to be a non-starter without subsidized overpayments from the government. These overpayments are percentage points above reimbursement levels through fee-for-service in Original Medicare, an obvious contradiction since overpayments don't save money. Private Medicare plans have to incur larger administrative costs than traditional Medicare for marketing and related activities, quite aside from the profits and return on investment that they require. Barbara Cooper and Bruce Vladeck of the Institute for Medicare Practice at the Mount Sinai School of Medicine in New York City summarize the problem in this way:[2]

"In a world of voluntary enrollment, managed care plans do not have to be just more efficient than FFS Medicare, they have to be a lot more efficient. To begin with, the administrative costs of Medicare's FFS program are small; combining Parts A and B, Medicare's retention is less than 3 percent. The traditional Medicare program has no marketing costs and it doesn't require any return on invested capital. So, for starters, setting aside for the moment problems of risk selection, capitated plans— with administrative expenses in the range of 8—25 percent—have to incur medical expenditures 10—20 percent less than FFS plans do just to break even. In most markets, capitated plans cannot attract enrollees unless they offer additional benefits, which also cost money, and some of the more effective devices for reducing utilization, such as tightly limited provider networks, also may discourage enrollment. Further, the administered prices Medicare sets for some of the services it buys on a piecework basis, such as inpatient hospital care, are sometimes lower than those that many plans can negotiate in the private market over time. Finally, the cycles of the federal budgetary process add a degree of instability in a field already characterized by high levels of entry and exit of plans from individual markets, which makes long-term profitability for private plans even more unreliable."

A report by Public Citizen has found that the federal government paid Medicare HMOs 13% more than traditional Medicare costs between 1998 and 2000.[3] Past efforts by Medicare to conduct competitive bidding for private plans "have been stopped dead in their tracks during the 1990s by someone in Congress, at the behest of the private health plans." A 2003 projection by the Congressional Budget Office (CBO) projected that private Medicare plans will cost 8-12% more than the traditional fee-for-service Medicare program.[4] If lower costs are factored in because of more favorable risk selection with healthier seniors enrolling in private Medicare plans, overpayments to private plans, including bonuses provided for in the 2003 MMA, are projected to be 25% more than traditional FFS Medicare.[5] Unfortunately, current methods to adjust payments by risk of enrolled populations in private plans are still inadequate.[6]

As a result of cost containment measures taken by Original Medicare over the last 20 years, it has been more successful in containing costs than private plans. Figure 6.1 compares the differences between Medicare and private plans since the 1980s in cumulative growth of per enrollee payments for personal health care.[7]

Figure 6.1

Cumulative Growth In Per Enrollee Payments For Personal Health Care, Medicare and Private Insurers, 1970-2000

Growth Index

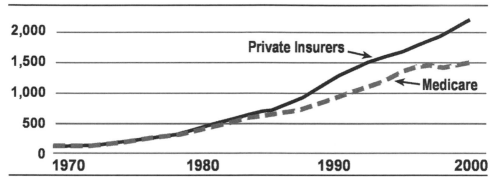

Source: Urban Institute analysis of National Accounts data from the Centers for Medicare and Medicare Services

Reprinted with permission from Boccuti C & Moon M. Comparing Medicare and private insurers: growth rates in spending over three decades. *Health Affairs (Millwood)* 22(2), 232, 2003.

Government agencies charged with oversight of the Medicare program have concluded that M + C plans cost more than Original Medicare. The General Accounting Office (GAO) issued this summary in 2000[8]

> *"The Medicare + Choice program has already been expensive for taxpayers... the vast majority of plans have gotten paid more for their Medicare enrollees than the government would have paid had these enrollees remained in the traditional fee-for-service program. Raising payment rates to a level sufficient to retain the plans leaving Medicare would mean increasing the excess that currently exists in payments for plan enrollees, relative to their expected fee-for-service costs. In areas of the country where there are few beneficiaries and providers are in short supply, no reasonable payment rate increase is likely to entice plans to participate in Medicare.... In our view, efforts to protect the viability of Medicare + Choice plans come at the expense of ensuring Medicare's financial sustainability in the long term."*

The Office Inspector General (OIG), based on its ongoing review of reports by private Medicare managed care plans of their adjusted community rates (ACRs) has found that:[9]

> *"(1) the estimated administrative costs on which reimbursement formulas are based exceed actual costs eventually incurred: (2) administrative costs that would not have been allowable under fee-for-service cost accounting have been charged to the program (including, for example, travel and entertainment costs and lobbying costs); (3) costs are charged to the Medicare program that should have been charged to commercial business, and (4) administrative costs included in the ACRs often cannot be documented under proper accounting principles."*

The Medicare legislation of 2003 continues with generous federal overpayments to private Medicare plans, under the new name Medicare Advantage (the successor to M + C) over the next 10 years. According to figures released by CMS in May, 2004, overpayments to private plans will amount to $4.7 billion in 2005 and $80 billion between 2004 and 2014. While rewarding Medicare Advantage plans for recruiting healthier Medicare beneficiaries, the federal government is not requiring risk adjustment of all payments (i.e., smaller payments for favorable risk selection.)[10]

MYTH OF COST CONTAINMENT THROUGH MARKETPLACE COMPETITION

Conservative policy analysts have argued for years to replace the solidarity of Medicare with a market-based approach. As Timothy Jost points out in his recent book *Disentitlement? The Threats Facing Our Public Health Care Programs and a Rights-Based Response*, this approach is grounded on several articles of faith—that there is a "moral hazard" created by too much insurance whereby people overuse health care services, that markets efficiently allocate the use of resources, and that health care costs can be contained by giving individuals more choice and personal responsibility for making prudent decisions about their own health care.[11]

Thomas Scully, who headed CMS until late 2003, fully subscribes to the promise of the private marketplace to restrain health care costs, despite incontrovertible evidence to the contrary, as reflected by these comments in a recent interview with Uwe Reinhardt, well-known health economist at Princeton University.[12]

> *"Medicare is a wonderful safety net, but it is a very flawed economic design, in my opinion. In many markets Medicare and Medicaid comprise over 65 percent of the payments to hospitals, and*

more than 80 percent in some physician specialties. When one payer is so dominant, it strangles competition and innovation and distorts the system. Allowing beneficiaries the choice to move to private plans (like PPOs [preferred provider organizations]) will give them more options, and that is the primary motivation for reform. But the ancillary benefit of increasing local market forces—generating multiple well-informed payers that will generate competition over price and quality—is an ancillary benefit that is nothing to sneeze at. Our aim in this reform is, basically, to place the administration of Medicare benefits on a competitive basis, in place of one big government-run program. We hope that once we're getting to the point where more local insurance companies make decisions and drive behavior, the entire Medicare system will be much more efficient."

A polar opposite view is taken, based on solid evidence of market dynamics around the world, by Robert Evans, a leading health economist at the University of British Columbia:[13]

"There is in health care no "private, competitive market" of the form described in the economics textbooks, anywhere in the world. There never has been, and inherent characteristics of health and health care make it impossible that there ever could be. Public and private actions have always been interwoven.

Current interest in market approaches represents the resurgence of ideas and arguments that have been promoted with varying intensity throughout this century. (In practice, advocates have never wanted a truly competitive market, but rather one managed by and for particular private interests.) Yet international experience over the past 40 years has demonstrated that greater reliance on the market is associated with inferior system performance—inequity, inefficiency, high cost, and public dissatisfaction. The United States is the leading example. So why is this issue back again? Because market mechanisms yield distributional advantages for particular influential groups:

1. A more costly health care system yields higher prices and incomes for suppliers—physicians, drug companies, and private insurers.

2. Private payment distributes overall system costs according to use (or expected use) of services, costing wealthier and healthier people less than finance from (income-related) taxation.

3. Wealthy and unhealthy people can purchase (real or perceived) better access or quality for themselves, without having to support a similar standard for others. Thus, there is, and always has been, a natural alliance of economic interest between service providers and upper-income citizens to support

shifting health financing from public to private sources. Analytic arguments for
the potential superiority of hypothetical competitive markets are simply one of
the rhetorical forms through which this permanent conflict of economic interest
is expressed in political debate."

A 2004 report of the Community Tracking Study, a nine-year study of 12 U.S. health care markets in major metropolitan areas, corroborates Evan's conclusion. It found widespread and deep skepticism that markets can improve efficiency and quality in our health care system, and identified these four major barriers to efficiency: (1) providers' market power; (2) absence of potentially efficient provider systems; (3) employers' inability to push the system toward efficiency and quality; and (4) insufficient health plan competition.[14]

Though the many M + C plans that have withdrawn from the market complain of inadequate reimbursement, they cost the government much more than it would have paid through Original Medicare even as they shift more costs to their enrollees through increasing premiums, co-payments, and deductibles. Figure 6.2 shows how average annual out-of-pocket

Figure 6.2

Beneficiaries' Costs Keep Rising

Medicare+Choice Members' Average Annual Out-of-Pocket Spending

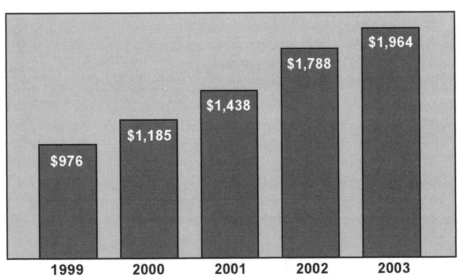

Source: Mathematics Policy Research Analysis of Medicare Compare

spending by M + C enrollees doubled between 1999 and 2003. For M + C beneficiaries in poor health, their out-of-pocket spending increased from an average of $2,631 in 1999 to $5,305 in 2003. By comparison, seniors in Original Medicare, who are sicker, on average, than M + C enrollees, spent $2,631 in 2003 (Mathematica Policy Research, 2003). Here are two patient stories that put a human face on these impersonal numbers.

- **_Ms. C,_** *now 80, retired from the Morgan Guaranty Trust Company, a unit of J. P. Morgan & Company, in 1986. The monthly deduction for her Medicare HMO from her $550 pension check almost tripled in 2002 from $50 to $129. She was forced to drop the HMO and take up a less expensive plan without any coverage for the drugs she needs for hypertension, diabetes, and high cholesterol.*[15]

- **_Ms. H_**. *62, lives in Forth Worth, Texas, where she is under treatment for leukemia. In January of 2002, her monthly costs under PacifiCare, a Medicare HMO, rose to over $1,000, Chemotherapy drugs can cost up to $500. She had to stop taking some medications. As she says: "The co-payments are killing us, literally. People will die because we're not able to get the treatments we need."*[16]

As we saw in Chapter 2, Medicare does not cover the costs of long-term care. Lower income seniors requiring this care need to explore coverage under Medicaid. Since almost 60% of seniors on Medicare have annual incomes less than $20,000, many millions cannot afford necessary health care, especially nursing home care, in a market of ever-increasing prices. There are several kinds of Medicare assistance programs (QMB, SLMB, Q1-1 and Q1-2) which can assist low-income Medicare beneficiaries in paying some or all of their premiums, co-payments, and deductibles if they qualify. Eligibility criteria include asset limits of $4,000 for an individual and $6,000 for a couple, with monthly income limits ranging from $716 to $1,238 for individuals and $958 to $1,661 for couples. However, there are a number of barriers which have prevented almost one-half of seniors who could qualify for these programs from taking advantage of this assistance. Many seniors who are frail or homebound cannot get to a Medicaid office or other location to inquire into these programs. Even if they can, they will encounter a burdensome application process which frequently takes as long as four to five months to receive benefits when eligible. A recent report found that only one-third of eligible seniors participate in the Qualified Medicare Beneficiary (QMB) program, and as a result commonly avoid physician visits, hospital visits, and filling of prescriptions because of inability to afford them.[17]

The Medicare Rights Center undertook a special project to educate Medicare beneficiaries about the Medicare Assistance Programs in New York State. In a later survey, they found that only 2% of eligible seniors actually applied for such assistance.[18] Many felt a stigma in going to a Medicaid office, as illustrated by this typical patient vignette.[19]

•   *__Mrs. B__ is 79 years old and lives in Yorktown Heights, N.Y. She has a monthly income of $850 and no savings. Mrs. B is enrolled in a Medicare HMO that charges a $50 monthly premium in addition to $45.50 for Medicare Part B. That was in 2000; premiums would be at least double that now. She is struggling to pay both premiums and still cover other basic expenses such as food and rent. Mrs. B learned that she would qualify for the SLMC program, but is reluctant to apply at a Medicaid office. She would rather struggle financially.*

EFFICIENCY OF M + C vs. ORIGINAL MEDICARE

Of all the claims made by M + C plans, the easiest to refute is their claim of greater efficiency over that provided by Original Medicare. The private Medicare plans are bloated with bureaucracy, duplication, higher administrative overhead, and inefficiency compared to the Medicare program, which reimburses providers of care for its beneficiaries through a single-payer mechanism. Original Medicare covers about 40 million American seniors, spending about 98 cents of every funded dollar on patient care, compared to about 80 cents for private plans.[20] While providing a stable and reliable benefit package to everyone 65 years of age and older, Original Medicare operates with an administrative overhead of about 3% compared to overheads five to nine times higher for private plans, as shown in Figure 6.3.[21] Major private plans in the U.S. employ 13 to 31 employees per 10,000 enrollees, compared to only one or two in the Canadian single-payer system.[22] The Community Tracking Study, after 9 years of study of 12

Figure 6.3

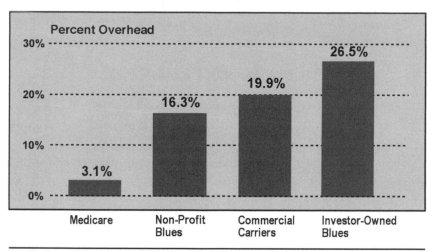

Private Insurers' High Overhead
Investor-Owned Plans are the Worst

Source: Schramm, Blue Cross conversion, Abell Foundation, and CMS

Adapted with permission from Geyman JP. *The Corporate Transformation of Health Care: Can the Public Interest Still Be Served?* Springer Publishing Co, New York, p 132, 2004

major metropolitan markets, has been unable to find efficiency in the private marketplace.[23] Here is one patient's story to illustrate the bureaucracy and duplication among M + C plans.[24]

- *Ms. W. called on behalf of her father who is trying to choose an HMO. He has a heart condition requiring him to take expensive medications and he lives in Queens, New York which has ten HMOs. Ms. W called a few of the HMOs to get a list of their formularies, but they all refused to send her the list. She was told by each HMO representative to call its Member Services Department and ask if her father's prescriptions were covered. However, when she did so, the first HMO she called left her on hold for almost 20 minutes before her questions were answered. Ms. W called MRC to see if there was a simpler way to find out if her father's medications were on the 10 HMOs' formularies. An MRC staff person informed Ms. W that unfortunately HMOs are not required to provide a list of their formularies to potential enrollees and, in fact, the formularies can change at any time. Therefore, even if her father's drugs are on the formulary today, they may not be tomorrow. The truth is that even though Ms. W's father is lucky to have a lot of choices, it is nearly impossible to understand them all.*

A MYTH EXPLODED

As we have clearly seen, despite the rhetoric about the supposed advantages of the private Medicare plans, M + C plans are less efficient than Original Medicare. Not only have they failed at cost-containment over the last 20 years, they have cost the government much more than it otherwise would have paid. Most M + C programs are for-profit; many are investor-owned national companies. They are in business to make money, and are accountable to their shareholders. In the next chapter, we will examine how much value Medicare beneficiaries receive in terms of benefits from M + C plans. In the meantime, this comment by Thomas Bodenheimer, internist and health policy expert at the University of California, San Francisco, is on target:[25]

> *"HMOs are businesses. We understand that businesses need to make business decisions. A business making business decisions is OK for selling TVs and automobiles. But a business making business decisions is not OK for providing health care to the least healthy people in the nation: our senior citizens. Health care for seniors should be based on their health care needs not a company's business decisions. Medicare privatization puts business decisions in charge."*

CHAPTER 7

BENEFITS IN PRIVATE MEDICARE PLANS: IS THE HYPE FOR REAL?

M + C plans typically market themselves as providing additional benefits and value compared to Original Medicare as a strategy to attract enrollees. But benefits are often changed over time, so that stability and reliability of benefits also need to be assessed. This chapter asks three questions: (1) what trends have been experienced over the years for benefits within M + C plans; (2) in what ways have M + C plans restricted benefits; and (3) can we anticipate that benefits provided by Medicare Advantage, M + C's successor, will be any better or more reliable than those of Original Medicare?

TRENDS IN BENEFITS OF M + C PLANS

A common pattern has emerged, especially during the 1990s whereby M + C plans market a broader set of benefits than Original Medicare in order to recruit enrollees, then steadily withdraw benefits while increasing premiums and cost sharing requirements for enrollees. A classic "bait and switch" tactic, it has been repeated over and over by for-profit Medicare HMOs. This practice is especially common among national investor-owned for-profit HMOs, which exhibit more commitment to their shareholders than the communities being served. Table 7-1 shows benefits not covered by Original Medicare in 2002.[1] Although several additional benefits have been added by Medicare since 2002 (egs., coverage of an initial physical examination at age 65, counseling for smoking cessation),[2,3] Table 7.1 accurately portrays currently available benefits under Original Medicare.

Based on CMS data, a recent report by the National Academy of Social Insurance found striking declines in benefits in M + C benefits across the country from 1999 to 2003. In 1999, 85% of M + C enrollees paid no additional premiums beyond their annual costs of enrollment; by 2003, that number had dropped to 29%. The average monthly cost-sharing burden on enrollees tripled between 2001 and 2003.

It isn't just that the cost of M + C plans skyrocketed. Their benefits also dropped as prices went up. Table 7.2 shows how many benefits decreased in M + C plans between 1999 and 2002, especially for preventive dental

Table 7.1

Products and Services Traditional Medicare Does Not Cover, 2002

• Outpatient prescription drugs (with limited exceptions)

• Routine or annual physical exams

• Hearing exams and hearing aids

• Routine eye care and most eyeglasses

• Dental care and dentures (in most cases)

• Screening tests (except for those specifically identified by Medicare)

• Routine foot care (with limited exceptions)

• Orthopedic shoes

• Vaccinations (except for those specifically identified by Medicare)

• Custodial care (help with bathing, dressing, using the bathroom, and eating) at home or in a nursing home

• Acupuncture

• Cosmetic surgery

• Health care received while traveling outside of the United States (except in limited cases)

Note: Medicare provides drugs not usually self-administered, oral anti-cancer drugs, drugs used following an organ transplant, erythropoietin for beneficiaries on dialysis, and injectable drugs used for treatment of postmenopausal osteoporosis. Screening tests covered by Medicare include bone mass measurement for some at-risk beneficiaries; colorectal cancer screening; glucose monitors, test strips, and lancets for all diabetics; diabetes self-management training for at-risk diabetics; glaucoma screening for at-risk enrollees; mammograms; Pap tests for pelvic exams (including clinical breast exams) for all women; and prostate cancer screening for all men age 50 and over. Vaccinations covered by Medicare include those for flu, pneumococcal pneumonia, and hepatitis B (for those at medium to high risk).

Reprinted with permission from King M & Schlesinger M (eds). *Final Report of the Study Panel on Medicare and Markets—The Role of Private Health Plans in Medicare: Lessons from the Past, Looking to the Future.* Washington, D.C., National Academy of Social Insurance, November 2003: p 55.

Table 7.2

Supplemental Benefits for Basic Plans in Medicare+Choice Contract Segments, 1999-2002

Weighted by Enrollment

Supplement Benefit	1999	2000	2001	2002
Prescription Drugs	83.9	78.0	70.2	71.4
Preventive Dental	69.9	39.0	28.6	14.3
Vision Benefits	97.8	96.2	94.7	86.7
Hearing Benefits	91.3	92.0	77.7	53.2
Physical Exam	100.0	100.0	100.0	100.0
Podiatry Benefits	26.9	28.20	29.4	26.0
Chiropractic Benefits	20.9	6.8	6.0	3.5
Number of Contract Segments/Number of Enrollees	6,254,616	6,094,767	5,577,787	4,937,106

Note: Enrollment for 1999-2001 is from March of each year. Enrollment for 2002 is from September 2001 and does not include enrollee switching due to changes in benefits, premiums, and/or withdrawals.

Source: Achman and Gold 2002b.

Reprinted with permission from King M & Schlesinger M (eds). *Final Report of the Study Panel on Medicare and Markets—The Role of Private Health Plans in Medicare: Lessons from the Past, Looking to the Future.* Washington, D.C.: National Academy of Social Insurance, November 2003: p 33.

and hearing benefits.[4] Prescription drug benefits fell from 84% of M + C enrollees in 1999 to 69% in 2003, and this drug benefit became less all the time, with 48% of enrollees having drug coverage less than $500 in 2003.[5]

HOW M + C PLANS RESTRICT BENEFITS

Recall that M + C stands for Medicare plus Choice, meaning recipients are to get more than they got under Original Medicare. That is the promise of privatization. Yet the reality is a narrowing of choice. The two main ways by which M + C plans restrict benefits are by progressive cuts in the menu of benefits for all enrollees or denying individual enrollee claims. Here are some examples which illustrate these practices, which unfortunately represent the norm, not the exception.

Cutting Benefits

Most M + C plans initially cover a range of services not covered by Original Medicare, often including free eyeglasses, dental care, and a limited prescription drug benefit. Then the cutbacks start.

* **Mr. M**, *a 81-year-old resident of Coalinga, California signed up for the California Blue Cross M + C plan in 1998 "to save ourselves some money and get the benefits." Three months later, the plan stopped his free drugs, eyeglasses and dental benefits and added a $65 monthly premium. His response: "We let our good (Medigap) policy go and signed up with this. We didn't think that after three months they were going to start raising prices." Mr. M then found himself facing prohibitive costs of restoring the previous coverage he once had.*[6]

It is little wonder that the number of people enrolling in M + C began to level off as news spread of the disappointments of many of those who had done so.

Mental health benefits are a particular problem throughout the health care system. Private insurers have long feared escalating demand for mental health services if too much coverage is offered, as well as adverse selection if they attract too many people needing mental health care. The Mental Health Parity Act was passed by Congress in 1996 as the Domenici-Wellstone amendment to an appropriation bill in an effort to alleviate disparities in coverage between general medical care and mental health services. For example, it prohibited employer-based health plans from imposing lifetime caps and annual reimbursement ceilings for mental health services, but there was still leeway for health plans to drop mental health coverage altogether or place annual day and visit limitations on covered services.[7]

Despite passage of the Mental Health Parity Act, there is still considerable evidence that many M + C plans severely restrict mental health benefits to the point of compromising access to necessary care. Mental health parity laws can be readily skirted by insurers through "carve outs," whereby an HMO contracts to provide mental health services, then subcontracts to a for-profit behavioral health company to provide that care. Commenting on this situation, Dr. Rodrigo Munoz, psychiatrist and president of the San Diego County Medical Society has observed: "The only way these firms can make money is by making it virtually impossible for those in need to get treatment, visits to psychiatrists are limited in number and time (typically just 20 minutes) and patients are often prematurely discharged from hospitals without arrangements for adequate follow-up."[8] As a result of systemic disparities throughout the health care system between mental health care and general medical care, it is estimated that up to two-thirds of older adults living in the community who need psychiatric services do not receive them.[9]

But whether in mental health or general medical care just how do M + C plans restrict or deny services?

Denial of Services

There are many iterations of how M + C plans restrict and deny services to their enrollees, even while increasing their costs, as illustrated by these varied patient experiences.

- *Mrs. W: I am the daughter of a Medicare HMO patient, Mrs. W. She was too sick to talk, so I will tell her story. She has incurable anemia which requires a special type of regular blood transfusions and which has now turned into leukemia. In our county there is an excellent hematologist who gave the transfusions without any problem. The HMO stopped contracting with this hematologist and my mother tried other hematologists with terrible consequences. Also, she had to go to a hospital which did not know how to use the special equipment needed for my mother's transfusions, creating numerous complications. I've learned that choice of doctor and hospitals are terribly important.*

  In 2002, the HMO started charging a $200 copayment for each transfusion; with at least 15 transfusions each year that cost us $3,000 last year that the HMO did not cover. In addition, medications last year cost $3,200 not paid for by the HMO. And the HMO didn't cover the chemotherapy she needed which was another $2,200 per month. All this is in addition to the HMO monthly premium and the Medicare Part B premium.

All the problems we have had with the HMO have left me, her daughter, exhausted. Once I was on the phone for 8 hours trying to talk to the HMO. Our family has worked hard all our lives and these HMOs have millions or billions in the bank.

Finally, we decided to leave the HMO because we weren't getting anything but trouble. My mother has switched to traditional Medicare plus a Medi-Gap plan at $373 per month without any drug coverage, but they do seem to pay for the chemotherapy that used to cost $2,200 each month. My mother has returned to the good hematologist, and she is feeling a lot better. We now have our choice, and we hope we can afford the cost. [10]

- *__Mr. K.__ I live in one of southern California's inland counties. I developed prostate cancer and went to the urologist in my Medicare HMO. He insisted on putting radioactive pellets in my diseased prostate, but that's not the treatment I wanted. I spent some time reading about the various treatments and talking to people who had experienced them. I chose a different treatment which I felt would work and have few side effects. Since the HMO wouldn't pay for it, it would have cost me thousands of dollars.*

  I left the HMO, joined a Med-Gap plan, and got the treatment I chose without having to pay. I feel fine now. The Medi-Gap plan costs $182 per month without any drug coverage. I spend an additional $200 per month for medications. In spite of these expenses, I'm satisfied. I don't like Medicare + Choice because it doesn't give you a choice. [11]

__Ms. J.__ I have multiple sclerosis and I use a wheelchair for mobility. My Medicare HMO threatened to leave this northern California county and changed its mind. But it doesn't matter much because each year its premiums go up and its coverage goes down. I was on a series of injections that many patients with multiple sclerosis use. Last year I was told the co-payment for the injections would go up from $30 to $200 per month. I'm on Social Security Disability and can't afford that. So I stopped the injections. I don't know *how that will affect my illness. I actually called up the HMO to complain and their response: "You're lucky we didn't leave the county yet."*

People with my disability need a lot of durable medical equipment. There is a device called a standing frame which helps me to stand up, it reduces the spasticity in my legs, and it allows me to bear weight which is crucial to preventing osteoporosis—a major problem for people with difficulty walking. The HMO wouldn't pay for it. A well-functioning wheelchair is one of the most important things in my life. The wheelchairs last a few years and then often need to be replaced. Thank goodness I got my wheelchair in 2001 when there was no co-pay. Starting in 2002, the HMO changed a co-pay of 20%, which would be $2,400.

Each year I calculate my costs with and without the HMO and then decide whether to re-enroll. It used to be an advantage to be in the HMO, but now, it may not be worth it.[12]

WILL MEDICARE ADVANTAGE PROVIDE BETTER BENEFITS?

In the aftermath of passage to the Medicare Prescription Drug, Improvement and Modernization Act of 2003 (MMA), as described in Chapter 3, new promises are being made by private Medicare plans for improved benefits and lower premiums. MMA will provide $46 billion in new subsidies to Medicare Advantage plans over the next ten years in an effort to reach a goal of enrolling 34% of Medicare beneficiaries in a private plan. Federal overpayments of $4.7 billion will be made to private Medicare plans in 2005 without any assurances that they will apply these payments to improved benefits.[13] CMS increased its payments to private Medicare health plans in early 2004 by a record 10.6% average increase. Reminiscent of promises made by M + C plans 10 and 15 years earlier, Karen Ignagni, president of the American Association of Health Plans, asserts "millions of beneficiaries will receive better benefits, lower premiums and expanded choices in 2004 as a result of the Medicare legislation."[14]

Many private Medicare plans, with their new subsidies in hand, have now announced plans to reduce premiums and consider increasing benefits.[15] But it is just a matter of time when these overly generous federal overpayments will end. Based on the track record of M + C plans, we can anticipate that Medicare Advantage plans will also cut benefits and increase premiums when that occurs. We need to recall that only a few M + C plans increased benefits or re-entered the market even after a $1 billion increase in Medicare payments in 2001.[16]

Early reports suggest that Medicare Advantage plans will fall far short of their subsidized claims. A recent study of PPOs by the Government Accountability Office (GAO), for example, found them to be more expensive for both patients and the taxpayer while limiting choice of providers offering routine physical examinations, dental care, skilled nursing and home health care. Medicare spent $650 to $750 more each year for each beneficiary enrolled in these private plans than it would have paid for the same patients under traditional Medicare.[17]

THE PROMISES OF PRIVATIZED MEDICARE RING HOLLOW

These last 4 chapters have exposed the rhetoric of greater choice, lower cost and greater efficiency through privatization to a harsh light of reality. Private enterprise was incapable of providing these promised advantages prior to 1965. Medicare was enacted as a solution to the problems wrought by "free enterprise." Today, 40 years later, the promises remain the same, and so unfortunately do the failures: patients left struggling with confusing options or who are shut out of care, or who face rising costs they can't afford. Meanwhile the government throws more and more money at the problems, in the vain hope that subsidizing private enterprise will one day achieve the promised efficiencies, choices and cost reductions. Having considered access, choice, costs and benefits, where we have not found clear-cut stable advantages of private Medicare plans over Original Medicare, it is now time to consider in the next chapter whether M + C plans have provided added value through better quality of care.

CHAPTER 8

QUALITY OF CARE: ANOTHER MYTH OF PRIVATIZED MEDICARE

"Our decade-old experiment with market medicine is a failure. Investor-owned plans have worse quality than non-profits, and non-profits are increasingly forced to mimic the for-profits. It's time to end our race to the bottom in health care and implement nationwide quality improvement and universal coverage through single-payer national health insurance." [1]

Ida Hellander, executive director of Physicians for a National Health Program (PNHP)

The centerpiece of the marketing message of private Medicare plans is that they can offer more choice and value, better customized to Medicare beneficiaries' needs than Original Medicare. The implication is also that quality of care may be improved through greater choice. We saw in Chapter 4 that increased choice in M + C plans is fictional, that choice is actually limited in these plans. But aside from choice, how has the quality of care fared? If it were improved, perhaps that would make up for less choice? But has it?

This chapter addresses two questions: (1) what is the track record of M + C, particularly for-profit plans, in terms of quality of care; and (2) how is quality of care frequently compromised in M + C plans?

QUALITY OF CARE IN M + C PLANS

While comparisons between quality of care in M + C plans and Original Medicare have not yet received the extent of study that the matter deserves, there is a substantial body of evidence that calls quality of care in M + C, especially investor-owned plans, into serious question. Here are some major studies which give reason for alarm:

• Undertreatment in for-profit HMOs was especially common during the 1980s; an administrator of a Florida-based Medicare HMO (International Medical Centers, Inc) was fired after blowing the whistle to his superiors about 130 major quality problems [2]

- Declines in physical health over a four-year period were found in 54% of chronically ill Medicare patients in HMOs, compared to 28% in traditional fee-for-service (FFS) Medicare[3]

- A large study in South Florida between 1990 and 1993 found that Medicare beneficiaries who were disenrolled from Medicare HMOs needed inpatient hospital care at 180% of the rate for beneficiaries enrolled in Original Medicare during the first year after their disenrollment (Figure 8.1). Conversely, M + C enrollees were hospitalized at only 66% of the rate for FFS Medicare as M + C plans took steps to avoid the costs of hospitalization.[4]

- A 1997 report of a study compared 19 Medicare HMOs in 12 states with FFS Medicare. It found that when seniors enrolled

Figure 8.1

Use of inpatient services by Medicare beneficiaries who switched from the Fee-For-Sevice System to HMOs (HMO Enrollment Group), and those who switched from HMOs to the Fee-For-Service System (HMO-Disenrollment Group).

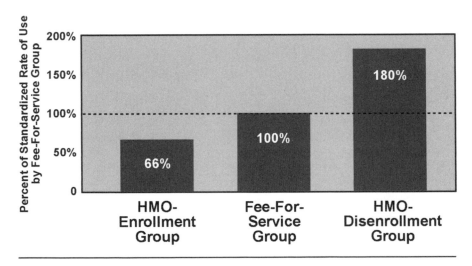

Rates of use are shown as percentages of the standardized rate of use by the fee-for-service group (100%).

Reprinted with permission from Morgan RO, Virnig BA, De Vito CA & Persily NA. The Medicare-HMO revolving door—the healthy go in and the sick go out. *New England Journal of Medicine* 337(3):173, 1997.

in the HMOs were hospitalized for stroke, compared to their counterparts in FFS Medicare, they were much more likely to be discharged to nursing homes instead of to rehabilitation hospitals or units for the preferred next stage of treatment.[5]

• A large national study of 329 U.S. HMOs, three-quarters of which were for-profit and investor-owned, analyzed the results of their reports to the National Committee for Quality Assurance (NCQA); investor-owned HMOs scored worse than their not-for-profit counterparts on all 14 quality-of-care measures, including a 27% lower rate of eye examinations for patients with diabetes and a 16% lower rate for use of beta-blockers, a critically important treatment after myocardial infarction. The more the profit incentive, the worse the care delivered, precisely the reverse of what was claimed by supporters of privatization.[6]

• Another national study of 182 private HMOs with Medicare contracts found that for-profit and nationally affiliated plans scored worse on most outcomes studied than other plans; ratings included consumers' overall ratings of the plan, personal physicians, overall care, and specialist care[7]

• Yet another study compared FFS Medicare against Medicare HMOs by 11 primary care indicators, including access, continuity and integration of care and quality of physician-patient interaction; for 9 of these 11 indicators, Medicare HMOs scored worse[8]

One recent study might appear to contradict the above trend. A 2004 report suggests that quality of care may be more comparable between for-profit and not-for-profit Medicare health plans. In a large study of over 3 million Medicare beneficiaries comparing the use of high-cost procedures, the investigators were surprised to find that the for-profit plans had higher rates than not-for-profit plans for 2 of the 12 procedures studied, and had lower rates for none. These procedures included such common procedures as cardiac catheterization, coronary artery bypass grafting, carotid endarterectomy, and total hip replacement.[9] Some may point to this one study favoring for-profit plans but it is skewed to compare only the highest quality ones against not-for-profit, weeding out those who would bring the averages down. Most studies of quality of care in M + C plans are based on analysis of <u>voluntary</u>

NCQA reports. A 2002 report found that NCQA reports are biased toward higher scores, since low-quality HMOs are more than three times as likely as higher quality HMOs to stop reporting quality data to the NCQA; non-reporters have been found to fall on the for-profit end of the spectrum.[10]

Despite this mountain of evidence some argue that not enough study has been done. In its comprehensive 2003 report, The Study Panel on Medicare and Markets concluded that not enough is yet known about quality of care in either Original Medicare or M + C plans. In the panel's words: "...none of the current mechanisms for monitoring quality under either original Medicare or M + C can measure certain crucial dimensions of practice, such as errors in treatment, selection of appropriate venues for treatment, or adequate coordination of care for beneficiaries with multiple chronic conditions."[11] At the same time, however, there is abundant evidence, as noted by the above examples, to conclude that there is a tendency for investor-owned HMOs, in their pursuit of financial bottom lines, to compromise quality of care compared to their not-for-profit counterparts. This pattern extends across the healthcare system to include hospitals, nursing homes, dialysis centers, and mental health centers (Table 8.1).[12]

Table 8.1

Investor-Owned Care

Comparative Examples vs. Not-For-Profit Care

Hospitals	Costs 3-13% higher, with higher overhead, fewer nurses and death rates 6-7% higher;[13-18] recent systematic review and meta-analysis found 19% higher costs in for-profit hospitals.[19]
Nursing Homes	Lower staffing levels and worse quality of care (30% committed [20] violations which caused death or life-threatening harm to patients.
Dialysis Centers	Death rates 30% higher, with 26% less use of transplants. [21-22]
Mental Health Centers	Medicare expelled 80 programs after investigations found that 91% of claims were fraudulent;[23] for-profit behavioral health companies impose restrictive barriers and limits to care (eg, premature discharge from hospitals without adequate outpatient care).[24]

Source: Geyman J.P The corporate transformation of medicine and its impact on costs and access to care. J Am Board Fam Pract 16(5): 449, 2003. Reprinted with permission from the American Board of Family Practice, Lexington, KY

HOW M + C PLANS CAN COMPROMISE QUALITY OF CARE

Here are some common ways in which M + C plans, especially those on the for-profit end of the spectrum, frequently compromise their quality of care.

Denial of services

As discussed earlier in chapter 7, this is an everyday task for physician administrators in many for-profit HMOs. As part of her orientation to a "medical consultant" job with a large investor-owned HMO in the 1990s, Dr. Linda Peeno, a general internist, received this orientation from an accountant with the HMO: "We take in a premium; we use about 10—15% to run the business, and we try to keep as much as possible of the rest. Your job is to help us do that." After four years in various administrative and executive positions for several HMOs, Dr. Peeno left the managed care industry to pursue a new career in medical ethics and has been actively involved since then in teaching and consultation in medical ethics.[25]

Here is one patient's experience with denial of a necessary procedure:

- **_Ms. G_**. *I am lucky to be alive. What happened to me should not happen to any human being. A few years ago I enrolled in one of the Medicare HMOs in my California coastal county. I had an excellent primary care physician who insisted on my having all the preventive tests. In doing so, he diagnosed colon cancer before it caused any symptoms. I had timely surgery, left the hospital after 5 days, was given radiation treatments, and felt fine.*

  Three years later, I noticed that my bowels were not working properly. My primary care physician asked permission from the HMO to authorize a colonoscopy. The HMO refused. Three months later a terrible pain appeared in my lower abdomen. I went to the hospital and had a ruptured colon due to recurrent cancer. All the germs in my intestine went into my peritoneal cavity. I developed peritonitis and septicemia and came close to death. I was in the hospital for a long time, had many complications, could not eat, required a feeding tube directly into my stomach, and needed intensive home care after leaving the hospital. The quality of care

*in the hospital was very bad, but the HMO didn't seem interested
in quality.*

*If the HMO had authorized the colonoscopy it would have spent
a few hundred dollars and would have saved tens of thousands
of dollars. Not only that, but the HMO cut off my home care and
I was charged $10,000 for home care services that I could not
do without, services I would not have needed if the HMO had
done what my doctor knew was needed. All this suffering was
unnecessary.*[26]

Undertreatment

The extent of undertreatment in for-profit private Medicare plans is
suggested by the findings of studies we have already noted—the greater
decline in physical health among Medicare beneficiaries enrolled in M + C
plans compared to Original Medicare[27] and the higher hospitalization rates
of seniors disenrolled from M + C plans.[28]

Lack of Mechanisms for Coordinated Care

Although some well established not-for-profit HMOs, such as Kaiser
Permanente and Group Health Cooperative, have developed innovative
systems of care, many for-profit M + C plans are not well organized. Marilyn
Moon of the Urban Institute, in testimony to the Senate Committee on Aging,
has made this observation: "Many managed care plans have relied upon
price discounts and do not even have the data and administrative systems to
attempt any care coordination."[29]

Physician Turnover

As we saw in Chapter 5, recruitment and retention of physicians by
M + C plans has been a serious problem for many private plans, with an
annual rate of physician turnover of 14% and some states having turnover
rates above 30%.[30] Here is how one patient has been adversely affected by
this problem.[31]

*   ***Ms. V****. In my southern California city, doctors are leaving because
    the HMOs don't pay them enough. I had 4 good physicians who
    have left. Not too many doctors know how to manage my condition,
    which is a rare dystrophy of the nervous system in my leg. My*

first internist, who was very good, left practice because he was unhappy with HMOs. I had foot surgery from a good podiatrist who then moved to Florida. I had knee surgery by an orthopedist who also left town and is now enjoying a satisfying practice without any HMO contracts. Now I am seeing an orthopedist who really understands my condition and has helped me a great deal. He just announced that he is moving to another county and I may not be able to continue with him. I have been told that physicians in town are discontinuing their HMO contracts so patients in Medicare HMOs will have fewer and fewer doctors to choose from. This is another way in which HMOs can hurt Medicare patients—they reduce our choices of good physicians by driving those physicians away.

Discontinuity of Care

About one-third of M + C plans across the country have faced disenrollment, many on multiple occasions.[32] As noted earlier, each time that patients switch from one M + C plan to another, there is only about a 50% chance of staying with their same physician.[33] Two-thirds of Medicare beneficiaries have multiple chronic conditions, and they are especially vulnerable to discontinuity of care.[34]

Lowering the Medical Expense Ratio

Higher overhead HMOs (some of the largest with overheads up to 33%) have been found to score lower on all 14 quality indicators submitted to the National Committee for Quality Assurance.[35-37] This should come as no surprise, since one would expect that the less an HMO spends on medical care, the lower its quality ratings will be. A 1998 study of 76 HMOs rated their quality of care on the extent to which they achieved five preventive goals established by the U.S. Public Health Service. Each plan was given a composite rating (four stars for best, one star for worst) as shown in Figure 8.2, which documents a consistent correlation between lower medical expense ratio and lower quality of care. That study also found that 80 percent of the not-for-profit plans received three or four stars, compared to just over one-half of the for-profit plans.[38]

Figure 8.2

Medical Expense Ratio, Administrative Expense Ratio and Quality Measures for 76 HMOs

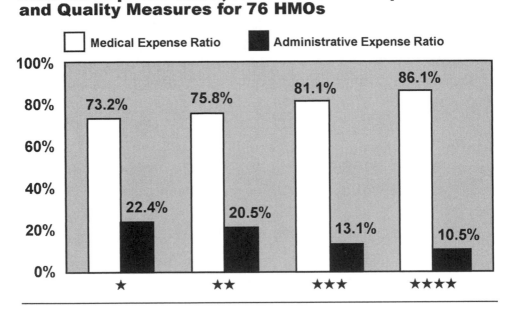

Reprinted with permission from Born P & Geckler C. HMO quality and financial performance: is there a connection? *Journal of Health Care Finance* 24(2):69, 1998.

THE CORROSIVE INFLUENCE OF PRIVATE, FOR-PROFIT PLANS

In his important 1998 article *Must Good HMOs Go Bad?*, Robert Kuttner warned us that the distinction between for-profit and not-for-profit HMOs can at times be blurred.[39] Aggressive "cherrypicking" by for-profit HMOs, by attracting healthier enrollees, put more value-driven not-for-profit HMOs in a difficult position through adverse selection. As the country's largest not-for-profit HMO, Kaiser Permanente is now confronting the challenges of providing care for an aging, sicker population in an intensely competitive marketplace. Kaiser's new CEO, George Halvorson, has observed: "These shifts in the marketplace will cause many of our healthiest members to leave us for lower-cost, lower-benefit plans. At the same time, employers will save money if their sicker patients voluntarily migrate to us."[40] As a result, even a Kaiser Permanente, which has pioneered many new improved systems of care as a leader in the industry, has occasionally emulated some of the practices of its for-profit competitors. An example is a pilot program conducted by Kaiser in California (since discontinued) whereby financial bonuses were given to telephone service representatives who spent the least amount of time on the telephone with patients and limited the number of appointments with physicians.[41] Nevertheless, as this chapter clearly shows, the track record of for-profit M + C plans falls far short of any claims of either comparable or superior quality of care as compared to FFS Medicare and not-for-profit Medicare plans.

CHAPTER 9

PUBLIC OPINION ON MEDICARE, PRIVATIZATION, AND THE ROLE OF GOVERNMENT

"Until now, the moderate majority has been slumbering, powerful in numbers but unaware of its own influence."

John P. Avlon, author of *Independent Nation: How the Vital Center Is Changing American Politics*[1]

"We have met the enemy, and he is us."

Pogo

W e have seen over the last five chapters that, contrary to marketing claims of for-profit M + C plans, they have under performed in comparison to Original Medicare with regard to access, choice, continuity, benefits, and quality of care. What then about public satisfaction and what can we learn from public opinion polls about the role of government in health care? This chapter asks three questions: (1) how does public satisfaction with M + C plans compare against Original Medicare; (2) what are the trends in public opinion concerning the role of government in health care and Medicare as a universal program; and (3) how has the public reacted to the Medicare Prescription Drug, Improvement, and Modernization Act of 2003 (MMA)?

M + C vs. ORIGINAL MEDICARE

A 1997 study conducted by Princeton Survey Research Associates for the Kaiser Family Foundation and Harvard University found that 54% of respondents believed that HMOs put their profits at higher priority than service to their enrollees.[2] A 2002 study conducted by the Medicare Rights Center found that 68% of Medicare beneficiaries surveyed felt the same thing.[3] A 2001 study by Mathematica Policy Research revealed that only 14% of Medicare beneficiaries who had the option to enroll in an M + C plan in that year either did so or seriously considered such a change.[4] Still another report found a wide variation in 1995 in complaints filed against M + C plans, with for-profit plans falling heavily on the high-complaint end of the spectrum. Thus, Humana's Florida plans recorded 4.58 complaints per 1,000 enrollees compared to only 0.82 for Kaiser Permanente and 0.18 for Group Health of Puget Sound, both not-for-profit plans.[5]

In its 2003 report, *The Role of Private Health Plans in Medicare*, the Study Panel on Medicare and Markets recognized that perceptions of M + C beneficiaries have received no careful study to date as they compare to seniors enrolled in Original Medicare. Such comparisons are made difficult by the great variation from one part of the country to another in the distribution of M + C plans. Some large metropolitan areas have multiple M + C plans, while many states and communities have no such programs. The Study Panel conducted one large survey of attitudes of M + C enrollees, and found that greater involvement in private Medicare plans, not unexpectedly, tends to undermine Medicare beneficiaries' connection and identification with the Medicare program itself. The Study Panel concluded that: "The more extensive the engagement with private insurance and market arrangements, the less important quality and equity are seen, relative to simply providing beneficiaries with adequate health insurance."[6]

According to a 2001 study by the Commonwealth Fund, Original Medicare is rated much more highly than private employer coverage by five criteria, as shown in Figure 9.1. These differences were found to be consistent across income and health status categories.[7]

PUBLIC OPINION ON ROLE OF GOVERNMENT

Contrary to the ceaseless rhetoric about Americans wanting privatized health insurance and multiple choice of insurers, a majority of Americans have long favored a substantial role of government in financing national health insurance (NHI) and assuring access to care for everyone. This public view is much stronger than advocates of the present market-based system are prepared to admit. Public support for NHI was 74% during the 1940s.[8] Sixty-one percent of the public supported the single-payer Medicare program as it was enacted in 1965. Over the last 25 years, one-half to two-thirds of Americans have favored "national health insurance financed by tax money, and paying for most forms of health care."[9]

This sustained high level of public support for government-financed health insurance comes down to the present day as well. A 2003 national poll by Republican pollster Bill McInturff and Democratic pollster Stanley

Figure 9.1

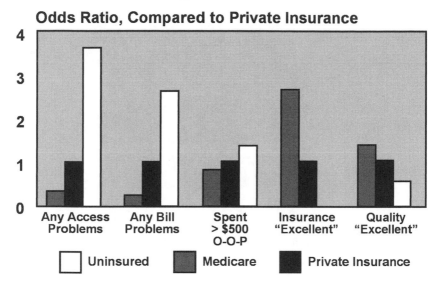

Medicare Coverage is Better Than Private

Source: Commonwealth Fund Survey - Health Affairs 2002; W311

Reprinted with permission from Physicians for a National Health Program (PNHP), Slide set. Chicago: 2003, source: Davis K. Medicare versus private insurance: rhetoric and reality. *Health Affairs* Web exclusive. October 9, 2002, W311-23.

Greenberg found that 70% of respondents are willing to pay a median amount of $200 a year if increased taxes were needed to support universal health care. Health care was tied with "terrorism and national security" as the highest priorities among voters for the Congress and Administration during the 2004 election campaigns.[10] A 2004 survey of 4,000 adult Americans found that 62% would be willing to give up the entire Bush tax cut in exchange for guaranteed health insurance for everyone, with 69% favoring that tradeoff if the tax cut were capped at $1,000 per person.[11]

When the matter of publicly financed health insurance is raised, the Canadian system is often brought into the discussion, either as a potential model for the U.S. or as a target for negative comment. Two common misperceptions then become part of that debate. First is the idea that the Canadian system is government-run. While the government finances health insurance, the delivery system of care is private. A second misconception is that the social ethic among Canadians is completely different from that

Figure 9.2

Public perceptions in U.S. and Canada

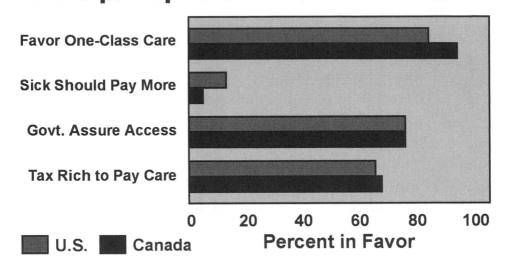

Reprinted with permission from *Health Management Quarterly* 3(2), 1991, cited in Chernomas R & Sepehri A (eds). *How to Choose? A Comparison of the U.S. and Canadian Health Care Systems.* Amityville, NY: Baywood Publishing Company, 1998, p 277.

held by Americans. The second issue was carefully studied by the Harris polling organization in 1991. More than 80% of people in both countries were found to favor one-class of health care (as opposed to a tiered health care system based on income level and class). More than three-quarters of respondents felt that government should assure access to care, and two-thirds agreed that the rich should pay higher taxes to support universal access to care. These similarities are shown in Figure 9.2[12] The pollsters concluded that Americans and Canadians hold similar views about their health care systems. The difference is that political leadership in the U.S. has not responded to popular will.[13]

Serial Roper polls between 1973 and 1990 in the U.S. revealed a shift in public opinion concerning health care reform. As Figure 9.3 shows, there was a major shift about 20 years ago toward a majority view that a new government-financed national health plan should replace the current marketplace system.[14] More recent studies have consistently confirmed this view. A 2003 survey by Harris Interactive found that two-thirds of respondents believed that health care should be a public good, not a private economic

Figure 9.3
Public Opinion and Health Care Reform in the U.S., 1973-1990

Percent
Agreement

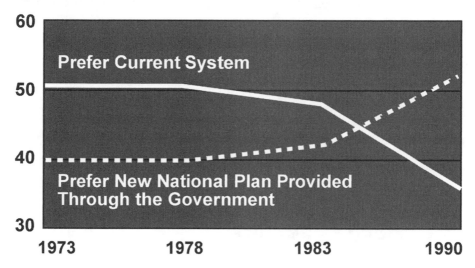

Reprinted with permission from Himmelstein DU & Woolhandler S. Public opinion and health care reform. In: Chernomas R & Sepehri A (eds). *How to Choose? A Comparison of the U.S. and Canadian Health Care Systems.* Amityville, NY: Baywood Publishing Company, 1998, p 281.

good.[15] Another 2003 national poll, conducted by the *Washington Post*, found that two-thirds of American preferred "a universal health insurance program, in which everyone is covered under a program like Medicare that's run by the government and financed by taxpayers."[16] If respondents had been told that a publicly-financed national insurance program like Medicare would assure greater choice of physicians and hospitals than in private plans, as we have seen with M + C, their support for universal coverage guaranteed by the government undoubtedly would have been overwhelming.

PUBLIC REACTION TO 2003 MEDICARE LEGISLATION

The 2003 Medicare law (MMA), summarized earlier in Chapter 3, has received little public support, especially among seniors, from the beginning. Even just before its passage, as details were being released for the House and Senate-passed versions, two-thirds of respondents age 55 and older viewed the drug plan unfavorably (65% to 26%), with the same number concerned about the large government subsidies to private plans as a worrisome move toward privatizing Medicare.[17] Several months later, public opinion to the new Medicare law remained negative. More recent surveys by the Kaiser Family Foundation found that three of four seniors who were aware of the bill's passage viewed it unfavorably, while many seniors were unaware of its enactment (Figure 9.4). More than three of

Figure 9.4

Impressions of New Medicare Law by Knowledge - Seniors

Given what you know about it, in general, do you have a favorable or unfavorable impression of this new Medicare law?

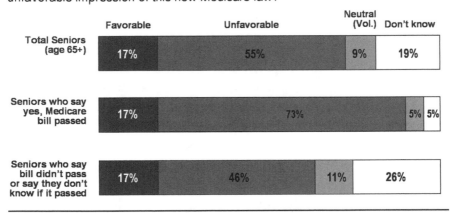

Source: Selected Findings on the New Medicare Drug Law, (#7040), Kaiser Family Foundation Health Poll Report survey, February 2004. This information was reprinted with permission of the Henry J. Kaiser Family Foundation. The Kaiser Family Foundation, based in Menlo Park, California, is a nonprofit, independent national health care philanthropy and is not associated with Kaiser Permanente or Kaser Industries.

every four seniors polled preferred that the new prescription drug benefit be managed by the government instead of private plans.[18]

In response to widespread disappointment and controversy over the Medicare bill, (accompanied as well by resignation of some 60,000 AARP members), the Administration launched an $80 million advertising and public relations campaign to improve the bill's public image.[19] Not surprisingly, during the 2004 political year, this campaign put a better face on the legislation than is the actual case, as previously mentioned, and the General Accounting Office found the ads "flawed but not illegal."[20] Misinformation and propaganda even extended to the release of the government's "Medicare & You 2005" booklet. Staff at the Medicare Rights Center found that document laden with confusing and inaccurate information, such as a blanket statement that "Medicare Advantage gives you more health care coverage choices and better health care benefits."[21]

There is now considerable evidence that a broad groundswell of public anger over soaring prices of prescription drugs in the U.S. is putting the Administration and the pharmaceutical industry on the defensive. Three-fourths of Americans recently surveyed by the Kaiser Family Foundation believe that drug company profit margins and marketing costs are the main drivers of rising costs of prescription drugs, not the costs of research and development.[22] Americans paid 67% more than Canadians for the same patented prescription drugs in 2003.[23] Although it is still illegal to import drugs from Canada, since the FDA has not yet pronounced that to be a safe practice, Americans are spending $350 to $650 million each year to import prescription drugs from Canada, whether by Internet, mail order, or driving across the border.[24] Despite the legal questions, some communities (e.g., Springfield, Illinois) and states (egs., Illinois, Wisconsin and Maine) are proceeding with organized plans to import Canadian drugs.[25,26]

Disregarding an intense lobbying and advertising campaign by the drug industry against Canadian imports, the House passed the bipartisan Gutknect-Emerson Bill in 2003 calling for legalization of drugs from Canada and some other industrialized countries.[27] In the Senate, Republican Senator Charles Grassley has been working toward a bipartisan bill to allow drug imports from Canada, with required inspections by the FDA to assure safety. A recent study by public health officials in New Hampshire compared medications reimported from Canada with the same drugs purchased in New Hampshire; a blind analysis found no differences between the two samples.[28] Meanwhile, the AARP is backpedaling with its new ads promoting legalization of Canadian drugs as "a drug war we can win."[29]

The reaction of Medicare beneficiaries to the new Medicare drug discount cards, authorized by the MMA for 2004 and 2005, has been tepid at best. By March 2005, only 25% of eligible low-income seniors had applied for Medicare discount cards offering $600 credit toward their 2005 drug expenses.[30] Touted by the Administration as providing drug discounts of 10 to 25% for many Medicare beneficiaries, the cards are much less useful than that. For example, in northwest Washington, D.C., discounts from Medicare-approved cards on the 10 most commonly used drugs averaged 13% in June 2004, no comparison with Canadian discounts averaging 41% and federal supply schedule discounts of 46%. Of the 31% of seniors over age 65, who have ever used the Internet, only 2% have visited the Medicare Web site comparing drug discounts.[31] Meanwhile, of course, continuing escalation of drug prices threaten to make potential future cost-savings from discount cards meaningless. Discounts and prices can change as often as weekly with drug discount cards while their holders cannot change cards more frequently than once a year. Fifteen of 30 prescription drugs tracked in a study by *Families USA* between January 2003 and January 2004 increased their prices more than once over that one-year period.[32] In 2003, retail prescription drug prices went up by 6.9%, more than three times the 2.2% inflation rate.[33]

THE M + C EXPERIMENT HAS FAILED, SO WHAT NEXT?

Most Medicare beneficiaries value reliability and predictability of coverage under Original Medicine more highly than the volatility of private M + C plans. Quite aside from polls, they have voted with their feet. Policymakers supporting the private Medicare plans hoped for 34% enrollment of U.S. seniors. From a peak enrollment in 1998 of 17%, however, that number has dropped to its present 11% as a result of M + C plan terminations and disenrollments. Today, private market advocates are again setting a goal of 31% enrollment for M + C's successor, Medicare Advantage. This chapter has offered little evidence that U.S. seniors will switch from Original Medicare in those numbers. Indeed, as these last six chapters have shown, the M + C experiment has been completed, and it is a policy failure, though still not recognized as such by its pro-market advocates.

For more than a decade, the U.S. has been largely run by the Republican Party, which maintains control over the legislative, judicial and executive branches of government. Their platform is one of steadfast support for the private sector and decreased government involvement in social services. To then have such a strong majority of the public favoring greater government intervention and reining in of corporate excesses speaks volumes about the chasm between our elected officials and policies favored by the governed. This disconnect will be revisited in the last chapter of this book, since the challenge is to awaken and energize this silent majority.

PART III

SOME CONTENTIOUS POLICY ISSUES

CHAPTER 10

CAN THE PRIVATE MEDICARE MARKETPLACE EVER OFFER MORE EFFICIENCY AND VALUE?

"Few trends could so thoroughly undermine the very foundations of our free society as the acceptance by corporate officials of a social responsibility other than to make as much money for their shareholders as possible."

Milton Friedman, leading advocate for free economic markets and author of *Capitalism and Freedom*, 1962[1]

"We've engaged in a massive and failed experiment in market-based medicine in the U.S. Rhetoric about the benefits of competition and profit-driven health care can no longer hide the reality: Our health system is in shambles."

Marcia Angell, M.D., Former Editor of *The New England Journal of Medicine* and author of *The Truth About Drug Companies: How They Deceive Us and What We Can Do About It* [2]

As we saw in Chapter 3, a meme is a self-replicating idea or slogan which through constant repetition makes its way into common language and culture regardless of its merits.[3] There are numerous memes in American culture, which many have come to accept with little question. One of these is the steady drumbeat over many years claiming greater efficiency of private markets in health care compared to public programs such as Medicare. Proponents of market-based health care promote these claims by arguing that a competitive marketplace exists in health care. At the same time, they suggest that public programs are less efficient because they are "government-run," while disregarding the fact that health care services in publicly-financed programs are delivered largely through the private sector. Although the last 5 chapters have documented under-performance by private M + C plans compared to Original Medicare, the supposed promise of private plans has re-emerged in the Medicare Prescription Drug, Improvement, and Modernization Act of 2003 (MMA) in the form of Medicare Advantage, the new name for M + C plans.

This chapter addresses two questions: (1) can Medicare Advantage be more efficient and offer more value than Original Medicare; and (2) can the private "competitive" marketplace function as efficiently under MMA 2003 as its supporters believe?

WILL MEDICARE ADVANTAGE PERFORM BETTER THAN M + C?

As we saw in Chapter 3, MMA 2003 provides for increased subsidies in 2004 and 2005 to Medicare Advantage plans and calls for a demonstration project starting in 2010 whereby private plans will "compete" against Original Medicare in six major metropolitan areas. Market advocates hope that about one-third of Medicare beneficiaries will opt for these private plans. Although the M + C experiment has been largely discredited as a model of efficiency and cost containment, MMA 2003 puts forward more flexible private Medicare plans, especially preferred provider organizations (PPOs) as a promising alternative to the more restrictive HMOs. Policy makers crafting MMA hope that Medicare Advantage PPOs will:[4]

- offer beneficiaries sustainable coverage options with more benefits or lower out-of-pocket costs than traditional Medicare;

- develop broad provider networks with substantial price discounts;

- expand private plan options across geographic areas, particularly rural areas;

- employ care management techniques that contain costs and improve quality; and,

- ultimately contribute to a slowing of Medicare cost trends."

As with earlier legislation, MMA 2003 has provided generous overpayments to Medicare Advantage plans during 2004 in an effort to expand enrollment in private plans. Federal payments in 2004 increased by an average of 10.9% over those in 2003. These are overpayments compared to costs in traditional Medicare. The average Medicare Advantage overpayment was 107% in 2004, (i.e., 7% more than Original Medicare), with some high-cost counties receiving 132% of FFS costs (e.g., San Francisco County). About one-quarter of Medicare Advantage enrollees are in counties receiving overpayments more than 110% of Original Medicare's costs.[5] The chief Medicare actuary recently reported to Congress that the government would spend $50 billion less over the next 10 years if private plans were paid at only 100% of the costs of traditional Medicare.[6] In return for these subsidies under the MMA, advocates claim that Medicare Advantage plans will provide additional benefits, reduce cost sharing with enrollees, or both. Critics contend that the private plans will just take the money and withdraw from the program whenever the business becomes less profitable.

MMA 2003 is scheduled to phase in its various components over a ten-year period. The 2004-2005 period offers Medicare-approved drug discount cards and incentive payments to encourage growth of Medicare Advantage plans. Starting in January 2006, the drug discount cards will be discontinued and Medicare beneficiaries can make one of three choices: (1) stay in traditional Medicare, a Medicare Advantage plan, or a retiree plan without signing up for the drug benefit; (2) stay in traditional Medicare and sign up for a stand-alone drug plan; or (3) enroll in a private Medicare Advantage plan that offers drug coverage. Table 10.1 lists time lines for phase-in of Medicare's prescription drug benefit, as summarized by the AARP.[7] A six-year premium support experiment will start in six cities in 2010 comparing subsidized private Medicare plans with Original Medicare.[8]

Some private Medicare plans are proposing to increase their benefits or reduce premiums. In New York, for example, Oxford Health Plans will increase its drug coverage from its current levels of $250 or $500 to $1,200.[9] Many private insurers, however, were reluctant to enter the Medicare market in 2004, fearing adverse selection and future cutbacks in federal overpayments to private plans as the government confronts budget deficits and cutbacks of domestic programs.[10] There is also no assurance that private plans will increase benefits on a stable basis over the long term. In June 2004, the CEO of Medco (now Express Scripts), a large pharmacy benefit manager (PBM) told its investors that private health insurers, fearing adverse selection, are not likely to underwrite stand-alone prescription drug benefits for individuals.[11]

So, based on available evidence to date, what can we expect from Medicare Advantage over the next 10 years, and will it perform any better than the failed M + C experiment? Though still early, there is little reason to believe that these plans will yield any better results.

TABLE 10.1

PHASE–IN DATES FOR MEDICARE'S PRESCRIPTION DRUG BENEFIT

June – August 2005:	Social Security Administration mails out applications to beneficiaries on limited incomes who may be eligible for special low-cost drug coverage. You can apply by mail, by phone at (800) 772-1213, at local SSA or Medicaid offices, or from early July online at www.socialsecurity. gov. From July onward, SSA lets you know if you qualify.
June 2005:	If you also receive Medicaid benefits or SSI or your Medicare premiums are paid by your state, Medicare informs you that you're automatically eligible for this extra help without having to apply.
Summer-Fall 2005:	If you have retiree health benefits, you may hear from your former employer or union about future drug coverage.
Late September-Early November 2005:	If you have a Medigap policy that covers drugs (plans H, I or J), you hear from the insurer about your options.
October 2005:	All beneficiaries receive the "Medicare & You 2006" handbook, with information on the drug benefit. From October 13, you can compare details of coverage options available in your area, by going to www.medicare.gov or calling (800) 633-4227.
November 15, 2005:	First open enrollment period for drug coverage begins. Enrolling is voluntary, but doing so after May 15, 2006, may incur late penalties in the form of higher premiums. Everyone—including those eligible for limited-income assistance—must enroll in a Medicare drug plan to get coverage. Income assistance—must enroll in a Medicare drug plan to get coverage.
Dec 31, 2005:	Temporary Medicare drug discount card program ends. You can use your card until May 15, 2006, or until you sign up for Medicare drug coverage (whichever is sooner).
Jan 1, 2006:	Drug coverage begins. Beneficiaries who previously got their drugs from Medicaid now get them from Medicare.
May 15, 2006:	First open enrollment period ends.

Figure 10.1

Medicare Advantage Enrollees as a Percent of Medicare Beneficiaries, by State, 2005

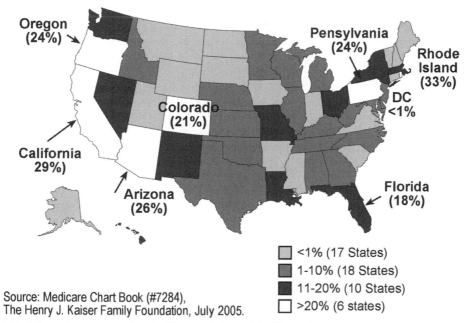

Oregon
(24%)

Pensylvania
(24%)

Rhode
Island
(33%)

DC
<1%

Colorado
(21%)

California
29%)

Arizona
(26%)

Florida
(18%)

☐ <1% (17 States)
■ 1-10% (18 States)
■ 11-20% (10 States)
☐ >20% (6 states)

Source: Medicare Chart Book (#7284),
The Henry J. Kaiser Family Foundation, July 2005.

Source: Medicare Chart Book, (#7284), The Henry J. Kaiser Family Foundation, July 2005. This information was reprinted with permission of the Henry J. Kaiser Family Foundation. The Kaiser Family Foundation, based in Menlo Park, California, is a non-profit, independent national health care philanthropy and is not associated with Kaiser Permanente or Kaiser Industries.

As a starting point in 2005, there were only 179 Medicare Advantage (formerly M + C) plans, down from a peak of 346 plans in 1998. They were poorly distributed around the country, as shown in Figure 10.1.[12] The vast majority of Medicare Advantage plans are HMOs. There were only 89,000 PPO enrollees concentrated in a small number of plans in February 2004, and less than 29,000 enrollees in private Medicare FFS plans.[13] Although Medicare Advantage plans made small gains in enrollment during 2004, Kaiser Family Foundation reported in April 2005 that they still accounted for only 12 percent of the entire Medicare population while receiving 15% of Medicare's budget.[14]

PPOs are a response by the insurance industry to field more attractive products to the public after the backlash of the 1990s to widespread abuses among HMOs, especially those that are investor-owned. Many PPOs see themselves more in the role of "arranging" care rather than managing care. Their administrative costs are often lower than in HMOs but still much higher than for Original Medicare.

The non-partisan policy research organization, Center for Studying Health System Change, conducted site visits to 12 nationally representative communities in 2002-2003: Boston; Cleveland; Greenville, S.C.; Indianapolis; Lansing, Mich; Little Rock, Ark.; Miami; northern New Jersey; Orange County, Calif; Phoenix; Seattle; and Syracuse, N.Y. These are this study's key findings:[15]

- "Most PPOs in the commercial market are not exercising much selectivity in network assembly and typically pay providers more than Medicare. Likewise, PPOs are more limited than HMOs in steering patients to some providers and away from others, weakening PPOs' ability to win substantial price discounts from providers or to coordinate care.

- The fact that traditional Medicare will remain an option for all providers and beneficiaries will undermine the potential leverage of PPOs. Some providers might consider accepting payments below traditional Medicare to expand market share, but experience to date—such as in the Medicare Select program that since 1998 has tried to encourage beneficiaries to use restricted hospital networks to enhance the value of private supplemental coverage—has been disappointing.

- A major attraction of the PPO option to policy makers is its broad geographic coverage. PPO options are widely available in the private sector, particularly beyond major metropolitan markets, and seem better positioned to serve Medicare beneficiaries in rural areas than did HMOs in the Medicare + Choice program. But discounts obtained in rural areas are greatly affected by provider market structure and (lack of) competition, so PPOs are likely to have to pay higher rates than traditional Medicare in these areas.

- The Medicare reform legislation imposes requirements on Medicare Advantage plans to offer quality improvement and chronic care management programs. Sponsors of many commercial PPO offerings are not strongly invested in care management and quality improvement techniques. To meet new Medicare requirements, many current PPOs would have to increase care management and information technology capacity—investments they may be reluctant to make in light of the history of private plan instability in Medicare."

The study investigators summed up their prognosis for Medicare PPOs as follows:[16]

> *"Much of the appeal of the PPO option lies in its asserted superiority relative to HMOs in terms of choice, limited medical management, accommodation of providers' preferences, and lower administrative expenses. However, the PPO arrangement enjoys none of these advantages relative to traditional Medicare. Moreover, as current trends indicate, much of the recent growth of the PPO is driven by its flexibility to enable employers to shift more costs to consumers and shrink benefit packages, not augment them. Finally, the fact that most PPO networks harbor limited aspirations to manage care, reward provider behavior, and promote aggressive quality improvement for participants makes it far from clear what it is that Medicare hopes to obtain from the PPO product."*

The transformation of Aetna U.S. Healthcare, once the country's largest managed care plan, sheds light on how Medicare Advantage plans are likely to evolve in the future. During the 1990s, its emphasis was on attracting growth in enrollment through attractively low premiums, increasing market share, and a one-size-fits-all approach to benefits and provider networks. It then encountered increasing public anger against its restrictive practices, revolt among providers, and litigation. The newly renamed Aetna Inc. then reassessed its goals and market strategies, re-committing itself to <u>profitable</u> growth, not just market share. Aetna has reduced its Medicare exposure by four-fold since 2000, withdrawing from the M + C program in counties accounting for 65% of Medicare enrollment. Its current emphasis is upon disciplined underwriting and pricing, and shareholders are again happy with more than a four-fold increase in earnings per share between 2000 and 2003. Aetna Inc. has retreated from its Medicare HMO business while it considers what to do with future PPO options. As Dr. James Robinson,

Professor of Health Economics and Policy at the University of California Berkeley, observes: "Aetna's improved ability to predict and price risk will expose it to obloquy as a failure at social insurance rather than to praise as a success at market insurance. In the health care sector, where no one agrees on the appropriate division of labor between the public and private sectors, no good deed goes unpunished."[17]

A recent publication, *Decision Maker News in Managed Care,* provides further indications as to how private Medicare plans are likely to approach the new Medicare prescription drug benefit. Based on a group discussion of managed care consultants at the Cambridge Healthcare Summit in 2004, recommendations were given to avoid adverse selection, lower "medical loss," and increase profits. These excerpts of recommendations are revealing:[18]

> *"One technique to minimize risk is to attract healthier senior citizens through benefit design, network configuration, and targeted marketing advertising. A low premium with a lean benefit, such as a yearly cap, a high co-payment, or co-insurance, may attract healthier senior citizens and discourage high-risk senior citizens. Other suggestions to attract healthy patients are to cover "lifestyle" drugs such as sildenafil and to provide health club reimbursements (both indicators of a more vigorous senior) and incentives for nonsmokers—targeted marketing and advertising (can also be used) to reach healthier senior citizens where they are and in what they read and see. An advertisement in the health club or the exercise room at a senior living community will reach active seniors who may not be high risk. Magazines and groups for people with active lifestyles (eg, Elderhostel, golf or running clubs) could reach low-risk seniors."*

As we saw in the last chapter, only 14% of Medicare beneficiaries who had the option to enroll in an M + C plan in 2001 either did so or seriously considered it.[19] In view of the negative experiences seniors have had with M + C, it seems unlikely that Medicare Advantage will fare any better. A 2004 survey by the U.S. Government Accountability Office (GAO) found that less than one percent of 10 million Medicare beneficiaries enrolled in a PPO demonstration which the CMS was promoting.[20] A ten-year projection by the Congressional Budget Office for Medicare Advantage plans between now and 2014, is shown in Figure 10.2, with estimated maximal enrollments of only 12% of Medicare beneficiaries.[21]

Figure 10.2

Share of Medicare Beneficiaries Enrolled in Medicare Advantage Plans

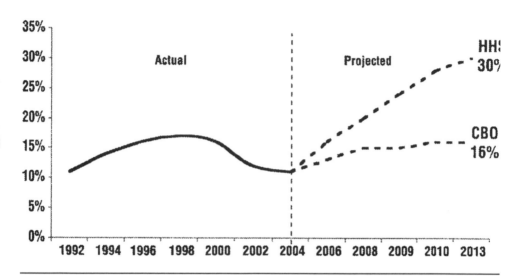

Source: Medicare Advantage (#2052-08), The Henry J. Kaiser Family Foundation, April, 2005. This information was reprinted with permission of the Henry J. Kaiser Family Foundation. The Kaiser Family Foundation, based in Menlo Park, California, is a non-profit, independent national health care philanthropy and is not associated with Kaiser Permanente or Kaiser Industries.

THE MEDICARE PRESCRIPTION DRUG BENEFIT: A CASE STUDY IN INEFFICIENCY

The massive Medicare prescription drug legislation enacted into law as MMA 2003 was largely deflected by industry lobbying into a gold rush for the drug industry (including brand-name, generic and biotech drug makers, select biomedical device makers, pharmacy benefit managers, and distributors) and the insurance and managed care industries. A June 2004 report by Congress Watch of Public Citizen, *The Medicare Drug War*, provides extensive documentation of how an army of almost 1,000 lobbyists assured a bonanza of future profits for special interests at the expense of Medicare beneficiaries and taxpayers. The drug industry hired a record 824 individual lobbyists in 2003, while PhRMA (the drug industry's trade group) fielded another 124 lobbyists and HMOs and health plans added another 222 lobbyists. Among the lobbyists working for the drug and managed care industries were 30 former U.S. senators and representatives.[22] The unseemly political process leading to the MMA's passage has been well documented by Congress Watch, including deception of Congress as to the bill's cost, bribery of a member of Congress, prolonged and unprecedented arm-twisting converting a 210-195 defeat of the bill to a 220-215 win, and multiple conflicts of interest through revolving doors.[23] In October 2004, the House ethics committee sternly admonished Rep. Tom DeLay (R-Texas) for three instances of unethical conduct, including offering rewards to a colleague in exchange for a favorable vote on the MMA.[24] The only efficient part of this legislation is how the relatively small lobbying expenses ($108 million and $32 million for the drug and managed care industries, respectively, in 2003) will be returned many times over with profits in the billions in future years. Table 10.2 summarizes this windfall for these industries.[25]

From the start, it is no surprise that the MMA is more aligned to corporate interests than to the needs of Medicare beneficiaries for cost savings on their prescription drugs. Here are some examples:

- the federal government is expressly prohibited from using its bargaining clout for 41 million beneficiaries in securing drug discounts, as it does so effectively for the Veterans Administration (about 45% discounts); instead, management of the prescription drug benefit is turned over to the drug industry, the most profitable of all U.S. industries

- seniors are limited to only one potential change of their drug discount card if they sign up for one during the 2004-2005 transitional period; while formularies and prices can change weekly, seniors are locked into their initial card selection without opportunity to change to another card until near the end of 2004

- As an incentive for Medicare beneficiaries to sign up for the prescription drug benefit when it becomes available from private plans in January 2006, they will be charged a premium penalty of 12% each year by failing to sign up in the first six months of 2006; many seniors find this inappropriate and unfair, though acknowledging the pressure to enroll in a private plan[26]

- Table 10.2

What Special Interests Got	Value
Drug Industry	Drug coverage is provided through HMOs and private insurance companies not the traditional Medicare program.	
	Expanded markets for drugs as more Medicare beneficiaries will have some drug coverage	No estimate available on net new drug spending
	Medicare is prohibited from using its bargaining clout on behalf of 41 million beneficiaries to directly negotiate deep drug price discounts.(a)	No estimate available
	An effective ban on the reimportation of prescription drugs from Canada and other industrialized countries, where drugs cost about 45% less than in the U.S.(b)	$40 billion over 10 years (c)
HMOs & Private Insurance Companies	Drug coverage is provided through HMOs and private insurance companies not the traditional Medicare program.	
	Enrollment in managed care plans (Medicare Advantage) is expected to climb from 12% in 2004 to 32% in 2009, according to the Medicare actuary.(d)	$531.5 billion increase in company revenues (2004-13) over the old Medicare + Choice program, according to the Medicare actuary.(g)
	Managed care plans wil get a windfall "due to the higher payment rates starting in 2004 and the re-structured payment formula in 2006 and later."(e) These changes were made to expand participation in HMOs despite the fact that they are already overpaid compared to the cost of delivering care under the traditional Medicare fee-for-service program.	$34 billion (h)
	Subsidies are provided to Preferred Provider Organizations (PPOs) to encourage them to establish plans in areas of low managed care enrollment.(f)	$12 billion(l)

(a) New 42 U.S.C. 1860D-11(i)as added bySec. 101 of H.R. 1.
(b) New 21 U.SC. 804(1)(1)(a) as added by Sec 1121 of H.R. 1; Congressional Budget Office, "Would Prescription Drug Importation Reduce U.S. Drug Spending?" p. 4, April 29, 2004.
(c) CBO p. 5, April 29, 2004; estimates range from 35 percent to 55 percent.
(d) Statement of Rick Foster, Chief Actuary, Centers for Medicare and Medicaid Services, Testimony Before the House Committee on Ways and Means, March 24, 2004, p. 11.
(e) Foster Ways and Means Committee testimony, March 24, 2004, p.. 11.
(f) New 42 U.S.C. 1858(e) as added by S. 221 of H.R. 1.
(g) Data provided by Centers for Medicare and Medicaid Services, Office of the Actuary, June 23, 2004. Baseline spending for Medicare+Choice was projected at $387.8 billion from 2004-2013. Projected Spending for Medicare Advantage is $913.3 billion over the same period.
(h) Foster Ways and Means Committee testimony, March 24, p. 11.
(i) Foster Ways and Means testimony, March 24, 2004, p.11.
(j) Figures include only companies and trade associations that lobbied on Medicare.
(k) Sum of lobbyists exceeds 952 because many worked for both the drug industry and HMOs.

Source: Reprinted with permission from Aaron C, et al. The Medicare drug war: an army of nearly 1,000 lobbyists pushes a Medicare law that puts drug company and HMO profits ahead of patients and tax payers. Washington, D.C.: *Congress Watch*, Public Citizen, June 2004, p 9.

The MMA calls for employers to be reimbursed for 28% of the cost of prescriptions of more than $250 per retiree, up to an annual subsidy of $1,330 per retiree, starting in 2006;[27] this subsidy will actually reward employers for cutting their retirees' benefits; as the Medical Rights Center has noted—"By reducing their contributions to roughly 40% to 50% of total costs—equal to the subsidy plus tax deductions—employers will be able to offer nominal drug benefits for free. By further slashing contributions beneath 40% to 50%, employers can pocket subsidy dollars as profit."[28]

- The MMA restricts importation of prescription drugs from Canada and other countries, where prices of the same drugs used in this country are less than two-thirds of U.S. costs; voicing safety concerns, the drug industry has been fighting fiercely against any importation of drugs as a threat to their pricing prerogatives, despite a recent study by the U.S. General Accounting Office finding that drugs purchased from Canada pose fewer risks than drugs obtained from online pharmacies in the U.S.;[29] according to IMS Health, Inc., there is a growing trend to reimportation of prescription drugs from Canada, which increased in 2003 from $500 million to over $1.1 billion[30]

If the initial experience of drug discount cards is any indication, as seems inevitable, of the inefficiency we can expect from the prescription drug benefit starting in 2006, then the promise held out by MMA's proponents will be largely discredited. Transitional drug discount cards are off to a poor start for these kinds of reasons:

- In April 2004, only weeks before discount cards were made available, only 18% of Americans over age 65 knew that the new law includes a low-income assistance program[31]
- Although the subsidies available to low-income seniors ($600 credit in each year, 2004 and 2005) would appear to be a "bulletproof" benefit for eligible seniors, many have been reluctant to apply for drug discount cards for fear of losing other benefits, such as food stamps and rental subsidies; the MMA is clear that drug subsidies will not jeopardize other federal benefits, but many

seniors and some staff members of other federal programs were not so informed;[32] by October, 2004, only 1.3 million low-income Medicare beneficiaries had qualified for the $600 credit on their cards, far short of the Administration's projection of 4.7 million eligibles[33]

• The more than 70 drug discount cards approved by Medicare pose a bewildering array of options for Medicare beneficiaries[34] more than one-half of whom have been found to have difficulty in making decisions about comparative differences in information.[35] This is not surprising since almost one-quarter of Medicare beneficiaries have cognitive impairments and 61% have a high school education or less.[36]

• Although the Medicare program has established a 1-800-MEDICARE hotline and a new Web site into which seniors can type in their zip code and drugs they take, and supposedly shop for best prices, it remains very difficult for Medicare beneficiaries to make informed choices among drug discount cards. The GAO found that customer service representatives gave the wrong answers 55 out of 70 times to questions about the $600 annual subsidy accompanying the Medicare drug discount card for low-income beneficiaries.[37] There were many errors in prices of drugs as the Web site was launched,[38] and prices continue to change frequently as invisible negotiations proceed among a large number of drug makers, pharmacy benefit managers, and pharmacies;[39] in addition, only 31% of seniors have ever used the Internet and only 2% have ever visited the Medicare Web site[40]

• Scams involving drug discount cards have been reported in 17 states, with con artists selling fake cards or attempting to get seniors' personal information[41]

• Initial interest among seniors in the drug discount cards has been low; while 2.8 million enrollees in private Medicare plans were provided cards automatically, only 4.4 million, little more than 10% of Medicare beneficiaries, had signed up almost a year after MMA was passed[42]

- Continued sharp increases in drug prices are eroding savings which might have been expected through the drug discount cards; for example, prices of these five commonly used drugs increased by 4.6 to 6.6 times the rate of inflation in 2003: Lipitor, Plavix, Fosamax, Norvasc, and Celebrex[43]

When the new Part D prescription drug benefit replaces the transitional drug discount cards in 2006, these are further reasons to expect that the drug benefit will be disappointing to many Medicare beneficiaries.

- By 2006, when seniors will be asked to select among health plans for their prescription drug coverage, the drug companies will have had more than two years since MMA 2003 to raise prices and limit the cost savings for many Medicare beneficiaries;[44] in the first two and one half months after the November, 2004 elections, 31 of the 50 top-selling drugs had price increases, compared to 22 of the top 50 drugs for the same period a year previously[45]

- Whether managed by private insurers or PBMs, the profit motive will be present all along the distribution chain for the new drug benefit, with transparency and accountability likely to be minimal

- According to a recent report by the Congressional Budget Office (CBO), premiums and deductibles for the benefit will vary by region; some states (eg., Indiana) are expected to have premiums over $50 per person per month despite the often quoted-average of $35 per month, and the CBO projects a 40% increase in cost sharing with beneficiaries by 2013[46]

- one in four Medicare beneficiaries are expected to incur higher out-of-pocket costs for their prescription drugs in 2006 as a result of the "doughnut hole."[47] Instead, had CMS been authorized by MMA 2003 to negotiate drug prices down to the level of Canada, France, or the United Kingdom, the "doughnut hole" in prescription drug coverage would have been closed and Medicare beneficiaries' out-of-pocket costs in 2006 would have dropped from an estimated $31 billion to $19.1 billion.[48]

- In 2006, 14.2 million seniors and people with disabilities, 35 percent of the entire Medicare population, will qualify for the low-income drug subsidy program; as a result, however, of complex screening and asset tests, as well as underfunded counseling services and the usual difficulties in reaching this vulnerable population, many will not receive this assistance with their premiums, deductibles, and co-insurance; in 2005, less than one third of eligible persons were enrolled in any of the Medicare Savings Programs.[49]

Because of all of these developments since the MMA was enacted, Figure 10.3 accurately portrays who the winners and losers are with this massive and expensive modification of the Medicare program.

CORPORATE WINDFALLS AND DOWNSIDES OF MEDICARE PRIVATIZATION

As is obvious from the foregoing, the most important problem concerning the access and affordability of prescription drugs for U.S. seniors is the unrestrained prices of drugs in this country. The MMA has gone to great lengths to assure generous profits for the drug and insurance industries. Based on previous experience with M + C plans, we can expect Medicare Advantage plans to cut back drug benefits in order to maximize their profits through such means as restricted formularies, tiered co-payments, and drug exclusions.[50] With its lack of cost containment measures, this bill has set the stage for corporate plunder on the backs of the most vulnerable groups in our society, while threatening the future fiscal viability of the Medicare program itself. Privatization of the prescription drug benefit for Medicare recipients, as well as potential future privatization of the overall Medicare program, rewards inefficiency and profit-taking without commensurate value. These two observations by leaders of Physicians for a National Health Program accurately portray the downsides of Medicare privatization:

> *"We don't need to import drugs from Canada; we need to import Canadian drug prices—Pharmacy benefit managers are no substitute for Medicare using its purchasing power on behalf of seniors. PBMs don't drive the best bargains for consumers; they switch patients' medications to boost profits—their own. Some PBMs are under investigation for taking tens of millions of dollars in "rebates" from pharmaceutical companies in exchange for increasing sales of "preferred" brands (regardless of their cost). Do they pass on the savings? Do pigs fly?"[51]*

Ida Hellander, M.D.
Quentin Young, M.D.

"Behind false claims of efficiency of privatization lies a much uglier truth. Investor-owned care embodies a new value system that severs the community roots and Samaritan traditions of hospitals, makes physicians and nurses into instruments of investors, and views patients as commodities. Investor ownership marks the triumph of greed." [52]

Steffie Woolhandler, M.D.
David Himmelstein, M.D.

Figure 10.3

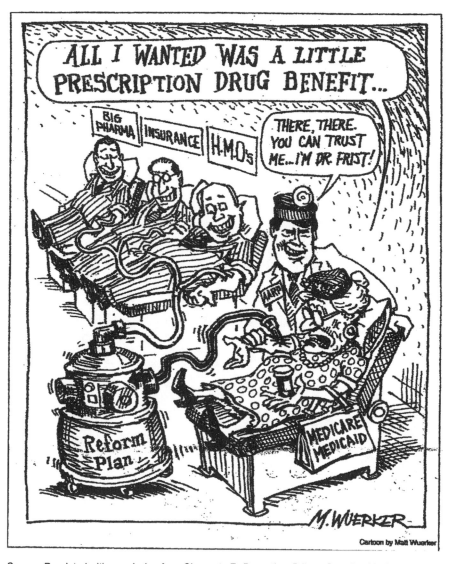

Source: Reprinted with permission from Clemente F. Deception, Bribery-Securing Medicare
law made for good theatre but bad policy. *Public Citizen News* 24(3), May/June 2004:1-5. and from
Matt Wuerker

CHAPTER 11

CAN SUBSIDIES CURE THE ILLS OF PRIVATIZED MEDICARE?

"The Medicare + Choice program has already been expensive for taxpayers... the vast majority of plans have gotten paid more for their Medicare enrollees than the government would have paid had these enrollees remained in the traditional fee-for-service program. Raising payment rates to a level sufficient to retain the plans leaving Medicare would mean increasing the excess that currently exists in payments for plan enrollees, relative to their expected fee-for-service costs. In areas of the country where there are few beneficiaries and providers are in short supply, no reasonable payment rate increase is likely to entice plans to participate in Medicare.... In our view, efforts to protect the viability of Medicare + Choice plans come at the expense of ensuring Medicare's financial sustainability in the long term."

Conclusion by General Accounting Office in 2000[1]

"No one will continue to pay you more [than fee-for-service Medicare] in the short term if you can't demonstrate better quality and cost down the road."[2]

Warning to private Medicare plans in 2004 by
Rep. Bill Thomas (R-CA), one of MMA's chief architects

As we have seen in earlier chapters, private Medicare plans have long claimed to provide greater choice, flexibility, value and efficiency compared to traditional FFS Medicare. In their initial years, they were reimbursed at 95% of FFS Medicare rates with the early assumption that they indeed could save the government money. Since they recruited healthier seniors through favorable risk selection, their costs to provide care were actually lower than those in FFS Medicare but their administrative costs much higher. Yet when their profits became less than hoped, they began to lobby the government for larger payments than traditional Medicare, threatening or actually leaving the market if these overpayments were not sufficient. Advocates of expanding private options for Medicare beneficiaries continue to press their case on the basis of claimed advantages of "competition" in the marketplace, despite the well-documented fact that these plans are more costly.

This chapter asks three questions: (1) to what extent has overpayment of private Medicare plans been established in national policy; (2) what is the history of competitive bidding among Medicare plans; and (3) why do overpayments to private plans continue despite the failure of these plans to be more efficient, provide more value, or save money?

PRIVATE MEDICARE OVERPAYMENTS AS NATIONAL POLICY

As we saw in Chapter 3, it was apparent to government auditors as early as 1989 that private Medicare HMOs were costing 15 to 33% more for the care of their enrollees than in FFS Medicare.[3] Still, many private Medicare plans lobbied the government for higher reimbursements, pushing Congress in 1989 to consider (but not pass) raising their reimbursement rates from 95% to 100% of FFS Medicare.[4] Even at 95% reimbursement levels, private Medicare plans should have been very profitable in view of these findings by investigators:

- Enrollments in Medicare HMOs were found by a 1997 study to have less than one-half as many individuals proportionally with both physical and cognitive problems as enrollments in FFS Medicare; sick individuals with both types of problems account for over 30% of total Medicare spending even though only 12% of the Medicare population[5]

- The healthiest 40% of Medicare beneficiaries accounted for only 1% of the overall program's costs in 2003[6]

- Federal payments to Medicare HMOs between 1998 and 2000 exceeded the costs Medicare would have paid in the traditional FFS program by an average of 13.2% each year[7]

- A 2000 report by the Office of the Inspector General found that Medicare paid hospitals $224 million between 1991 and 1996 for inpatient services required within three months by people disenrolled from their HMOs, $204 million more than it would have paid the HMOs through capitation payments had these sick individuals not been disenrolled.[8] This strongly suggests that the HMOs were avoiding the costs of hospitalization of sick enrollees, then dumping them on Original Medicare so sick that they then required expensive hospitalizations

In response to political pressure from the managed care industry, the Balanced Budget Act of 1997 (BBA) set in place an explicit policy of increased overpayments to private Medicare plans. The 95% payment rate was discarded in favor of rates at least 100% of FFS levels as determined through a complex new reimbursement formula by which private plans were paid the highest of three different amounts for each county—a 50-50 blend of local and national rates, a minimal "floor rate" (set higher in an effort to attract plans to non-metropolitan areas), and the minimal increase authorized by law.[9]

The 2003 Medicare legislation (MMA) revised its reimbursement formula to private plans with even more generous overpayments to private Medicare plans. As noted previously, the new law paid private plans an average across all counties of 107% of FFS costs in 2004; some counties saw an increase of 40% in their payments.[10] Medicare now pays 116% of FFS spending for beneficiaries in floor counties in large urban areas and 123% of FFS payments in floor counties in other areas.[11]

When favorable risk selection by private Medicare plans is factored in these federal overpayments to private plans are even higher. On the basis of data submitted to CMS by private Medicare plans in 2003, it was determined that they had an aggregate risk score of 0.92 percent (i.e., their predicted costs should have been 8 percent lower than the costs for the average beneficiary in FFS Medicare).[12]

Only 30% of plan payments are risk-adjusted now, with full risk-adjustment not scheduled until 2007.[13] Additional overpayments because of favorable risk selection are expected to add another 2.3 percent in 2004 and 4.0 percent in 2005.[14] According to 2004 projections by CMS, overpayments to private Medicare plans in 2005 will be about $4.7 billion, and will total $80 billion between 2004 and 2014.[15]

HISTORY OF COMPETITIVE BIDDING

Advocates of the private sector in Medicare consistently tout the advantages of competition in the marketplace on the theory that it produces efficiency. It is therefore ironic that private interests galvanize their resistance to competitive bidding demonstrations whenever and wherever they are attempted by the Medicare program. Since the late 1980s, there has been only one competitive-pricing demonstration that has reached the point of evaluating bids and paying for services—a durable medical equipment (DME) demonstration in Polk County, Florida. Even in that case, the DME industry lobbied Congress and brought suit to block the demonstration.[16] That demonstration achieved aggregate savings of 17% without reduction in access or quality of services.[17]

The first two demonstration projects to test the efficacy of setting payments to M + C plans competitively were carried out by the Health Care Financing Administration (HCFA) in Baltimore in 1996 and Denver the next year. Both were disastrous failures as a result of fierce opposition by private stakeholders, who mounted a political and legal counterattack to block the demonstrations. Some local beneficiary groups were persuaded to resist the demonstrations by threatening that their benefits could be put at risk. Opponents argued that the FFS program be included in such demonstrations, that the method to determine the Medicare contribution be announced before the bidding, and that HCFA pay more attention to the views of local communities before selecting the sites.[18]

BBA 97 again called for competitive pricing demonstrations for M + C plans, this time to be designed and overseen by an independent body, the Competitive Pricing Advisory Committee (CPAC), composed of 15 mostly private-sector experts and stakeholders. Area Advisory Committees (AACs) were also established, with representatives from major local stakeholders, to recommend to HCFA how to tailor the demonstrations to local communities. In 1999, CPAC selected Phoenix and Kansas City for the next demonstrations. HCFA concluded that it lacked the authority to include FFS Medicare in the demonstrations, but went to considerable lengths to address concerns raised in Baltimore and Denver. In spite of these efforts, strong political opposition again emerged in Phoenix and Kansas City, resulting in prohibition by Congress of any further spending on those demonstrations and a moratorium on demonstrations until 2002.[19]

Several comments by researchers reviewing these failures are instructive concerning lessons to be learned. Len Nichols and Robert Reischauer, both from the Urban Institute and members of CPAC, had this to say in retrospect:[20]

"Although all businesses like to purchase their inputs in highly competitive markets with low prices, most would prefer to sell their

outputs in a monopolistic market or in one with an administered price well above their costs. In short, it was not in the interest of the American Association of Health Plans (AAHP) to have HCFA learn how to become an effective health plan purchaser."

" It turned out that the health policy leadership had insufficient leverage, and the overall leadership deferred to a few vocal members who were allowed to operate outside the committees with jurisdiction over Medicare policy. Congress as a whole did not kill the demonstrations it had approved in the BBA. Rather, the leadership on both sides of the isle and the White House allowed a few members to kill them, for reasons that had precious little to do with long run Medicare reform policy."

"If CPAC could have prepared the press and the members (of Congress) for the kinds of arguments the health plans would make before they made them, it may have been somewhat harder to kill the demonstration in the dark of night or during the end-of-session chaos, for then the leadership could be made to pay a public price by obviously retreating from the policy agreement they implicitly promised to enforce with passage of the BBA. As it happened, few people outside the Beltway and the elite media even noticed."

Barbara Cooper and Bruce Vladeck, both of the Institute for Medicare Practice at the Mount Sinai School of Medicine in New York City, have added this perspective.[21]

"Everyone wants market competition until they don't like the results. Real markets have losers. Without them, it is difficult to achieve much efficiency. In a democratic political system, losers, potential losers, and even those who feel that they might someday be losers often seek redress from their elected officials."

The AAHP has found itself giving lip service to the abstract concept of competition in the marketplace, while fighting against it tooth and nail. AAHP's objections in Baltimore and Denver included these defensive reactions, among others—participation should be voluntary, sites should be selected where there are no Medicare plans, FFS Medicare should be included in any demonstration, and any participants should be protected from any adverse effects. AAHP has long objected to basing reimbursement of private plans on FFS payment formulas. Although it has proposed that "market-based" methods be used to determine reimbursement, it has never come up with such a plan, even after being requested by HCFA to do so in the mid-1990s.[22]

After completing its comprehensive study and report on the role of private health plans in Medicare, the National Academy of Social Insurance (NASI) drew this conclusion about competitive pricing demonstrations.[23]

> *"That the program conduct competitive bidding demonstrations to test whether market forces can control costs and improve the stability of plan participation and benefits. Most panel members recommended that traditional Medicare be excluded from the demonstrations to provide vulnerable beneficiaries with greater stability, but that view was not unanimous."*

The Medicare legislation of 2003 (MMA) includes plans starting in 2010 for FFS Medicare to compete directly with private plans in up to six metropolitan areas where at least 25% of Medicare beneficiaries are in private plans. If past experience with cherry picking healthier enrollees and self-serving politics in the private sector is any indication of how these will fare, however, their outcomes are not likely to be much different from the failed pricing demonstrations described above.

In 1980, Arnold Relman, then Editor of *The New England Journal of Medicine*, called attention to the emergence of a medical-industrial complex as a threat to formulation of health policy in the public interest. Judging from the large role played by industry in the passage of MMA in 2003 and the veto power against real competition in the marketplace as illustrated above, Relman's words of 25 years ago are precisely on target:

> *"the medical-industrial complex creates the problems of overuse and fragmentation of services, overemphasis on technology, and 'cream-skimming,' and it may also exercise undue influence on national health policy"*[24]

WHY DO WE SUBSIDIZE PRIVATE "COMPETITORS" TO MEDICARE?

In view of all of the evidence presented in this and previous chapters that private Medicare plans offer no advantages over Original FFS Medicare by any measure—efficiency, access, cost containment, value, quality, or reliability—the question remains as to why they continue to be subsidized with ongoing federal overpayments. Three reasons stand out.

First, the claimed advantages of "competition" in the private marketplace lives on as an article of faith blinded by political ideology. As a meme, it does not require supporting evidence, which is lacking in health care markets. The Medicare plus Choice experience of the 1990s was discredited as a failure. As we saw in Chapter 6, the recently completed Community Tracking Study, after nine years of study of health care markets in 12 major metropolitan areas, found an absence of potentially efficient provider systems and insufficient health plan competition.[25] Both the General Accounting Office and the Office of Inspector General have concluded that private Medicare plans are more costly than FFS Medicare, and that protecting their viability threatens the financial sustainability of Medicare in the long run.[26,27]

Second, conservative pro market advocates have been very effective for many years in advancing the interests of stakeholders in the private sector while working to limit the role of government. We saw an example of this in Chapter 3 with the $30 million media campaign carried out by the Heritage Foundation between 1995 and 1997 to discredit Original Medicare as an "inferior program" and promote market-based solutions to the "Medicare problem."[28] The Heritage Foundation is but one of many neo-conservative think tanks which have emerged since the 1970s in the U.S. They are well funded, sponsor or produce studies and reports supporting their own interests, and lobby legislators effectively for competitive open markets.[29] Over the years, these think tanks have been very influential in shaping language patterns of the media and public opinion.[30]

Third, a more cynical but probably true reason for why private interests still promote their interests without supporting evidence is their longer-term goal to dismantle Medicare itself, convert it to a smaller welfare type program, and limit the obligations of government to the nation's elderly and disabled As we saw in Chapter 3, the new Republican majority in Congress, as part of its Contract with America in 1995, brought a bill forward (later vetoed by President Clinton) which would have privatized the Medicare program and shifted it to a program with defined contributions instead of benefits defined by law.[31] At that time, Newt Gingrich, as Speaker of the House, predicted that this kind of "reform" might result in "solving the Medicare problem" and lead it to "wither on the vine."[32,33] The ongoing conservative agenda is still to privatize Medicare as much as possible, segmenting the risk pool of healthier seniors into private plans, leaving sicker Medicare beneficiaries in traditional FFS Medicare where they will face increasingly unaffordable premiums, and then restrain government spending by a strategy of "premium support" with defined (and increasingly limited) federal contributions. That would promote a two-tiered system, with healthier seniors gravitating to the "better" private plans, shrinking the Medicare program to a smaller but high-risk pool of sicker seniors requiring high costs of care. To the extent that that agenda is carried out, the winners would be the corporate stakeholders in the private marketplace, the losers the most vulnerable groups in our society—the elderly and disabled.

SUBSIDIES AS CORPORATE WELFARE vs. THE PUBLIC INTEREST

We have seen in this and previous chapters how private Medicare plans cost more and provide less value and stability to Medicare beneficiaries compared to the traditional FFS program. Despite all the rhetoric by proponents of the private health care marketplace, real competition is more fiction than reality. With the first "age wave" of retiring baby boomers due to impact Medicare in only five years, demands on Medicare's resources will become even more strained. The health of the nation's elderly and disabled is too important to allow administrative waste and private corporate profiteering to drain Medicare's treasury away from patient care. These two observations are pertinent to the question of whether or not private Medicare plans should be subsidized:

> "Subsidizing private health plans is anathema to the Republican concept of using competition to ensure value. Private plans should be funded at no more than the same level as the traditional fee-for-service Medicare program, with appropriate adjustments for risk. The plans have already indicated that they would not participate without the subsidy to cover their greater administrative costs. But that should be their independent decision. It is immoral to grant them extra Medicare Trust Funds in a phony effort to create a mirage that they are somehow competitive. Take away the extra subsidy and then let them compete if they dare to. Removing the subsidies would meet the Republican goal of reducing waste of Medicare funds, and would meet the Democratic goal of being certain that the traditional Medicare program receives at least the same level of public funding, risk adjusted, as the Medicare + Choice (now Medicare Advantage) options." [34]

Don McCanne, MD, 2004,
Past President, Physicians for a National Health Program

"Initial higher payments to private plans may jump start this migration (to PPOs) but will not produce savings to Medicare if the payment rates are set above costs in the traditional Medicare program. When cost containment concerns in Medicare are reasserted, as they inevitably will be, payments to private plans will be targeted for reconsideration and refinement, potentially triggering a new round of instability that discredited Medicare private plan options in the late 1990s. " [35]

Issue Brief on Medicare Advantage
Center for Studying Health System Change, 2004

CHAPTER 12

COST-EFFECTIVENESS AND MEDICARE COVERAGE DECISIONS: THE (MUFFLED) BANG FOR OUR BUCKS

"Health interventions are not free, people are not infinitely rich, and the budgets of [health care] programs are limited. For every dollar's worth of health care that is consumed, a dollar will be paid. While these payments can be laundered, disguised or hidden, they will not go away."

David M. Eddy, MD, PhD Senior Advisor for Health Policy and
Management, Kaiser Permanente Southern California[1]

The U. S. has by far the most expensive health care system in the world, representing about one-seventh of the entire national economy. Americans spend more per capita on health care each year than any other industrialized Western country (nearly twice the per-capita spending in Canada and almost three times that in the United Kingdom in 2000).[2] Health care costs have been rising at double-digit levels in the U.S. over the last five years (by 16% in 2003) despite annual increases in the cost of living of only 2 to 3%.[3] Unfortunately, much of this spending is for health care services of marginal value, even at times harmful.[4,5] Against that background, it is now time to ask to what extent Medicare, as the largest single purchaser of health care in the country, has embraced the concept of cost-effectiveness in its coverage decisions.

This chapter addresses four questions: (1) how have Medicare coverage decisions been made since 1965; (2) what is the state of the art of cost-effectiveness analysis; (3) to what extent do politics complicate, or even supercede, evidence-based coverage decisions; and (4) should cost-effectiveness become an explicit consideration in future Medicare coverage decisions?

HOW MEDICARE COVERAGE DECISIONS ARE MADE

Over the 40-year period of Medicare's life, the major criterion used in its decisions about what services to cover is medical necessity, as defined by the words "reasonable and necessary." The original mandate by Congress in the 1965 Medicare legislation called for coverage decisions to be based on this principle: "Notwithstanding any other provision of this title, no payment may be made… for any expenses incurred for items or services which… are not reasonable and necessary for the diagnosis or treatment of illness or injury." That language left wide latitude in determinations of medical necessity, and payers generally accepted physicians' judgments at that time.[6]

As a result of continued inflation of health care costs over the years, triggered in large part by expansion of medical technology, together with the growing unaffordability of health care services by a sizable part of the population and concerns about quality of care, there have been further efforts to refine the process used in medical coverage decisions. An independent Medicare Coverage Advisory Committee (MCAC) was established in 1998 to assist in developing coverage policies. This interdisciplinary group includes clinicians, methodologists, industry representatives, and consumer advocates, and its meetings and reports are open to the public.[7] There are six panels within the MCAC: Medical/Surgical, Drugs/Biological/Therapeutics, Laboratory and Diagnostic Services, Medical Devices, Durable Medical Equipment, and Diagnostic Imaging. Decisions made through Medicare's national coverage process are made in one of four categories: national non-coverage; issue left to contractor discretion; national coverage with coverage limitations; and national coverage without coverage limitations.[8]

The Medicare program has at times attempted to address cost and value concerns in some of its coverage decisions. In 2000, for example, Medicare published a Notice of Intent (NOI) proposing that technologies must demonstrate "medical benefit" as well as "added value." The NOI proposed that four questions be added as part of a new application for coverage:[9]

"1 *Medical benefit*—Is there sufficient evidence to demonstrate that the product or service is medically beneficial for a particular population?

2 *Added value*—Does Medicare already cover a medically beneficial service that is in the same clinical modality for the same condition?

3 *Added value*—Is the new product or service substantially more beneficial, substantially less beneficial, or just about as beneficial

as the same modality product or service that is already covered?

4. *Added value*—Does the new product or service "result in equivalent or lower total costs for the Medicare population than the Medicare-covered alternative?""

In addition, the NOI suggested that Medicare cover only the lower-cost option among alternative treatments or services of equal efficacy.[10]

These proposed changes brought immediate and intense opposition from industry. This reaction to HCFAs proposed use of cost-effectiveness in coverage decisions was soon issued by the Pan Industry Group on Medicare Coverage, which includes such associations as the Advanced Medical Technology Association (Adva Med), the Medical Device Manufacturers Association, and the National Electrical Manufacturers Association, among others.[11]

> *"HCFA has no authority to deny coverage for a treatment because of issues related to cost effectiveness, and as a policy matter, it should not do so. If economic factors are to be considered, it is more appropriate to do so in the context of payment. HCFA should rely on market data in setting (and adjusting) payment levels."*

Another example of a heated response to Medicare's NOI of 2000 is this response from the Cancer Leadership Council, which describes itself as "a patient-centered forum of national advocacy organizations addressing public policy issues in cancer:"[12]

> *"The Notice assumes, without discussion or justification, that the Medicare program is authorized to make coverage determinations on the basis of cost-effectiveness or cost comparisons among different technologies. It is by no means clear that this approach was intended by Congress. Certainly, if the views of those charged with implementing the statute at the outset were taken into account, there would be no reason to believe that cost should be a consideration in coverage decisions, and in fact for most of the life of the Medicare program cost has not been a factor. Only in the failed Notice of Proposed Rulemaking in January 1989—25 years after the initiation of the program—did agency officials suggest that cost-effectiveness might be considered, and of course that proposal sat unfinalized for more than a decade and was ultimately withdrawn in April 1999. The assumption that cost-effectiveness is inherent in the statutory standard requiring coverage of items and services "reasonable and necessary" for medical care will*

not go unchallenged. Many would argue—and the agency's own history of interpreting the statute would support—that, so long as financial resources are available (as they clearly are in an entitlement program), the reasonableness of treatment for a life-threatening disease like cancer should not depend on its cost. If the agency insists on retaining cost-effectiveness as a coverage criterion for life-threatening diseases when and if it publishes a proposed rule, we will have much more to say then with respect to the appropriateness of this approach."

In other words, industry believed that cost and cost-effectiveness of their products are irrelevant to Medicare coverage decisions.

As chief clinical officer at CMS and director of the Office of Clinical Standards and Quality, Dr. Sean Tunis has this to say about Medicare's inability to set more specific rules for better defining "reasonable and necessary" and of adding considerations of cost-effectiveness to coverage decisions:[13]

"The failure to issue regulations defining" reasonable and necessary" reflects, in part, the inability of the primary stakeholders— employers, drug and device manufacturers, private payers, patient advocates, and organizations representing medical professionals—to reach a consensus. Among the most controversial issues addressed in past discussions has been the potential role of cost effectiveness in coverage decisions."

Nevertheless, despite the absence of explicit criteria concerning cost-effectiveness, Medicare has begun in recent years to move cautiously toward more cost-consciousness in its coverage decisions within the framework of its existing authority. An example is Medicare's 2003 rejection of Amgen's application for higher reimbursement for its anemia drug, Aranesp, on the basis of its "functional equivalence" to an older, less expensive drug.[14]

COST-EFFECTIVENESS ANALYSIS: STATE OF THE ART

Cost-effectiveness analysis (CEA) is the main method of measuring the costs and clinical consequences (i.e., efficacy and safety) in order to estimate the "economic value" of alternative treatments or services. The goal of CEA is to compare the relative value of different interventions in leading to better health and/or longer life. Its results are typically measured in terms of quality-adjusted life years (QALYs), and are derived from the following kind of equation, which captures both costs and outcomes:

$$\text{Incremental cost effectiveness, therapy A} = \frac{\text{Cost}_A - \text{Cost}_B}{\text{Effectiveness}_A - \text{Effectiveness}_B}$$

In this case, two interventions are compared—A (usually the new intervention) and B (the established one). Four outcomes of this comparison are then possible, which can better inform choices by policy makers. (Figure 12.1). Outcomes in Quadrant B should clearly be rejected, while Outcomes in Quadrant C should be accepted. Outcomes in Quadrants A and D involve tradeoffs calling for judgments of clinicians, patients and payers as to whether the improvement or loss in health outcomes are worth the additional costs or cost savings.[15]

In 1993 the U.S. Public Health Service convened a multidisciplinary panel of economists, ethicists, psychometricians, and clinicians to study and make recommendations for the use of CEA in health care policy. The panel's work was summarized in the 1996 book *Cost-Effectiveness in Health*

Figure 12.1

Depiction of Possible Outcomes of Pharmacoeconomic Studies.

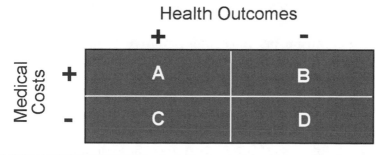

Notes: (A = higher costs, improved outcomes [trade-off]; B = high costs, worsened outcomes [reject]; C = lower costs, improved outcomes[accept]; D = lower costs, worsened outcomes [trade-off].) (Adapted from P Ellwood. Outcomes management: a technology of patient experience. NEngl J Med 1988; 318:1549-1556.)

Reprinted with permission from Ramsey SD & Sullivan SD. Weighing the economic evidence: Guidelines for critical assessment of cost-effectiveness analysis. In: Geyman JP, Deyo RA & Ramsey SD. *Evidence-Based Clinical Practice: Concepts and Approaches.* Woburn, Mass: Butterworth-Heinemann, 2000, p 104

and Medicine, which serves as the gold standard for conduct and quality of CEAs. The panel recognized early on that choices among health care interventions, no matter how informed by science, are also value judgments with distributive consequences.[16]

CEAs can vary widely in their quality and relevance to health policy based on many factors, especially the perspective taken, sponsorship, and assumptions made. The interpretation of a CEA requires some background. Ramsey and Sullivan[17] have provided us with a helpful approach by asking seven essential questions to interpret a particular CEA. Gold and her colleagues draw these distinctions with respect to sponsors' various perspectives and definitions of the term "cost-effective:"[18]

> *"Purchasers of health care use the term to convey a careful assessment of the relative value of different health care services; producers of health care technologies and programs use the idea to support marketing claims; advocates for particular illnesses or constituencies use the term to garner resource investments. All of these parties are agreeing to the notion of value for money that is connoted by the term, and this notion does allow for common conceptual ground to be found. However, notions of what is cost-effective held by the pharmaceutical industry, by managed-care organizations, or by other participants in the health care system may well be at variance with each other, or with what is thought of as cost-effective by society at large."*

For the purposes of Medicare coverage decisions, of course, the societal perspective is required.

CEA's can be confusing or even counterintuitive, even when rigorously and well done. Here are three examples of commonly held misperceptions about CEA.

- "Low technology" or inexpensive services are not necessarily cost effective (e.g., one CEA found that the cost of detecting a new case of colon cancer was $1,200 with the first stool guaiac test, but rose to $47 million if six one dollar guaiac cards were used)[19]

- Some expensive "high technology" interventions can be very cost-effective (e.g., coronary bypass surgery, costing about $30,000, has a cost-effectiveness ratio of about $2,300 to $5,600 per year of life saved for patients with left main coronary disease)[20]

• Faced with limited resources, the most responsible choice among competing interventions for care of a population is to cover an intervention that provides the greatest benefit to the most people; in some cases this may require rejection of an intervention that is more effective but costs more (i.e., has a lower cost-effectiveness ratio); this can appear counter-intuitive through the perspective of the individual patient or physician, but obvious from a population or societal view[21]

CEA clearly has no role to play in informing policy judgments for ineffective interventions, nor is it needed for new interventions that are already demonstrated to be both less expensive and equally or more effective than an older intervention in common usage. CEA's are most useful to assess new interventions that are both more expensive and more effective than standard interventions.[22]

Although there is still no broad consensus of what levels of cost-effectiveness are acceptable, there is a ballpark of societal acceptability which has gained currency. Interventions that cost less than $50,000 per QALY are generally accepted as cost-effective (renal dialysis for patients with end-stage renal failure costs $50,000 per QALY). Interventions in the range between $50,000 and $120,000 per QALY are considered questionable in terms of cost-effectiveness, while those over $120,000 per QALY are challenged and often not adopted on a wide scale.[23,24]

COST-EFFECTIVENESS AND MEDICARE COVERAGE: POLITICS vs. SCIENCE

As we have already seen, fierce opposition is engendered from industry each time that Medicare proposes to consider cost-effectiveness in its coverage decisions. From a business standpoint, that opposition is certainly understandable. Indeed, the stakes to industry of prompt and positive coverage decisions are high, and even more so because many other payers follow Medicare's lead.

Here are three examples of high-stakes Medicare coverage decisions which are not cost-effective by CEA measures, but had sufficiently strong political constituencies to gain coverage.

• <u>Left ventricular assist devices</u>. Initially used as a temporary stopgap measure in patients with severe heart failure awaiting heart transplantation, left ventricular assist devices were later used as a definitive treatment for patients who were not candidates for heart transplants because of age or other illness. A 2001 report of a randomized study found that the device did decrease mortality, but still with survival rates at one year of 52% and at two years of only 23%. There were modest improvements in quality of life noted at one year.[25] After careful review by the MCAC, the procedure was approved by CMS if performed in selected heart-transplantation facilities after a rigorous process of informed consent.[26] A CEA for this procedure, computed by Blue Cross-Blue Shield, estimated its cost-effectiveness between $500,000 and $1.4 million per QALY for the population for whom it was approved by CMS.[27] About 5,000 Medicare patients are initially expected to qualify for the left-ventricular assist device, but this number could rise to 100,000 at a cost of $7 billion per year.[28]

- Lung-volume-reduction surgery. A five-year multicenter random-ized clinical trial was reported in 2003 for lung-reduction-surgery as a treatment for patients with advanced chronic obstructive lung disease. Although the procedure achieved no improvement in survival, exercise capacity was increased in 16% of surgically-treated patients compared to those receiving medical treatment.[29] CMS recently approved this procedure for three selected groups of patients, for which CEA's were also reported in 2003—patients with upper-lobe disease and low baseline exercise capacity ($98,000 per QALY); patients with upper-lobe disease and high exercise capacity ($240,000 per QALY); and patients with diffuse disease and low exercise capacity ($330,000 per QALY).[30] It is anticipated that 10,000 to 20,000 Medicare patients will be candidates for this procedure each year, at a cost of between $600 million and $1.2 billion.[31, 32]

- Pedicle screws for spinal fusion. In the five-year period between 1996 and 2001, spinal fusion surgery in the U.S. increased by 77%, more than five times the increase for either hip replacement or knee arthroplasty.[33] The indications for spinal fusion are controversial and highly variable from one part of the country to another. For most patients having surgery for low back problems, there is little evidence that fusion improves their outcomes;[34-36] Some studies show much higher complication rates for fusion compared to laminectomy without fusion.[37] However, the market for various kinds of spinal implants and devices has been growing by about18 to 20% each year for use in spinal fusion procedures.[38] Not only do pedicle screws cause more complications than fusion procedures without the hardware, but they also do not give more pain relief or improved function.[39] Nevertheless, spinal fusions with pedicle screws are still approved for Medicare patients, as they have been for some years, even with a CEA of over $3 million per QALY reported in 2000![40]

In each of these instances, high-cost treatments became covered by Medicare without evidence of cost-effectiveness. Legislators and payers are under heavy political pressure by industry and allied groups to approve coverage and reimbursement, as illustrated by these examples:

- After publication of two research papers in the early 1990s which found that lumbar spinal fusion procedures were less effective than surgery without fusion,[41,42] the Agency for Health Care Policy and Research (AHCPR) published clinical guidelines for managing low back pain favoring non-surgical approaches. Concerned about a decline in spinal surgery as a result of AHCPR's new guidelines, the North American Spine Society criticized the guidelines and lobbied Congress through an advocacy group formed by a Society Board member (the Center for Patient Advocacy) to eliminate funding for the AHCPR. The House of Representatives actually voted to cut off AHCPR funding, and it was only after industry's tactics were exposed that the Senate restored partial AHCPR funding. The FDA, which had not approved the use of pedicle screws beyond narrow indications, was also the target of a lobbying campaign. In an effort to protect its market for pedicle screws, one manufacturer sought (unsuccessfully) a court injunction to block the AHCPR from publishing and disseminating its guidelines for treating low back pain.[43]

- According to its Web site, AdvaMed is the largest medical technology trade association in the world, representing more than 1,200 medical device, diagnostic products, and health information systems manufacturers of all sizes. AdvaMed member firms manufacture 90 percent of the $75 billion of health care technology products purchased annually in the U.S. and more than 50 percent of the $175 billion purchased annually around the world. Among its activities, AdvaMed "works for responsible legislation to address industry concerns on Capitol Hill and for appropriate administrative policies affecting the industry in agencies such as the Food and Drug Administration (FDA) and the Centers for Medicare and Medicaid Services (CMS), formerly the Health Care Financing Administration (HCFA), by using all the tools of modern political advocacy." As part of its ongoing lobbying campaign for the industry's interests, largely invisible to the public, AdvaMed promotes these goals:[44]

> —"Faster coverage and payment determinations by CMS.
>
> —Comprehensive Medicare reform based on market-based principles
>
> —Patient access to medical technologies and appropriate payment for medical technologies around the globe.
>
> —Reasonable Medicare coverage criteria.
>
> —Recognition of AdvaMed as a global authority in technology assessment."

The collective impact of favorable coverage decisions by Medicare and other payers is enormous and certain to exacerbate health care inflation and unaffordability of health care by a growing part of the population. Just one other example conveys some idea of the magnitude of this problem. A 2002 report of a study funded by industry found an absolute survival benefit of 5.6% for the prophylactic use of an implantable cardiac defibrillator (ICD) in patients with myocardial infarction and reduced cardiac ejection fraction.[45] Guidant, the leading manufacturer of ICDs, submitted an application to CMS in 2002 for coverage by Medicare of the prophylactic use of ICDs in this population of patients. Coverage for that population could have involved up to 400,000 patients each year at a cost of $12 billion a year, three times the 2003 budget for the Centers for Disease Control and Prevention (CDC).[46] After careful review of other studies and further consultation, CMS recently approved this procedure for a small subgroup of patients with inducible ventricular tachycardia for whom the CEA is probably in the range of $30,000 to $85,000 per QALY.[47,48] That coverage decision remains hotly contested, however, and the medical device industry continues to lobby for broader coverage criteria in order to expand the market for its products.[49]

SHOULD COST-EFFECTIVENESS BECOME AN EXPLICIT PART OF MEDICARE COVERAGE DECISIONS?

From the foregoing, we have seen how intense the resistance has been from market-based industries to the introduction of cost-effectiveness considerations in Medicare coverage decisions. This reaction is reminiscent of the drug industry's powerful (and successful) lobbying against any price controls for the new prescription drug benefit established by MMA 2003. We continue to see profiteering by corporate stakeholders at the expense of the Medicare program and its beneficiaries. As we have also seen in earlier chapters, rising prices, together with increasing cost-sharing requirements pose formidable barriers to access and affordability of essential health care for Medicare beneficiaries. As a single-payer program for 40 million Americans, Medicare therefore has the opportunity and the responsibility to introduce more cost-consciousness into its coverage and reimbursement policies.

Privatization is the most serious challenge facing the Medicare program. As long as private interests exert such undue influence on prices, coverage and reimbursement policies, Medicare will have a hard time serving the best interests of its beneficiaries. The U.S. has by far the highest prices and most expensive health care system in the world, and has been the least successful in reining in these costs. In their excellent recently reported study of the reasons for this country's unabated inflation of health care costs, Gerald Anderson and his colleagues at the Bloomberg School of Public Health at the Johns Hopkins University documented that the two most important reasons for this are higher medical care prices and higher incomes of our citizens. Despite misperceptions to the contrary, Americans on a per-capita basis have less access to hospital beds, physicians and nurses, and both magnetic resonance imaging (MRI) and computed tomography (CT) than most other Organization for Economic Cooperation and Development (OECD) countries, which spend so much less on health care than the U.S.[50] Thus, it is the prices, not the amount of health care delivered, that on a per-capita basis Americans are responsible for large differences in health care costs between the U.S. and other industrialized countries.[51]

Stakeholders on the provider side of the health care system have promoted their interests while fueling consumer concerns about the R-word, "rationing." Legislators at both state and federal levels have been receptive to lobbyists' efforts, and on many occasions have mandated the coverage of disputed services. In the ensuing debates, tension repeatedly arises between the whole population perspective and the individual patient perspective inherent in clinical practice.[52, 53]

Despite persistent resistance by stakeholders in our market-based system to explicit cost-effectiveness policies, it appears likely that it is only a matter of time before pressure will build to implement such policies. Two recent developments are noteworthy, and should be helpful as that transition inevitably takes place.

The American Medical Association (AMA) has taken a leadership role by sponsoring the Ethical Force Program, a collaborative project led by the AMA's Institute of Ethics. With a focus on fairness in health care coverage decisions, the Ethical Force Program brought together leaders representing practitioners, patients, health plans, government, unions, employers, and other organizations to develop consensus and plans of action. After two year's of study and dialogue, its consensus report was published in 2004. One of its five content areas deals with the need for coverage decisions to be sensitive to value. Among their recommendations to organizations involved in coverage decisions are the following:[54]

- "Employ cost-effectiveness analysis (CEA) using standardized methods when comparing two treatments or tests that are expected to have similar clinical efficacy but substantially different costs.

- Give priority to the most cost-effective service or treatment option when more than one similarly effective alternative is available. Exceptions should be made for individuals for whom alternatives

Table 12.1

Recommendations of Ethical Force Program for Coverage Decisions

Expectations of All Organizations Involved In Designing Covered Benefits

4.1 In determining whether to include proposed new services, technologies, or modalities in a health benefit package, the organization considers their value for the covered population by assessing:

4.1a Their benefits, harms, and risks using the best available clinical and scientific data;

4.1b Their net health benefits compared to those of the best existing alternatives.

4.2 When the net health benefit of a proposed new service, technology, or modality significantly exceeds that of the best existing covered alternative, the new service is covered.

4.3 When the net health benefit of a proposed new service, technology, or modality is comparable to that of the best existing alternative, the organization reviews (or performs, if necessary) cost-effectiveness analyses to compare the new technology to the best existing covered alternative(s). Services that are more cost-effective are covered preferentially as first-line services for the population, but exceptions may be made in individual circumstances.

4.4 Cost-effectiveness analyses, when performed, are performed using standard and consistent methodologies.

4.5 When previously performed cost-effectiveness analyses are reviewed, they are assessed for whether they were performed using standard and consistent methodologies."

4.6 In assessing the overall cost-effectiveness of proposed interventions, the organization considers the health of all relevant communities, including communities outside the covered population.

4.7 The organization periodically reviews cost-effectiveness assessments when:
4.7a Relevant new information arises that might significantly impact previous analyses;
4.7b More than 5 years pass.

Expectations of All Organizations Involved In Administering Covered Benefits

4.8 Financial and other costs and benefits that may lie outside the immediate organization (including costs and benefits to the patient, his or her caregivers, employer, family members, and so on) are considered in assessing whether to cover proposed interventions for individuals.

4.9 For conditions and categories of service that are included in the covered benefits, a specific technology or modality is covered when its net benefit significantly exceeds that of the best-existing alternative for the given individual, taking the unique clinical and functional needs of the individual into account.

Expectations of Some Specific Parties Involved In Administering Covered Benefits

4.10 Practitioners and provider organizations give the most accurate information available

Reprinted with permission from Ethical Force Program. *Ensuring Fairness in Health Care Coverage Decisions.* Chicago: American Medical Association, 2004 p 8.

would provide unique benefits or who face unique harms from the preferred option."

Table 12.1 lists ten recommendations made by the Ethical Force Program in order to facilitate value-sensitive coverage decisions.

Another project that sheds light on how consumers will respond to a value-based criterion for clinical and coverage decisions is the Visible Fairness project conducted by Sacramento Healthcare Decisions in 2000. Twenty-five groups of consumers, totaling more than 250 participants were presented with various scenarios illustrating medical interventions that provide small benefit at high cost. As expected, several concerns were expressed about using cost-effectiveness in coverage and care decisions, including worries that technological innovation might be compromised and an unwillingness to admit that any treatment may be too expensive to be worth doing. However, most of the participants thought that the present skyrocketing costs and co-payments are not sustainable, and that a cost-effectiveness criterion for coverage and care decisions would be reasonable if three conditions are met:

1. the key to patients' acceptance of cost-effectiveness lies in their trust of their physicians, (i.e., that the physician has their best interest at heart)

2. coverage guidelines should have some flexibility and be based on scientific evidence, be created by an independent body without conflicts of interest, and be able to demonstrate that cost savings are redistributed to improve patient care

3. there must be fairness and consistency to coverage decisions, with a national standard involving all health plans likely to be most fair[55]

In view of the virtual absence of CEA in Medicare coverage decisions to date, together with the strong political pressure by market-based stakeholders to maintain the status quo, what can we expect concerning the role of CEA in future Medicare coverage policy? Here are two assessments of this question by experienced health policy experts.

"To Medicare, CEA has been an elephant in the living room, officially ignored despite its obvious importance. A decade of failed

attempts to integrate CEA has revealed the strength of reluctance in the United States to openly confront resource constraints. If Medicare officials—and politicians—learned anything from the ordeal, it is the political folly of trying to ration honestly. Despite rising Medicare expenditures and the impending retirement of the baby boomers, prospects for the adoption of CEA remain dim. Physicians are already angered and frustrated by CMS. Politicians will not risk antagonizing elderly voters.

At the same time, Medicare cannot avoid difficult decisions about costly new technology. What's a $400 billion-agency to do? Most likely, it will stumble along with one hand tied behind its back, evading the tough choices by delegating authority, cutting payment rates, and handling expensive new technology through coding and payment policy, all the while reassuring beneficiaries that they will maintain access to important advances."[56]

Peter Neumann, ScD,
Program on the Economic Evaluation of Medical Technology,
Harvard School of Public Health

"Cost-effectiveness analysis is a decades-old technique that has been studied more than it has been applied. Although it is not without flaws, it was never widely applied to U.S. coverage decisions because there was neither a consensus about how it should be used nor strong enough incentives to adopt it. The erosion of commercial health insurance and the growing burden of public health insurance programs may transform it from an academic curiosity to an essential tool for health care decision making."[57]

Alan Garber, MD,
Director of the Center for Health Policy,
Stanford University

CONCLUDING COMMENTS

As we have seen, politics driven by stakeholder self-interest often trumps evidence-based science in health policy. The use of cost-effectiveness considerations in coverage policies has lagged way behind its need, largely due to resistance from special interests and the disinclination of legislators to address the problems. Like it or not, however, real limits are already here.

As a large and growing program, Medicare coverage decisions affect not just its 40 million elderly and disabled beneficiaries, but their families and generations to follow. Everyone therefore has a stake in its coverage decisions to assure that they best serve the public interest. Thus coverage policies should be decided through an informed and open political process, not through behind-the-scenes lobbying of special economic interests.

Increased awareness among health professionals and the public is an urgent need whereby coverage policies can be framed from a societal perspective, not the economic self-interest of stakeholders in a largely unfettered market-based system. Richard Lamm, former governor of Colorado, reminds us "In public policy, everything we do prevents us from doing something else."[58] We will need to develop the political will to make health policy choices which benefit the largest number of people within limited resources. As controversial as cost-effectiveness is in Medicare coverage policy, so too is the level at which such policy is set, and that is the subject of the next chapter.

CHAPTER 13

HOW SHOULD MEDICARE COVERAGE AND REIMBURSEMENT DECISIONS BE MADE: LOCAL vs. NATIONAL?

As we saw in Chapter 2, there was widespread opposition initially to the enactment of Medicare throughout the medical, hospital, and insurance industries. In order to gain passage of the statute, the federal government needed a buffer between itself and these industries. Blue Cross, closely affiliated with the hospital industry, stepped forward to fill that role. Through this political compromise in 1965, the federal government ceded much of its regulatory authority over Medicare to the private sector and launched a complex and cumbersome decentralized administrative structure that has come down to this day. It has become apparent to many health policy experts over the years that this structure perpetuates serious inequities of coverage and access, together with wide geographic variations in costs and quality of care. This decentralized structure has also impaired national efforts to contain costs and assure quality in the overall program.

This chapter addresses five questions: (1) how has this decentralized administrative system evolved over the last 40 years; (2) how are coverage and reimbursement decisions made today; (3) do geographic variations in coverage and reimbursement policies matter; (4) what are the political forces which have so far made reforms impossible; and (5) what are some new proposed directions to decrease geographic variations and improve coverage and reimbursement policies for the Medicare program?

HISTORICAL PERSPECTIVE

The Medicare statute defined two different contractual structures in 1965. Under Part A, fiscal intermediaries (FIs) would contract to set coverage and reimbursement policies for hospitals, extended care facilities, and home health agencies, as well as provide utilization review and auditing services. Under Part B, the federal government would contract with private insurers (carriers) to carry out the same functions for physician services. The American Hospital Association (AHA) selected the Blue Cross Association as the prime contractor for all of its member hospitals, which then subcontracted to its local plans around the country to serve as FIs.[1] By 1970, Blue Cross was serving 91% of hospitals, 54% of extended care facilities, and 78% of home health agencies.[2] Blue Shield plans held contracts to work with physicians serving about 60% of Medicare beneficiaries in over 30 geographic areas of the country, with commercial carriers covering the rest.[3] Thus, in the case of both Parts A and B, local decision-making resulted from the decentralized nature of FIs and carriers, not from any requirements in the Medicare legislation itself.

From the early years of Medicare, its national Office of Coverage Policy was only rarely involved with coverage policy. Instead, it relied on local contractors to mediate disputes and set policy. As the program grew and its costs mounted, however, a need developed for more effective and efficient ways to evaluate coverage of costly new technologies, such as computed tomography (CT) scanning and heart transplantation. There have been repeated efforts by HCFA over the last 30 years to establish mechanisms to centralize more Medicare coverage and reimbursement decision making. All of these efforts have generated intense opposition, led especially by the medical device industry. Susan B. Foote, a leading expert on Medicare coverage policy, coined the term regula mortis for the stalemate which has persisted between industry and the federal government which has effectively thwarted a strong shift to national coverage decision making. As she observed in a 2002 case study of regula mortis in Medicare:[4]

> "From the 1970s into the 1990s, HCFA tried a variety of tactics to enact an explicit national coverage rule. In 1997, HCFA abandoned the rule making strategy and opted to carry on with development of criteria without engaging in rule making. When HCFA changed tactics, industry turned the tables in response, demanding rule making when faced with informal agency action imposing potentially undesirable standards. HCFA once again flirted with rule making in 2000 by publishing a Notice of Intent (NOI) to Engage in Rulemaking (HCFA 2000a). Now that HCFA is positioned to engage in a new round of rule making, the industry has opposed the substantive provisions in the notice. Regula mortis—the stalemate continues."

Each time that HCFA has attempted to set new rules or criteria for national coverage decision making, the medical device industry has orchestrated vigorous lobbying and letter-writing campaigns to members of Congress in opposition to centralized coverage decisions. As we saw in the last chapter, industry has steadfastly opposed any efforts to bring cost-effectiveness into such decisions. Over the years, these campaigns have played a large role in countering federal efforts to establish effective national bodies for technology assessment, such as the National Center for Health Care Technology (NCHCT) (1978-1981) and the Technology Advisory Committee (TAC 1997-1998). The power of the medical device industry to influence coverage policy behind the scene is well illustrated by its successful lobbying, in the waning moments of the 106th Congress, to make important changes in the decision-making process of the Medicare Coverage Advisory Committee (MCAC). As part of the 2000 reconciliation package, the Executive Committee of MCAC could no longer reverse panel decisions, industry MCAC representatives would become voting members, and appeals provisions for dissatisfied parties would be expanded.[5,6]

About 90% of Medicare coverage decisions are made by almost 50 local contractors, which posted more than 9,000 separate coverage policies on the local medical review policies (LMRPs) Web site in 2001. Each of these policies apply only in its local jurisdiction. Some contractors develop many LMRPs while others develop only a few. There is little consistency in coverage policies from one area to another, as illustrated by 35 separate policies for deep brain stimulation.[7]

HOW ARE COVERAGE AND REIMBURSEMENT DECISIONS MADE?

Until recently, little was known about what takes place across the country in the formulation of Medicare policy by local contractors. We have Foote and her colleagues to thank for learning more about that process. They analyzed 6,900 carrier and FI LMRPs as of May 2001, downloaded from the CMS-sponsored Web site. Two physician consultants, acting independently, in order to increase the validity of their reviews, classified all of these LMRPs into one of three categories—new technology (NT), extensions of covered technology (TE) and utilization management (UM). They agreed upon 84% of policies, with UM the most common category (73 to 88%), followed by NT (8 to 16%) and TE (3 to 10%). Their study found wide variations among local contractors, however, in resources, productivity, use of evidence, and timelines.[8]

Local contractors vary considerably in size and scope, ranging from smaller single-state programs to larger multi-state networks. Staff involved in LMRP development range from one-half time person to 9 full-time staff. Many contractors lack access to external assessment expertise and have limited internal expertise in technology assessment. Of special concern, especially for NT and TE evaluations, is the finding that many contractors fail to cite evidence in support of their LMRPs. Less than one-half of LMRPs are based on journal articles or medical texts.[9] This means that decisions are often made at the local level to cover services of little or no value to patients.

The vast majority of Medicare coverage and reimbursement decisions are made by local contractors. This is a very large task. Local contractors employed 21,000 people in 2001, processed a billion claims, and provided administrative services to 33 million people.[10] By contrast, only 10 to 12 national coverage decisions (NCDs) are made each year that apply to all Medicare beneficiaries across the country.[11]

In view of the major differences in size, resources, and expertise in technology evaluation among local contractors around the country, it is no surprise that their coverage decisions also vary widely. These differences have not yet received much analysis, but two examples make the point, both contentious in their areas. Oxygen is considered a drug in some states, but not in others; it is subject to different state laws, and its use is regulated and reimbursed differently.[12] Intravenous vitamin D replacement therapy is covered by some local Medicare contractors for patients on kidney dialysis, while others restrict such therapy to oral vitamin D. The irrationality of many coverage differences becomes obvious when restricted services are covered for other Medicare beneficiaries who live just minutes away in another LMRP jurisdiction.[13]

Industry recognizes that local coverage decisions are based on less vigorous evidence-based review compared to national decisions, and are more likely to give them favorable coverage decisions. Steven Ubi, executive vice president, federal government relations for the Advanced Medical Technology Association (AdvaMed, a large trade organization) observes:[14]

"For most manufacturers, it makes sense to first try the local determination process, in which carriers make determinations for their regions. Requesting a national coverage decision can be a gamble.

> *Besides the lengthy process, if the agency opts against coverage, that decision holds nationwide, with no local carrier leeway."*

Thus, many stakeholders have a vested interest in keeping this cumbersome and inefficient process of making Medicare coverage decisions.

In addition to making Medicare coverage decisions, local contractors also develop evidence and coding requirements for reimbursement of covered services. For example, Empire Medical Services, a local contractor covering New York City and New Jersey, had 216 effective posted policies in 2001 in New Jersey with more than 2,600 unique Healthcare Common Procedure Coding System (HCPCs) codes.[15] Not only do billing codes vary considerably from one local jurisdiction to another, but reimbursement levels for Medicare services have varied widely across the country since the program's early years.

Since Medicare was designed to follow local practice patterns instead of being a monolithic program, Medicare payments were based initially on health care costs existing in Medicare beneficiaries' counties of residence. These costs varied widely from one part of the country to another, and later years have seen continuing wide geographic differences in Medicare reimbursement levels.[16] For example, Medicare spending levels in 2000 ranged from a low of $3,053 per capita in Iowa to a high of $10,373 in the District of Columbia. Many factors influence these differences, of course, including average age of a county's population, physician supply, local styles of practice, and variations in costs of living. However, geographic variation in Medicare spending is only partly related to price variations, since counties with high hospital wage indexes do not necessarily have high Medicare spending levels, and vice versa.[17] Although many efforts have been made by Medicare over the years to reduce geographic disparities in reimbursement levels, this has turned out to be a very difficult problem to manage, particularly for political reasons. We will return to politics shortly after asking a critical question.

DO GEOGRAPHIC VARIATIONS MATTER?

The important overriding policy question is whether and how these persistent geographic variations impact the care of Medicare beneficiaries. One might expect that higher levels of Medicare spending could lead to better access and quality of care. Unfortunately, however, there is now a solid body of evidence that no such improvements result from increased Medicare spending, and that some impacts are on the negative side of the ledger.

John Wennberg and colleagues at the Center for Evaluative Clinical Sciences at Dartmouth Medical School have done landmark studies of the geographic variation issue in the U.S. They have found more than two-fold differences in Medicare spending from one part of the country to another. Per capita Medicare spending in 2000, for example, was $10,550 in Manhattan, New York but only $4, 823 in Portland, Oregon, even after adjusting for age, sex, and race.[18] Spending differences have been found to be mostly unrelated to differences in illness or price[19] but instead due to differences in patterns of practice, which are more specialist oriented and inpatient-based in higher spending areas.[20] Medicare beneficiaries in Manhattan spent twice as many days in the hospital in 2000 than their counterparts in Portland, had twice as many physician visits that year, and were three times as likely to spend a week or more in a hospital intensive care visit in their last six months of life.[21]

It is now clear that more medical care is not only not better, but it also is often worse. The Dartmouth group has analyzed health care patterns in 306 Hospital Referral Regions (HRRs) around the country. They have compared health care across these HRRs in terms of three criteria—effective care, preference-sensitive care and supply-sensitive care. An effective care index was determined as the sum of 11 evidence-based indicators of good practice, such as vaccination for pneumococcal pneumonia, mammography screening for breast cancer and use of beta-blockers after myocardial infarction. Preference-sensitive care occurs when there are two valid treatments available with differing risks and benefits, typically surgical vs. non-surgical; the index for preference-sensitive care is the sum of rates for 10 surgical procedures profiled in the 1999 Dartmouth Atlas of Health Care. Supply-sensitive care refers to services which increase with the supply of providers, especially specialists and specialized facilities. These indices are brought together in Figure 13.1, which compares Medicare spending and patterns of care in four HRRs. The important point revealed by these data is that higher spending areas have more specialist visits, more hospitalizations, and more use of ICUs, while lower-spending areas provide equally effective care.[22]

In other analyses, the Dartmouth group compared all HRRs across the

Figure 13.1

Comparison of Medicare Spending, Supply Sensitive Care, Preference-Sensitive Care and Effective Care For Orange County, Miami, Minneapolis, And Portland Hospital Referral Regions, 1995-1996

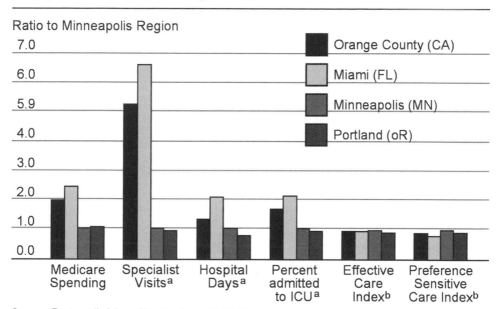

Source: Dartmouth Atlas of Health Care, 1995-96 database
Notes: Rates are given as ratio to Minneapolis hospital referral region (valued as 1.0)
[a] Care provided per decedent in the last six months of life.
[b] See Exhibit 2 for definitions
Reprinted with permission from Wennberg JB, Fisher ES & Skinner JS. Geography and the debate over Medicare reform. *Health Affairs* Web Exclusive W103, February 13, 2002.

country by quintiles of Medicare spending for end-of-life (last 6 months) care. Cost and outcomes of care were examined for hip fracture, colorectal cancer, and acute myocardial infarction. Table 13.1 shows lower quality of care in the highest-spending HRRs for both preventive services and care of myocardial infarction, while Table 13.2 shows lower access to care as well in higher-spending HRRs.[23,24]

The Dartmouth group has shown beyond any doubt that higher Medicare spending does not improve health, patient satisfaction, or quality of care, and can even be harmful.[25] It estimates that about one-third of this

Table 13.1

Quality of Care according to Level of Medicare Spending in Hospital Referral Region of Residence*

Variable	Quintile of EOL-EL					Test for Trend ‡
	1 (Lowest)	2	3	4	5 (Highest)	
Acute MI cohort ‡						
Received reperfusion within 12 hours	55.8	55.3	52.3	53.3	49.8	↓
Received aspirin in the hospital	87.7	87.0	84.8	85.3	83.9	↓
Received aspirin at discharge	83.5	82.5	79.8	78.5	74.8	↓
Received ACE inhibitors at discharge	62.7	60.0	56.6	58.3	58.5	↓
Received b-blockers in the hospital	61.5	61.0	54.3	61.5	63.9	↑
Received b-blockers at discharge	52.7	53.2	47.1	53.5	53.7	>0.05
MCBS cohort						
Preventive services						
Received influenza vaccine	60.3	56.3	54.3	50.0	48.1	↓
Received pneumonia vaccine	29.4	28.7	27.2	25.3	19.7	↓
Received Papanicolaou smear (among women without hysterectomy)	40.8	36.9	39.6	39.8	33.6	↓
Received mammography (among women age 65-69 y)	48.7	46.9	46.2	47.5	47.6	>0.05

* ACE = angiotensin-converting enzyme EOL-EI=End-of-Life Expenditure Index; MCBS Medicare Current Beneficiary Survey; MI myocardial infarction.
　Arrows show the direction of any statistically significant association ($p \leq 0.05$) between the percentage of patients receiving a specified service and regional EOL-EI differences. An arrow pointing upward indicates that as spending increases across regions the percentage of patients receiving a specified service increases. A p value greater than 0.05 was considered not significant.
‡ Values are for patients who were ideal candidates for the specific treatment, defined as having no absolute or relative contraindication.

Reprinted with permission from Fisher FS, Wennberg DE, Stukel TA, et al. The implications of regional variations in Medicare spending. Part 1: The content, quality, and accessibility of care. *Annals Internal Medicine* 138:283, 2003a.

spending is wasteful without benefit to patients.[26] A 2004 report corroborates and adds to its findings, showing that states with higher levels of Medicare spending use more expensive, higher intensity care of lower quality. States with more generalist physicians were found to provide more effective care at lower cost.[27] The full extent of this wasteful use of unnecessary care is

Table 13.2

Access to Care according to Level of Medicare Spending in Hospital Referral Region of Residence*

Variable	Quintile of EOL-EL					Test for Trend ‡
	1 (Lowest)	2	3	4	5 (Highest)	
Acute MI cohort						
	←———— % ————→					
Procedures within 30 days of admission ‡						
Angiography among all patients	48.2	50.3	49.3	50.2	47.4	↓
Angiography among appropriate patients	55.8	57.6	56.0	57.2	53.7	↓
Coronary bypass surgery	13.8	14.2	14.6	15.0	14.5	↑
Percutaneous coronary interventions	19.8	20.7	18.9	19.5	18.5	↓
Cardiac stress test	17.9	15.2	14.0	15.7	14.7	↓
Use of services after discharge ‡						
Physician office visit within 30 days of discharge	71.3	70.0	67.5	69.4	69.6	↓
Hospital readmission within 30 days of discharge	19.4	20.2	10.0	21.2	21.8	↑
Physician visits within first 30 days ‡						
Family or general practitioner	33.9	31.9	32.4	24.3	21.2	↓
General internist	47.7	50.0	52.1	49.9	52.6	↑
Cardiologist	70.1	76.4	72.5	78.3	81.3	↑
Other medical specialist	23.1	27.6	28.2	32.9	42.2	↑
Surgeon	20.9	24.7	25.9	25.9	28.9	↑
MCBS cohort						
Has usual source of care	87.8	89.7	89.0	86.0	86.5	↓
Specific visits received and waiting times at visit						
Emergency department visit	15.8	19.7	17.8	17.7	18.2	>0.05
Waited >30 min	28.4	28.8	29.3	33.8	34.0	↑
Outpatient department visit	28.5	26.2	26.3	26.5	25.3	↓
Waited >30 min	22.9	30.1	35.7	34.9	39.3	↑
Physician visit	81.1	81.0	82.4	83.1	84.5	↑
Waited >30 min	24.8	29.3	29.9	30.3	31.9	↑
Barriers to access						
Had trouble getting care	2.5	2.9	3.4	3.0	3.1	>0.05
Had a problem but did not see MD	8.7	9.9	11.4	11.5	10.1	↑
Delayed care because of cost	9.3	10.2	10.9	11.0	8.9	>0.05

* EOL-E1 = End-of-Life Expenditure Index; MCBS = Medicare Current Beneficiary Survey; MI = myocardial infarction.
↓ Arrows show the direction of any statistically significant association ($p \leq 0.05$) between the percentage of patients with a given attribute and regional EOI-EL differences.
An arrow pointing upward indicates that as spending increases across regions, the percentage of patients with a given characteristic increases. A p value greater than 0.05 was considered not significant.
‡ Percentage of patients receiving one or more.

§ *Appropriate* is defined as patients with class I disease by American Heart Association-American

Reprinted with permission from Fisher FS, Wennberg DE, Stukel TA, et al. The implications of regional variations in Medicare spending. Part 1: The content, quality, and accessibility of care. *Annals Internal Medicine* 138:285, 2003a

illustrated by one patient's experience who lives in an affluent area with many specialists in South Florida. A retired manufacturer of flight simulators went to a physician for a shot of cortisone for a finger. He received much more: " I had diathermy. I had ultrasound. I had a paraffin massage. I had $600 worth of Medicare treatments to get my lousy $35 shot of cortisone."[28] This kind of anecdote is unfortunately part of a well-documented and entrenched national pattern. Wennberg brings this perspective to the problem:[29]

> *"Greater per capita spending buys more intensive intervention among patients with chronic illness: Those who live in high-cost regions experience more visits to medical specialists, tests, hospitalizations, and ICU stays than their counterparts living in low-cost regions. And because of the way Medicare is financed, regions with low costs end up subsidizing a sizable proportion of the care for those living in high-cost regions."*

In earlier chapters we saw how unabated escalation of prices in the overall health care system threatens access to care and affordability of essential care for many millions of Americans, with the elderly and disabled an especially vulnerable population. That we at the same time have high-spending areas of the country which provide too much health care at much higher cost and without improvement in quality points to how difficult it has been to manage the Medicare program in the best interests of all of its beneficiaries. In short, we continue to have two kinds of problems—overuse of care, including unnecessary and lower quality care in areas of excess capacity, and underuse of necessary care due to access barriers, especially in areas of the country with fewer resources. Both problems need to be addressed, but to do so will require much more effective management than has yet been possible within the current decentralized Medicare structure of governance.

LOCAL vs. NATIONAL DECISION-MAKING: A TUG-OF-WAR STALEMATE

We have seen in the foregoing how this debate has persisted over the last four decades as an "accident of history" since the political compromise of 1965 whereby private insurers were established in a buffer zone between the federal government and local communities. The duplicative and inefficient system of local coverage decisions that we have would hardly have been the intended design for a rational system of governance and administration of a large and growing national program. Foote and her colleagues have labeled the political dynamics involved in continuation of this inefficient system as a stalemated tug-of-war.[30] It may also be seen as an unresolved tension between private interests and government. Here are some of the major forces and interests on each side of the debate.

Industry advocates of local decision-making welcome the flexibility and less rigorous reviews of coverage and reimbursement decisions for their products and services more highly while worrying about a more rigorous and binding review process at the national level which may go against them. If they can gain favorable local coverage decisions, they can proceed to market their products while seeking coverage in other local jurisdictions. Federal officials at the Department of Health and Human Services (HHS) also support continuation of the present system. Dr. Stephen Phurrough of CMS's Office of Clinical Standards and Quality recently acknowledged at a meeting of AdvaMed that "if your (scientific) evidence is not mature, it's better to go local, at the national office, we want mature evidence that's fairly consistent." A recent HHS report went further: "Medicare was designed as a regionalized program that could accommodate local variations in treatment, utilization of care, and the needs of unique beneficiary populations."[31]

On the other side of this impasse, the Medicare Payment Advisory Commission (MedPAC) has called for elimination of the local decision-making process in order to "reduce current complexity, inconsistency, and uncertainty."[32] The U.S. General Accounting Office (GAO) has recently recommended that the local coverage process be abolished.

> *"Because contractors can determine coverage for beneficiaries being treated in their jurisdictions, coverage inequities for beneficiaries with similar medical conditions have resulted"; and further "because of inequities and inefficiencies resulting from divided authority to develop coverage policy among CMS, carriers, and fiscal intermediaries, we are recommending that CMS eliminate claims administration contractors' development of new local coverage policies for procedures and devices that have established codes."*[33,34]

The AMA and Medicare Rights Center have also weighed in on a shift to national decision-making in order to achieve more equity and uniformity of Medicare coverage policy.[35]

The Medicare Prescription Drug, Improvement, and Modernization

Act of 2003 (MMA) calls for HHS to develop a plan to determine the need for "greater consistency and less duplication among local Medicare contractors." There is no evidence to date, however, that the political stalemate between local and national levels will be resolved any time soon. Minnesota gives us an example of how cumbersome and dysfunctional Medicare governance still is. Minnesota's new PPO region includes six other states—Montana, Wyoming, North Dakota, South Dakota, Nebraska and Iowa. These states are served by five different Fiscal Intermediaries for Medicare Part A and four different carriers for Medicare Part B. All of them issue different coverage policies.[36]

CAN GEOGRAPHIC VARIATIONS IN MEDICARE BE FIXED?

As is quite apparent from the foregoing, the long-standing current system of largely decentralized decision-making for Medicare policy results in problems of equity, access, cost containment and quality. These problems have been insoluble for many years, in large part due to the fragmented system of governance and accountability. In view of ongoing political realities, the question then becomes whether and how these problems can be remedied.

Based on their extensive studies of the local vs. national Medicare policy-making issue, Foote and her colleagues offer these promising new approaches to break present and past political gridlock:[37]

1.   The CMS should classify all policies into NT, TE and UM categories, as is commonly done with regard to medical technologies[38]

2.   Coverage and reimbursement policies for NT and TE should be made at the national level. This would avoid duplication of effort by many local contractors and allow more efficient evaluation by CMS with its greater availability of technology assessment expertise.

3.   The CMS should oversee and assist local contractors in their ongoing UM functions in administering policies, paying claims, and working with providers on utilization issues.

4. CMS contracts with local contractors should be redesigned, including redrawing of regional contractor jurisdictions in order to better equalize local resources.

5. The national coverage process should be expanded and reformed, including more explicit use of evidence in coverage decisions, cost-effectiveness and value-of-information analysis, and expanded use of "coverage under protocol" tied to ongoing clinical studies.

As we saw in Chapter 6, despite its inefficiencies as illustrated by this chapter, Medicare operates with an administrative overhead of only about 3 percent compared to overheads five to nine times larger for private insurers.[39] It has also been much more successful in cost containment over the years than private plans. Between 1970 and 2000, for example, Medicare demonstrated continuously more effective containment of per-enrollee personal health spending than private insurers.[40]

Concerning future cost containment of Medicare, Tom Bodenheimer at the University of California San Francisco notes the important differences between painful cost containment (e.g., denial of appropriate therapies to patients) and painless cost controls, such as cutting prices instead of volume of services, and eliminating administrative waste and unnecessary medical services.[41] Although Medicare is already far more efficient than private plans, there are still many areas where painless cuts can be made without compromising patient care. Indeed, it is a central premise of this book that the excesses of privatization themselves are too expensive for this vital program to afford. Privatization serves private interests more than the public interest, and is an obvious place for painless cuts while simultaneously strengthening the program.

ARE GEOGRAPHIC VARIATIONS AND DISPARITIES INEVITABLE?

The focus here is by no means anti-technology. Quite the opposite, advances in medical technology have contributed greatly to the strengths of the U.S. health care system. However, a substantial amount of medical technology is misguided to unnecessary wasteful services, at times even harmful, serving providers more than patients. As we saw in the last chapter, we can no longer afford to ignore cost-effectiveness in health policy decisions.

As called for in MMA 2003, Medicare has a new opportunity to revisit its governance structure in an effort to decrease inequities of access, increase quality of care, better contain spiraling costs, and eliminate waste. As a result of recurrent political compromises since its origins in 1965, Medicare continues to be a maze of private contracts and micromanagement through an inefficient and decentralized bureaucracy of governance. The question, as always, remains whether we can muster the political will in our democracy to deal with these problems. We will address that question in the closing chapters of this book. But now we have another contentious and divisive issue to consider in the next chapter—whether or not Medicare should be a means-tested program

CHAPTER 14

MEANS TESTING AND MEDICARE: MORE FAIR OR ANOTHER THREAT TO THE PROGRAM?

"Means testing for Medicare coverage is fiscally misleading, programatically threatening, and—if taken to its natural extreme, as advocates desire—philosophically at odds with the ideals that have made Medicare such a popular and successful program.[1]

Jacob Hacker, author of *The Divided Welfare State*
Theodore Marmor, author of *The Politics of Medicare*

Should all Medicare enrollees pay the same, regardless of their income, for the same benefits? Or should the more affluent pay more while others pay less? This controversy has recurred throughout the history of Medicare and remains a central battleground. On the surface, it may seem appropriate, even fairer, for individuals with higher incomes to pay more for these benefits. But behind this seemingly obvious assumption, the issue is far more complicated, cutting to the core of the philosophic goals of the program, with implications for the structure and vitality of the program itself.

This chapter is intended to better understand this controversial issue by addressing three questions: (1) what are some historical highlights concerning the use of means testing by Medicare; (2) what are the main philosophic differences over Medicare; and (3) why is universality important in determining the future shape and viability of Medicare?

SOME HISTORICAL HIGHLIGHTS

Four time periods provide good examples of the intensity and dimensions of controversy engendered by the means testing issue for Medicare.

Early and mid-1960s

Whether health care of the elderly should be an entitlement earned by contributions over the years or a charity program based on financial need as measured through means testing was a hotly debated issue in the period leading up to Medicare's enactment in 1965. The landslide victory of Lyndon

Johnson in the presidential election of 1964, combined with large Democratic majorities in the Senate (68-32) and the House (295-140), brought enough liberals and progressives into Congress to break the conservative coalition which had blocked any federal health insurance initiative since the New Deal.[2] Passage of some sort of government program for the elderly then became not only possible but also inevitable. Republicans and the AMA still opposed the contributory model, but the final Medicare bill embraced the concept of earned eligibility without means testing. Kaiser leaders saw Medicare as giving wage earners the opportunity to "make a dignified contribution in advance for the medical care he will need when he becomes 65."[3] *Business Week* saw contributory financing as the only way "of keeping old people from feeling that they are beggars living off society's handouts."[4,5]

The health care legislation which was enacted in 1965 was a political compromise by which Medicare became a contributory program for Part A hospital coverage through an earmarked payroll tax on employers and their employees. Part B physician services were covered by voluntary insurance and was financed by equal contributions from general revenues and premiums paid by beneficiaries. Medicaid, on the other hand, was designed as a means tested charity program.[6] In his 1970 book *The Politics of Medicare*, Theodore Marmor described Medicare as a middle-class program serving a broad demographic population without means testing but with earned, non-comprehensive benefits, in marked contrast to unearned, more comprehensive benefits in a means-tested charity program like Medicaid.[7]

1986-1989

As we saw in Chapter 2, in an effort to expand hospitalization coverage, Congress passed the Medicare Catastrophic Coverage Act in 1988. These new benefits were to be financed entirely by Medicare beneficiaries themselves, with additional premiums linked to their income levels. With premiums ranging up to $800 per year, 40% of the nation's elderly would pay over 80% of the costs of catastrophic coverage. A firestorm of protest was engendered after Congress passed this Act, including an ugly scene in Chicago. Dan Rostenkowski (D-Ill), then chairman of the House Ways and Means Committee, had his chauffeured car surrounded by about 50 angry seniors who beat on it with signs protesting the Catastrophic Care Act, pounded on the car windows, and hurled epithets at him.[8] The intensity of this reaction, widely covered by the media, took Congress and the AARP by surprise. As a result, Congress was forced to repeal the Act in 1989, even before it could take effect and the principle of universality of Medicare was strengthened and extended.[9,10] Table 14.1 shows how rapidly support for this Act eroded among seniors during that period.

Table 14.1

Support for and Opposition to the Medicare Catastrophic Coverage Act among Elderly Americans Age Sixty-five and Over

Position of Respondents

	Number Holding Position (%)		
	DECEMBER 1988	FEBRUARY-MARCH 1989	AUGUST 1989
Low income:			
Support	70	52	47
Oppose	13	23	27
Difference	+57	+29	+20
Moderate income:			
Support	62	49	38
Oppose	23	33	45
Difference	+39	+16	-7
High income:			
Support	63	47	38
Oppose	31	43	57
Difference	+32	+4	-19

Source: Richard Himmelfarb, Catastrophic Politics: The Rise and Fall of the Medicare Catastrophic Coverage Act of 1988 (University Park: Pennsylvania State University Press), 63, using AARP survey data.

Reprinted with permission from Oberlander J. *The Political Life of Medicare*. Chicago: University of Chicago Press, 2003, p 68.

1994-1997

As Jonathan Oberlander has described in his excellent book, *The Political Life of Medicare*, a bipartisan consensus on the universality of Medicare eligibility as an earned right prevailed from 1965 to 1994. That consensus broke down with the 1994 mid-term elections, when Republicans gained control of both houses of Congress for the first time since 1954. The new congressional majority soon passed the Balanced Budget Act of 1995, which would have privatized the Medicare program and converted it from a program of defined benefits to one of defined contributions.[11] Although it was vetoed by President Clinton, the Senate passed a plan for means testing of Part B premium payments in 1997. However, it soon ran into vehement opposition in the House. AARP and other seniors and labor groups opposed means testing, and brought pressure on legislators. The Administration rejected the Senate's provision for DHHS to collect and compute the increased premiums, proposing instead that the Internal Revenue Service (IRS) perform those functions. Republican backers of means testing reacted against any such involvement of the IRS, and bipartisan support for tabling that effort soon prevailed. Remembering the united opposition among seniors to the Catastrophic Coverage Act nine years earlier, many legislators feared another backlash from seniors and allied groups that Republicans were trying to "cut Medicare to pay for tax cuts."[12]

THE MEDICARE PRESCRIPTION DRUG, IMPROVEMENT, AND MODERNIZATION ACT OF 2003 (MMA)

As we saw in Chapter 3, MMA 2003 added means testing for Part B Medicare premiums, for the first time in four decades, as well as for the new prescription drug benefit for low-income beneficiaries. Starting in 2007, seniors with incomes above $80,000 a year ($160,000 for couples) will be required to pay higher premiums for health care services. The National Committee to Preserve Social Security and Medicare argues, however, that higher income workers have already paid higher taxes during their working years and also pay higher general tax payments in support of Medicare, so that means testing results in decreasing their benefits and compromising the principles of universal coverage.[13] Since MMA 2003 barely gained passage in a disputed extended voting procedure amid intense controversy and bipartisan opposition, it remains to be seen how extensive the backlash will be this time. As noted earlier, because the AARP supported the legislation in opposition to many of its members' interests, 60,000 AARP members resigned in protest in the first few months after its passage, while many Democrats vowed future efforts to delete some of MMA's more objectionable provisions.[14]

OPPOSING PHILOSOPHIES CONCERNING MEDICARE

Means testing for Medicare is a complex issue, and one that is not entirely of partisan politics. While Republicans have promoted means testing for many years, some Democrats have also endorsed it. On the surface, asking affluent seniors to pay more sounds egalitarian and fair. The real question, however, is not whether higher-income seniors can afford to pay more, but what the effect of means testing will be on the overall Medicare program.

Advocates for means testing point to Medicare's future fiscal challenges and the need to offset projected costs of the new prescription drug benefit. Some note that other ways of containing Medicare's costs are less acceptable, such as raising premiums for all seniors, cutting benefits, or raising payroll taxes. Three different perspectives illustrate the logic of this approach.[15]

"I do not believe that someone with a $200,000 income living in a gated community should have exactly the same subsidy as someone struggling along on $25,000 or $30,000 of income."

Rep. Nancy Johnson, R-Conn

"I don't see an objection to having an income-related premium,"—
"I am opposed to varying Medicare benefits according to the income of the recipient, but I find it completely acceptable to have people with higher incomes pay more for those benefits."

Robert Ball, a former Social Security Administration Commissioner

"This is one of the most reasonable, most justifiable, least painful changes you could make,"—"It does not do violence to Medicare as a program that provides the same coverage and benefits to everyone."

Robert Greenstein of the Center on Budget and Policy Priorities

Other advocates for means testing Medicare come at the issue from a different standpoint based on a libertarian preference for small government and the belief that people should save during their working years and take responsibility for their own health care costs without depending on an entitlement program. In the first year of George W. Bush's first term, Paul O'Neill, then Secretary of the Treasury, had this to say on the subject:

"Able-bodies adults should save enough on a regular basis so they

can provide for their own retirement and, for that matter, health and medical needs. "[16]

Milton Friedman, Nobel laureate and conservative economic guru, has even extended this view to Social Security. As early as 1980, he was advocating that Social Security be ended, since unfettered market forces would give people enough incentive to save during their working years.[17] He argued that:

> *"The winding down of Social Security would eliminate its present effect of discouraging employment—[and] would add to personal saving and so lead to a higher rate of capital formation and a more rapid rate of growth of income."* [18]

Opponents of means testing for Medicare recipients worry about the threat to universality and political support for the Medicare program. They point to the increased administrative costs of implementing means testing, which may not return much in the way of cost savings, as well as its complexity (egs, what income figures will be used—gross or adjusted gross? will earnings from equities be counted as income? etc).[19] A 2005 study of the impact of means testing for the new prescription drug benefit found that widowed Medicare beneficiaries will be especially hard hit by this approach. Widows are already vulnerable in tending to be older, to live alone, to have more chronic illnesses and less family support than other seniors. This study raised questions about the equity of means testing, noting also the irony that those with modest means who have saved for retirement are not eligible for low-income subsidies and have little except their Social Security income to fall back upon.[20] Most other countries have rejected the means testing approach in publicly-financed health care programs, though many provide reduced cost-sharing for lower-income people.[21] Here are three further perspectives by opponents of means testing:

> *"Medicare Part B is entirely voluntary. And if Part B is not financially attractive, people who can afford it will go elsewhere. Charging higher premiums, no matter the rationale, really means cutting benefits for Part B premiums are part of the beneficiary package, which means the affluent will net less."* [22]

Don McCanne, MD,
Past president, Physicians for a National Health Program

> *"—when we have to make tough choices, we should look at*

whether people should pay more. But I don't think that the price of holding taxes exactly where they are should be borne solely by people who are really firmly middle and lower middle class seniors"—" to call thirty-thousand-dollar-a-year households as being well off and able to bear a substantially higher burden that over time will lead them to be spending half or more of their income on health care is not the right approach."[23]

Marilyn Moon, Ph.D.,
vice president and director of the health program,
American Institutes for Research

"The means-testers on the right have found a political wedge issue that splits Medicare advocates on the left. But those worried about low-income citizens should not fall into the trap.... This seemingly sensible step forward represents a fundamental step backward, should be rejected, as it was by Medicare's founders."[24]

Ted Marmor, PhD,
Medicare policy expert at Yale University

In order to sort through the pro's and con's on the means testing controversy, we need to consider more fully how universality remains important to Medicare.

WHY IS UNIVERSALITY SO IMPORTANT?

As we saw in Chapter 2, Medicare was designed as a social insurance program, not a social welfare program. Mandatory contributions by wage earners in their working years partly fund the program, which then provides a defined set of benefits to all eligible individuals as an earned right regardless of their health condition. This social contract has received continuing broad public support across age groups since 1965. For example, a 1998 survey by the Kaiser Family Foundation found that 77% of respondents over the age of 18 felt that it is "very important" that Medicare be preserved as a health care program for everyone over 65.[25]

The major force driving the enactment of Medicare in the 1960s was the failure of the private health care market to meet the needs of many millions of elderly Americans. As earlier chapters fully attest, this problem is at least as serious today as it was 40 years ago. In 1963 Kenneth Arrow, leading American economist at Columbia University, called attention to uncertainty as the root cause of market failure in health care. Patients have no way of knowing what services they will need, insurers face the same problem, and health professionals cope with clinical uncertainty every day.[26] The insurance industry, largely for-profit, turns to "experience rating" and medical underwriting to select healthier enrollees and increase its profits, thereby segmenting and shrinking the insurance risk pool.

The concept of social health insurance for the elderly and disabled depends for its integrity upon preserving a broad risk pool (e.g., everyone age 65 and older) through its universality. As we have seen in earlier chapters, adverse selection has been a major problem in this population when healthier and more affluent seniors opt out of traditional Medicare for a private program. Figure 14.1 shows that about one-third of Medicare beneficiaries have disabling physical and/or cognitive health problems which account for 60% of Medicare spending.[27] According to the Century Foundation's Task Force on Medicare Reform's recent report, Medicare spent almost $32,000 on average in 1996 for the 10 percent of beneficiaries with the highest costs compared to only about $1,700 on average for the other 90 percent.[28]

After years of study of the Medicare program Hacker and Marmor contend that higher Part B premiums charged to affluent seniors will cover only 1 to 2 percent of Medicare's total program costs, that many of these seniors will inevitably move to private plans which they can readily afford, and that less affluent and sicker patients remaining in traditional Medicare will find themselves facing higher costs for threatened benefits. The more that universality of Medicare coverage is compromised, the more that adverse selection becomes an increasing problem and the more likely that broad political support for the program will erode.[29] Jost further notes: "Only universal access undergirds the sense of solidarity necessary to sustain health-care entitlement programs in the long term."[30] Robert Reich, former Secretary of Labor in the Clinton Administration and author of *Reason: Why Liberals Will Win the Battle for America*, adds this important observation about social solidarity:[31]

> *"(Social Security and Medicare) were created for Americans as a system of insurance, not welfare. The basic idea was that we are all in the same boat together. Misfortune can happen to anyone. The result was*

Figure 14.1

Beneficiaries with Disabling Health Conditions as a Percentage of Beneficiary Population and Total Medicare Expenditures, 1997

Percentage of Enrollees

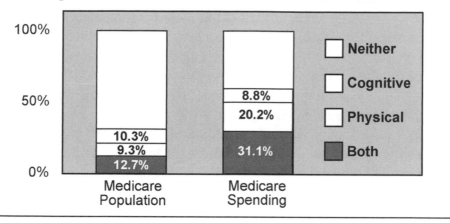

Note: All figures exclude ESRD beneficiaries and the Medicare expenditures also exclude HMO beneficiaries.

Source: Moon M & Storeygard M. *One-Third at Risk: The Special Circumstances of Medicare Beneficiaries with Health Problems, The Commonwealth Fund,* September 2001.

Reprinted with permission from *The Commonwealth Fund.*

a giant system of redistribution—mostly from young to old (the typical retiree now takes out three times more Social Security and Medicare than he or she ever put into the system), but also from healthy to sick, employed to unemployed, people who didn't suffer a natural disaster to people who did. But it didn't feel like redistribution because the money didn't go from "us" to "them." It went from us to us.

These programs remained popular because they were based on "it could happen to me" thinking. Any one of us could fall out of the boat. Unless we promised to rescue one another, some of us would drown. And—here's the important part—there was no way to know in advance which of us might need the rescuing."

MEANS TESTING MEDICARE: ANOTHER STEP TOWARD DISMANTLING THE PROGRAM

Although means testing in Medicare may seem like a reasonable and egalitarian approach, its effects on the program would be detrimental. It is being promoted by its advocates as part of a larger conservative agenda to further privatize Medicare by applying means testing, peeling off more affluent seniors to private plans, and converting Medicare from a defined benefits program to one of defined contributions. The end result would be a smaller Original Medicare program for lower-income sicker Americans requiring higher cost sharing for less benefits. That outcome would cancel out the advantages of a broad risk pool—the idea behind social insurance all along—and result in an underfunded and stigmatized public welfare program. Such an outcome would also tear asunder a 40-year social contract with elderly and disabled Americans for an earned entitlement program into which people have paid until they became 65 or disabled.

While it may be difficult to ascribe definitive motivation to the conservative agenda for Medicare, it seems reasonable to presume that it is to exploit the program while it survives, but kill it as a large federal program under the claim of "saving" it. As the chief architect of the Republican's Contract with America in 1995, recall from Chapter 11 then House Speaker Newt Gingrich's prediction that Medicare will "wither on the vine" if its Medicare bill could be passed that year.[32] In an excellent recent chapter on the mix of public and private payers in the U.S. health care system, Uwe Reinhardt, Professor of Political Economy at Princeton University and a leading health policy analyst, considered the question of motivation. He concluded that the most likely primary goal of conservative legislators and politicians, though not explicitly acknowledged, is to "reduce the taxpayer's exposure to Medicare spending, even if it increased total health spending per Medicare beneficiary."[33] Concerning the conservative agenda, one also cannot help but see through the "fairness" disguise of means testing as disingenuous, since it would contribute to further privatization and dismantling of Medicare as we know it. In view of the proven superior track record of Original Medicare for efficiency, cost containment, and reliability compared to private Medicare plans, this effort seems duplicitous.

There is no question but that various reforms will be needed for Medicare to remain viable and true to its mission in future years. The pressing issue is what direction these reforms take, which is the subject of the next chapter.

PART IV

THE FUTURE OF MEDICARE

CHAPTER 15

OPTIONS FOR MEDICARE REFORM: CAN A PERFECT STORM BE AVERTED?

"The care of human life and happiness, and not their destruction, is the first and only legitimate object of good government."

Thomas Jefferson,
To the Republican Citizens of Washington County, MD
March 31, 1809.

"One of the most striking features of Medicare's political evolution is how the ideological cleavage that attended its birth reappeared, in a different guise, more than three decades later. Most reform advocates, for obvious reasons, claim an interest in "saving Medicare." But the equally obvious truth is that the program still excites fundamental differences about the proper role of government in health insurance. For those who embrace its social insurance purposes, this would be satisfaction. For those who reject those principles as inappropriate, the fight over "reforming" Medicare is in fact about changing it fundamentally."[1]

Theodore Marmor, author of *The Politics of Medicare*

There is no question but that Medicare needs reform. It was modeled in the 1960s after employer-sponsored insurance with an emphasis on acute care, especially in the hospital. The world has changed since then. The management of chronic illness in an aging population has become a dominant priority, medical technologies have advanced rapidly, hospital stays have become short with many conditions previously requiring hospitalization now managed as outpatients, and information technology now provides for effective new ways of communication, patient monitoring, and quality assurance. Christine Cassel, who chairs the Department of Geriatrics and Adult Development at Mount Sinai Medical Center in New York City, with her colleagues, had this to say in 1999:[2]

"Medicare has not kept pace with medical advances, new care strategies, and accompanying coverage needs, including interventions for sensory impairment and psychiatric care. Optimal management of chronic illness requires close coordination with long-term care

services, but today's financing policies encourage fragmentation and cost shifting. Excluded services, including basic medications, often are unaffordable. Supplemental insurance cannot adequately bridge these gaps, particularly for lower-to-middle-income populations."

There is already an extensive literature proposing many ways of reforming Medicare. A contentious policy debate is being waged across a wide gulf of polarized, strongly held ideological views, as illustrated by the passage and aftermath of the Medicare Prescription Drug, Improvement and Modernization Act of 2003 (MMA). Unfortunately, however, most of the reform literature deals with financing issues alone, assuming continuation of Medicare's structural, content, and administrative problems.

We cannot make that assumption. As a result of corporate compromises all along the line over the years since the 1960s, Medicare has persisting, unresolved structural, governance, and accountability problems which require correction if the program is to be sustained for future generations. A large part of Medicare spending still goes to wasteful inefficiencies and profits to an enormous *private* administrative bureaucracy, siphoning off taxpayer dollars from patient care. I will argue here that corporate profiteering at public expense is the single biggest problem of Medicare, and will have to be dealt with despite the political obstacles. Medicare is too important to fall prey to the perils of the private marketplace.

This chapter takes a broad approach to the issue of Medicare reform, starting with two assumptions which should have wide consensual support: (1) health care is a basic human need, not just another commodity for sale; and (2) whatever reforms are undertaken should meet primarily the needs of patients themselves, not the economic self-interests of providers and services. This chapter addresses three objectives: (1) to describe the major problems of the current Medicare program; (2) to outline major reform alternatives, together with their strengths and weaknesses; and (3) to offer a value and problem-based approach to reform of Medicare.

WHAT ARE THE MAJOR PROBLEMS OF MEDICARE TODAY?

The sheer size of Medicare can be intimidating to considerations of its reform. As we saw in Chapter 2, it is the largest public purchaser and payer of U.S. health care services. It is the major source of coverage for one in seven Americans—41 million people, including 6 million non-elderly people with disabilities. Medicare's reach is enormous. A 1999 HCFA report listed involvement with over 6,000 hospitals, 830,000 physicians, 167,000 clinical laboratories, 3,500 end-stage renal disease facilities, 3,500 rural health clinics, 2,600 ambulatory surgical centers, 2,500 outpatient physical therapy facilities, 2,300 hospices, 700 portable x-ray units, and 600 outpatient rehabilitation facilities.[3] Its total expenditures in 2005 were about $325 billion, and its costs are expected to increase by 30% from 2005 to 2007 as the new prescription drug benefit is implemented.[4] Medicare accounts for about one-fifth of total personal national health expenditures and one-third of hospital and home health services.[5,6]

Looking at the elephant of Medicare as a whole, these six problems stand out as especially challenging. All are important and inter-related, but the first is the most important since it is a major contributor to the other five problems.

1. <u>Transformation by the for-profit medical industrial complex</u>

This transformation inflates health care prices, and transfers large amounts of money from patient care to corporate profits. Examples abound to confirm this point.

• The long tradition of Blue Cross for not-for-profit socially responsive and community-rated health insurance has gone by the wayside. Indianapolis-based Anthem and California's Wellpoint Health Networks are now the largest owners of Blue Cross-Blue Shield (BCBS) plans. They are investor owned and have merged to create the nation's largest health insurer. Each reported a 34% increase in net revenues for the second quarter of 2004.[7] In California, with an eye to the bottom line and constraining its medical loss ratio, Blue Cross spent only 76% of each premium dollar on patient care in 2002 compared to not-for-profit Kaiser's 96%.[8] The administrative overhead of investor-owned BCBS plans averages 26.5% compared to only about 3% for Medicare.[9] Blue Cross and other private insurers stand to profit handsomely through marketing health savings accounts (HSAs), as created by MMA 2003, to relatively healthy people as a vehicle for tax-sheltered savings.

* MMA 2003, while providing a meager drug benefit and preventing price controls for prescription drugs, rewards the inefficiencies of private plans with large over-payments and subsidies, and allocates $139 billion over 10 years to private interests to administer the drug benefit.[10]

* For-profit, investor ownership now accounts for 85% of the nation's renal dialysis facilities, 70% of nursing homes and home health agencies, and 64% of HMOs.[11]

* The distribution chain to hospitals for medical supplies is dominated by for-profit group purchasing organizations which pad their expenses and maximize profits with little oversight or disclosure.[12,13]

This transformation of U.S. health care has led Arnold Relman, for many years Editor of *The New England Journal of Medicine*, to this observation:[14]

> *"My conclusion from all of this study is that most of the current problems of the U.S. system—and they are numerous—result from the growing encroachment of private for-profit ownership and competitive markets on a sector of our economy that properly belongs in the public domain. No health care system in the industrialized world is as heavily commercialized as ours, and none is as expensive, inefficient, and inequitable—or as unpopular. Indeed, just about the only parts of U.S. society happy with our current market-driven health care system are the owners and investors in the for-profit industries now living off the system."*

2. Growing Problem of Affordability

The average out-of-pocket health care spending among seniors in the U.S. now takes up 22% of their annual income, double that if in poor health, and even higher if low-income (Figure 15.1). According to a 1999 report of the National Academy of Social Insurance, the majority of seniors depend on Social Security for the bulk of their income. A 2003 report by the Employee Benefit Research Institute found that Social Security was the largest source of income, 41.9% on average, for people 65 and older.[15] Three

Figure 15.1

Projected Out-of-Pocket Health Care Spending as a Share of Income, 2000 and 2025

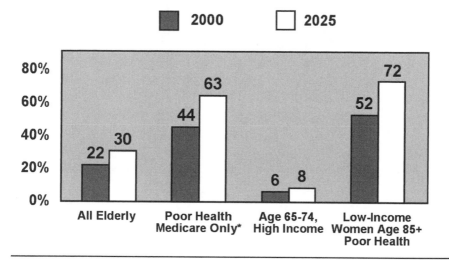

Note: All figures exclude ESRD beneficiaries and the Medicare expenditures also exclude HMO beneficiaries.

Source: Maxwell, S et al. *Growth in Medicare and Out-of-Pocket Spending: Impact on Vulnerable Beneficiaries,* The Commonwealth Fund, December 2000

Reprinted with permission from The Commonwealth Fund.

out of five Medicare beneficiaries with incomes below the poverty level are not eligible for Medicaid, and spend 50% of their income on health expenses.[16] Recall by comparison from Chapter 2 that the average out-of-pocket health care spending among seniors when Medicare was enacted in 1965 was 15% of their average annual income. Out-of-pocket spending for health care by seniors is certain to increase in future years, as shown in Table 15.1.

All current trends, including increasing health care costs much above the cost-of-living, problems of fixed income among retirees, diminishing retiree coverage, and increased cost-sharing for Medicare costs, all point to further difficulty for seniors to afford essential health care. Five other major factors also contribute to placing essential health care services beyond the reach of many, even most seniors.

Table 15.1

Out-of-Pocket Expenses as a Percentage of Illustrative Social Security Benefit for 65 Year Old, 2006-2050

CY	Part A Out-of-Pocket expenses	Part B Premium	Part B Copayments	Part B Out-of-Pocket expenses	Part D Premium	Part D Copayments	Part D Out-of-Pocket expenses	TOTAL Out-of-Pocket expenses
2006	2.6%	8.7%	7.2%	16.0%	4.1%	14.6%	18.6%	37.2%
2010	2.6%	8.7%	6.4%	15.2%	4.7%	16.7%	21.4%	39.2%
2015	2.6%	9.2%	6.6%	15.8%	5.5%	19.8%	25.4%	43.7%
2020	2.6%	10.4%	7.1%	17.4%	6.2%	22.6%	28.8%	48.9%
2025	2.7%	10.9%	7.5%	18.4%	6.8%	24.7%	31.4%	52.6%
2030	2.9%	11.5%	7.9%	19.5%	7.1%	25.8%	32.9%	55.3%
2035	3.2%	12.3%	8.5%	20.8%	7.4%	27.1%	34.5%	58.5%
2040	3.5%	13.1%	9.1%	22.2%	7.9%	28.7%	36.6%	62.2%
2045	3.8%	14.0%	9.7%	23.7%	8.4%	30.5%	38.9%	66.4%
2050	4.0%	14.8%	10.3%	25.1%	8.9%	32.5%	41.3%	70.5%

Source: Adapted from Table II-C14-SMI Out-of-Pocket Expenses as a Percentage of Illustrative Social Security Benefit. 2003 Annual Report of the Boards of Trustees of the Federal Hospital Insurance and Federal Supplementary Medical Insurance Trust Funds. Centers for Medicare and Medicaid Services. Baltimore.

- The recently announced increase of 17.4% for Medicare Part B premiums charged to the consumer is the largest premium increase since Medicare was enacted in 1965 and could prompt some healthier beneficiaries to switch to more volatile and less reliable subsidized private plans.[17] Recent government estimates suggest that prescription drug benefits will be reduced or eliminated for 3.8 million retirees when Medicare offers that coverage in 2006.[18]

- The Equal Employment Opportunity Commission (EEOC) ruled in 2004 to allow employers to decrease or stop altogether health benefits for retirees when they become eligible for Medicare at age 65, asserting that this decision does not violate the civil rights law banning age discrimination.[19]

- In 1984, three of four Medicare beneficiaries also had some form of supplemental insurance;[20] today, only one-quarter of seniors have such coverage. There are 10 types of MediGap plans (Plans A through J), each providing different benefits at different rates. Prices for these plans often vary by as much as 10-fold from one market to another for the same benefits (up to $11,000 per year in one market for an H plan providing prescription drug coverage). Although MediGap plans are required by law to offer guaranteed coverage during a six-month period of open enrollment when seniors turn 65 years of age, insurers can hike their rates later based on claims experience or discontinue coverage altogether.[21]

• The cost of nursing home care in the U.S. continues to rise much more rapidly than the cost of living. According to a recent national survey by MetLife, Inc., the average cost across the country of a day in a nursing home is $192, with the highest rates in Alaska, where they average $561 a day. Since the average stay in a nursing home is 2.4 years, a typical bill would be about $170,000.[22] There is a 100-day limit on coverage for skilled nursing care under Medicare Part A with a coinsurance rate of $96 per day for days 21 to 100. Medicaid covers most costs of nursing home care, but only after seniors have spent down to poverty levels.

• Social Security will likewise become a slippery rock for assistance with health care costs, as shown by Table 15.1. A 65-year-old-senior in 2006 will spend 37% of his or her Social Security benefit on Medicare premiums, co-payments, and out-of-pocket health care expenses; by 2025 that figure will exceed 52% for the same individual.[23,24]

3. Threats to Access

Current Medicare coverage and reimbursement policies limit access to Medicare services in a number of ways. These examples illustrate the extent of this problem.

• 37% of Medicare beneficiaries have annual incomes below 150% of the federal poverty ($13,470/single; $18,180/couple in 2003);[25] they have particular difficulty in affording increasing costs of essential services

- 6.4 million Americans who are "dual eligible" for both Medicare and Medicaid will lose whatever prescription drug coverage they have under Medicaid when the Part D Medicare drug benefit takes effect on January 1, 2006; that safety net is threatened in a complex administrative transition which will put many sick and cognitively impaired individuals at increased risk.[26]

- As a result of reimbursement cuts which for many physicians do not even cover the costs of providing care, the number of physicians no longer willing to take new Medicare patients continues to increase; 22% of family physicians nationally now refuse to accept new Medicare patients,[27] while the percentage of physicians accepting new Medicare patients in Seattle dropped from 71% in 1997 to only 54% in 2001.[28]

- Private Medicare plans have proven volatile and unreliable for Medicare beneficiaries; as we saw in Chapter 4, about one-third of Medicare beneficiaries enrolled in M + C plans were dropped when many of these plans abandoned the market between 1999 and 2002, forcing 2.4 million seniors to find other physicians.[29]

4. Gaps in Coverage

Medicare coverage policy is biased toward acute hospital care and has not adapted to a new paradigm for care of chronic illness. Medicare payments are still skewed to the costs of hospitalization, covering about 90% of inpatient stays for Medicare beneficiaries, as compared to 75% of Part B physician services and 60% of outpatient hospital services.[30] About one-quarter of all Medicare spending is for care in the last year of life.[31] There is a pressing need to update Medicare benefits to the changing needs of an aging population. These are some of the most obvious gaps in coverage which need to be revisited:

- Without price controls on prescription drugs, MMA 2003 is estimated to cover no more than 22% of Medicare beneficiaries' costs of these drugs[32]

- Interventions to detect or treat functional loss, including most routine foot care and sensory impairment through visual or hearing loss, are not covered by Medicare; sensory impairments can be effectively treated by eye glasses and hearing aids, which can prevent depression and delay functional decline[33]

- One in five seniors has a mental health condition,[34] as do more than one-half of Medicare beneficiaries with disabilities.[35] Medicare pays only 50% for covered mental health services, a disparity from the usual 80% coverage for most Part B services. There continues to be a stigma attached to mental health conditions, perpetuated by this reimbursement policy, which causes many patients to forego needed treatment.[36]

- About four of five Medicare beneficiaries are living with at least one chronic condition, in many cases requiring some level of home care. However, Medicare coverage for home care services is very limited. A strict definition of "homebound" is applied in order to qualify for up to 35 hours of care a week, usually a combination of skilled and personal care. Care in a nursing home (skilled nursing facility) is very expensive. Medicare coverage is limited to 100 days (average length of stay 2 1/2 years), and seniors have to spend down to poverty in order to qualify for Medicaid coverage.[37]

- It takes 29 months from the time a person is certified as disabled and unable to engage in any "substantial gainful activity" for that individual to receive coverage under Medicare. This waiting period extending well past 2 years is often devastating for the newly disabled at a time of their greatest need. Based on tabulations of Social Security Administration data from nine states, about 4 percent of SSDI beneficiaries die each year during this waiting period.[38] Only 8 percent of disabled Americans less than 65 years of age have Medicaid coverage. Once again, Medicaid is the ultimate safety net for the disabled, but only after they have become impoverished.[39]

- The M + C experience has shown that private Medicare plans have a poor track record in terms of a stable benefit package. "Bait and switch" tactics are used by many for-profit plans to build enrollment, followed by systematic cuts in benefits as financial bottom lines take precedence. As examples, the proportion of M + C plans providing hearing benefits dropped from 91% to 53% between 1999 and 2002, while those offering preventive dental services fell from 70% to 14%.[40]

5. Inconsistent Quality of Care

Quality of Medicare services is highly variable, and quality management is still rudimentary. Apart from necessity, appropriateness and competence in providing health care services, there are many other factors which can compromise quality of care, including barriers to care, discontinuity of care, and neglect of quality of life and psychosocial issues. There are wide disparities in quality of care for Medicare beneficiaries from one part of the country to another, with areas of higher reimbursement and excess capacity often providing suboptimal care.[41] Excessive use of inappropriate hospital-based services for terminally ill patients is especially common in high capacity areas of the country even though Medicare-funded hospice care has been shown to provide optimal care for those who have used it.[42] A 2000 study found wide variation in the quality of Medicare services from place to place, with a median difference across states for various quality performance indicators of 33 percentage points.[43] Although an elusive figure, it is estimated that up to 30% of Medicare spending could be saved each year if overuse of services in some parts of the country were corrected.[44] As we saw in Chapter 8, the track record of investor-owned hospitals, HMOs, nursing homes, dialysis centers and mental health centers is especially worrisome in terms of inconsistencies in quality of care.[45] A 1999 national study of HMOs, for example, showed that investor-owned HMOs scored worse, compared to not-for-profit plans, on all 14 quality indicators reported to the National Committee for Quality Assurance (NCQA).[46] Since NCQA reporting is voluntary and many HMOs with less quality of care fail to report their scores, published report cards by the NCQA are misleading on the high side.[47]

6. Ineffective Care and Administrative Redundancy

There is substantial waste through ineffective care as well as through administrative redundancy in the Medicare program. Although Medicare has demonstrated much more efficiency than private insurers in terms of administrative overhead (3% vs. 16—26%),[48] resources are still wasted on both the service and administrative sides. These three areas stand out as high priorities for painless cuts, which if made, could extend Medicare's limited resources to more effective coverage of seniors and the disabled.

- <u>Overuse of ineffective services</u>. As Wennberg and his colleagues at Dartmouth have shown, overuse of ineffective services are much more common in more highly reimbursed parts of the country with excess capacity. These examples are striking—the average number of visits to medical specialists during 1995-1996 ranged from two in Mason City, Iowa to over 25 in Miami, Florida, for Medicare patients in their last six months of life; intensive care unit admissions during the last six months of life varied from only 14% of decedents in Sun City, Arizona to almost one-half in Miami, Florida and Sun City, California; cardiac bypass surgery rates adjusted for age, sex, and race vary from three per thousand in Albuquerque, New Mexico to more than eleven in Redding, California.[49] According to a 2002 report by the Commonwealth Fund, more than 40% of cardiac bypass procedures and angioplasty procedures carried out each year are either questionable or inappropriate.[50]

- <u>Limited Use of Cost-Effectiveness Criterion in Coverage Decisions</u>. As we saw in Chapter 12, industry has consistently and strongly opposed considerations of cost-effectiveness in coverage and reimbursement decisions, whether for drugs, medical devices or procedures. Despite a recent CEA estimating the cost-effectiveness of left ventricular assist devices between $500,000 and $1.4 million per QALY,[51] it was approved for 5,000 Medicare patients, with possible expansion to up to 100,000 patients in the future.[52] We are still in an era of deregulation, and Congress has yet to mandate application of cost-effectiveness as an essential criterion for approval decisions by the FDA. Industry funds about one-half of the FDA's annual budget for review of marketing applications,[53] and has obvious conflicts of interest as active participants in the review process.[54]

- <u>Duplicative Technology Assessment Reviews</u>. We saw in Chapter 12 how, for reasons of history, most Medicare coverage decisions are made at the local level, often without sufficient rigor and with limited expertise and resources. Industry presses to preserve the status quo, with concern over more rigorous "all or none" decisions at the national level. However, more evidence-based rigor is needed in coverage decisions for new technology (NT) and technology extensions (TE) if the level of effective care is to be improved and ineffective wasteful services reduced.

Based on the foregoing discussion, our problem-oriented medical record for the Medicare program today is shown in Table 15.2. Since privatization in our deregulated private marketplace itself has been found in earlier chapters to be more expensive, less efficient, less equitable and less reliable than Original Medicare, it stands out as an obvious target for reform.

REFORM ALTERNATIVES FOR MEDICARE AT A CROSSROADS

Here, in view of the experience of private plans and traditional Medicare over the years as discussed in earlier chapters, we will consider the merits of each end of a spectrum from polar opposites—Original Medicare as a social insurance program vs. largely or fully privatized Medicare. As we have seen, of course, Medicare is already partly "privatized," for historical and political reasons, in terms of its delegation of administrative responsibility to local and regional private insurers, management of the new prescription drug benefit by the drug industry, and M + Cs managed care successor, Medicare Advantage. The conservatives' goal for many years has been to fully privatize Medicare, transforming it to a defined contribution program in the private marketplace and transferring responsibility from the government to individuals for any shortfalls. We saw in Chapter 2 how the Republican majority in Congress, led by House Speaker Newt Gingrich, pushed that agenda with a legislative proposal in 1995 as part of the Contract with America.[55] Although BBA 1995 failed to pass that year, the tension over how much to privatize Medicare remains. Table 15.3 compares the typical features of both ends of this spectrum.

Table 15.2

PROBLEM LIST FOR MEDICARE PROGRAM

1. Corporate profiteering at public expense
     Investor-owned insurers
     Investor-owned managed care plans
     Drug manufacturers and distribution chain
     Medical devices industry
2. Growing unaffordability of essential services
     Escalating health care costs
     Underused bulk purchasing power (e.g., prescription drugs)
     Decreasing supplemental insurance coverage
     Increasing cost sharing on fixed income
3. Barriers to access
     Low reimbursement of providers
     Lack of mental health parity
     Limited choice in private plans
     Discontinuity in private plans
     29-month waiting period for the disabled
4. Gaps in essential coverage
     Focus on acute hospital care more than chronic illness
     Care of sensory impairment
     Care of chronic illness
     Long-term and home care; rehabilitative services
     Underutilization of hospice
5. Variable quality of care
     Suboptimal quality in excess capacity areas
     Unnecessary supply-sensitive services
     Decreased quality in many investor-owned private plans
6. Ineffective care and administrative waste
     Non-use of cost-effectiveness in coverage decisions
     Duplicative and inefficient local coverage decision process

The strengths of Original Medicare as a social insurance program include its guarantee of a defined set of benefits with universal coverage, maintenance of a broad insurance pool to equitably share risks, as well as more reliability, choice, and efficiency compared to the private marketplace. As we have seen, however, its integrity is under attack by recurrent efforts to privatize the program. At some point along a spectrum toward full privatization, cream-skimming and adverse selection will precipitate a "death spiral" of the public program with attendant underfinancing and increased

Table 15.3

COMPARATIVE FEATURES OF PRIVATIZED AND

PUBLIC MEDICARE

PRIVATIZED MEDICARE	ORIGINAL MEDICARE
Experience -rated eligibility	Universal coverage
Managed competition	Social insurance as earned right
Defined contribution	Defined benefits
Segmented risk pool	Broad risk pool
Market pricing to risk	Administered prices
More volatile access & benefits	More reliable access & benefits
Increased cost sharing	Less cost sharing
Less accountability	Potential for more accountability
Less choice of provider & hospital	More choice of provider & hospital
Less well distributed	Well distributed
Less efficiency, higher overhead	More efficiency, lower overhead

cost-sharing for sicker Medicare patients remaining in the program. There is no question that Medicare needs reform for the 21st century. The urgent question, of course, is how, especially concerning the future extent of market-based changes.

Further Privatization Strategies

Most "reform" approaches being proposed by conservatives and many moderates are incremental steps to further privatize the program and limit the role of government while preserving the status quo of the program's structure. Advocates of privatization tout the Federal Employees Health Benefits Program (FEHBP) as a market-based solution to the "Medicare problem."[56,57] The FEHBP contracts with three kinds of plans: national fee-for-service plans, with PPO options and uniform premiums; fee-for-service plans offered by employee organizations; and comprehensive medical plans available only to employees living in specific areas, with community-rated premiums. Loose arrangements are made by the federal Office of Personnel Management (OPM) with participating plans. Minimal benefits requirements are established by OPM, less than those set by Medicare, and OPM lacks authority to contract with plans on the basis of price or quality. Since premiums are not risk-adjusted, there is risk of a "death spiral" in higher benefit, higher premium plans if healthier enrollees leave these plans for lower cost lower benefit plans, forcing costs still higher and less affordable in higher cost plans.[58-60] From the standpoint of cost containment, the FEHBP was able to contain costs as well as Medicare in the mid-1990s, but its track record from 1985 to 2002 shows that traditional Medicare has

Table 15.4

Annual Per Enrollee Growth in Medicare Spending And in Private Health Insurance And FEHBP Premiums, Calendar Years 1985-2002

| | All Benefits (%) | | | Common benefits[a] (%) | | |
| | NHE | | | NHE | | |
Calendar year	Medicare	Private health insurance	FEHBP	Medicare	Private health insurance	FEHBP
1985-1991	7.0	10.8	11.7	6.4	11.2	12.1
1991-1993	8.6	8.7	8.4	6.8	7.6	7.3
1993-1997	7.5	4.3	0.3	6.5	2.6	-1.3
1997-1999	0.1	5.2	8.1	1.3	3.5	6.3
1999-2002	6.4	10.0	12.0	6.2	8.7	10.7

Sources: Centers for Medicare and Medicaid Services, Office of the Actuary; and Office of Personnal Management. Office of the Actuary.

Notes: Per enrollee includes primary policy holder plus dependents. Federal Employees Health Benefits Program (FEHBP) spending excluding certain benefits was estimated based on the share of total premiums these benefits accounted for in private health insurance overall. NHE is national health expenditures.

[a]Benefits commonly covered by Medicare and private health insurance: hospital services, physician and clinical services, other professional services, and durable medical products.

Adapted with permission from Levit K, Smith C, Cowan C, et al. Health spending rebound continues in 2002. *Health Affairs (Millwood)* 23(1): 153, 2004.

been considerably more effective in this area (Table 15.4).[61] Between 1997 and 2002, FEHBP's costs increased by 50%,[62] while its premiums increased by over 10% in 2004.[63]

The concept of premium support, whereby beneficiaries would receive a defined contribution from the government to help them purchase a health plan of their choice, was first proposed as an alternative to defined benefits under Medicare by Aaron and Reischauer in 1995.[64] By this approach, Medicare would pay only a specified amount toward the purchase of private coverage by Medicare beneficiaries (i.e., defined contribution instead of defined benefits). The theory behind this concept is that beneficiaries would be more likely to select lower-cost plans, and that health spending could be better contained over time. A study by HCFA in 1999 found that most of the 2.5% savings to the federal government associated with premium support resulted in cost shifting to beneficiaries, who ended up paying more.[65] However, the conservatives' policy agenda sees premium support as a way to attract more Medicare beneficiaries away from traditional Medicare, thereby segmenting the risk pool and limiting the federal government's obligation to Medicare recipients under the guise of personal responsibility and choice. Original Medicare would end up with a sicker, high-risk population compared to healthier populations in private plans. At the same time, the government's defined contribution to beneficiaries' care could readily be scaled back as more costs are shifted to individual beneficiaries and their families.

Defined contribution can be accomplished by various means. Two currently popular approaches being advocated by those who want to further privatize Medicare are vouchers and health savings accounts (HSAs). As established by the MMA of 2003, individuals can contribute up to $2,600 a year tax-free to their HSA (up to $5,150 for families) as long as their deductible is at least $1,000 for individuals and $2,000 for families. Withdrawals are tax-free if they are used for medically necessary services or for retiree health insurance. Yearly out-of-pocket caps are set at $5,000 for individuals and $10,000 for families. Employers can contribute to their employees' HSAs, who in turn can take their accounts with them if they change jobs.[66]

HSAs will transfer financial risk from the government to individual Medicare beneficiaries, and will keep the private insurance industry well supported and happy. MMA 2003 allocates $6.4 billion over the next 10 years to establish tax-free HSAs through a system of tax rebates. Both employer and employee contributions to HSAs, when accompanied by a high deductible policy, will be protected from taxes. The conservatives' goal is to transfer Medicare and our health care system to one of high deductible coverage, not for everyday routine health care needs.[67] The wide use of HSAs would shift responsibility for financing health care away from collective pools and towards individual patients. Proponents of HSAs hope that they will delay or prevent a political movement toward universal insurance. As the head of the conservative National Center for Policy Analysis observes "It's going to be hard to socialize the system if everybody has their own account."[68]

Since HSAs are being touted as the centerpiece of the Bush health care plan under his concept of an "ownership society," they warrant further consideration here. They may be attractive to younger, healthier individuals and families, who have less health care costs and can use HSAs as investment accounts. However, critics argue that HSAs will fragment the risk pool, help the affluent healthy, and discriminate against the sick, especially if lower income.[69] Lower-and middle-income families with sick or chronically ill members will find little solace in purchasing private health insurance (*if* they can qualify for over $9,000 a year for insurance premiums after they have put aside $5,150 in their HSAs).[70]

So far individuals, families and employers have been slow to take up HSAs, despite their marketing hype by the private sector and the government. A recent survey conducted by America's Health Insurance Plans (AHIP), the industry's trade group, found that two-thirds of respondents are not planning to exchange their current coverage for HSAs. United Health Group, the nation's largest health insurer representing employers who cover more than 18 million workers, anticipates that only about 150,000 of those employees will opt for HSAs in 2005. By May of 2005, fewer than 5,000 of the 8 million enrollees in the Federal Health Benefits Program (FEHBP) had signed up for HSAs.[71] The low level of interest in HSAs is readily explainable. Uwe Reinhardt, the well-known Princeton health economist, sums up HSAs as "a bum deal for people with chronic illnesses, but for chronically healthy people it's another 401 (K) savings account, and Wall Street is licking its chops at the prospect of managing the money."[72]

Changing Age for Medicare Eligibility

Reform proposals have been brought forward in both directions concerning eligibility ages for Medicare. Some have advocated raising the eligibility age from 65 to 67, based on the premise that people are living longer and generally in better health than they were in 1965. The counter arguments, however, include the detrimental impact on sick individuals at 65 and 66, many of whom would be left without health insurance, the small savings to the program that would result, and the availability and affordability of health insurance.[73] Others have proposed that people should be able to buy into Medicare between the ages of 55 and 64. However, individuals with many pre-existing conditions will be denied insurance or find the premiums unaffordable, especially if lower-income.[74]

Still others have proposed folding Medicare and other programs into a single-payer system of national health insurance (NHI). A strong case for NHI has been made by the Physician's Working Group for a National Health Program, endorsed by over 12,000 U.S. physicians, and proposed in the 109th Congress as the United States National Health Insurance Act, H.R. 676.[75,76] NHI under such a plan would provide universal coverage for necessary health care for the entire population while saving more than $280 billion a year through more efficiency and lower administrative costs than the current market-based system.[77] Recent economic projections from the nation's largest health care consortium, the National Coalition on Health Care, lend further weight to the case for single-payer NHI. Professor Kenneth Thorpe of Emory University analyzed the total change in health care spending under four scenarios for the years 2006 through 2015:

> *(1) employer mandate supplemented by individual mandate; (2) expand on existing programs to expand coverage; (3) develop new program modeled after the FEHBP, and (4) universal publicly financed single-payer NHI. Over that ten-year period, options 1 through 3 could realize savings ranging from $320 to $370 billion while option 4 would save $1,136 trillion ($1,136 billion).*[78]

As a very large segment of the entire U.S. health care system, the problems of Medicare, which we have seen, mirror the problems of the system itself. The two are so closely intertwined that obstacles and approaches to reform are similar. Indeed, it is difficult to resolve the major problems of one without tackling those of the other.

A single-payer system under NHI could effectively address larger system problems, including those of Medicare, *if* political compromises are not once again allowed to subvert the system to private for-profit interests. Together with a growing number of health professionals and others involved in our chaotic health care system, I have become convinced that NHI is the only alternative which can successfully resolve larger system problems. These are some of the reasons, which are compelling.

- With by far the most expensive health care system in the world (for which annual per capita spending in the U.S. was $6,167 in 2004),[79] administrative bureaucracy and profits of the private health insurance industry siphon off 31 percent of the health care dollar from direct patient care.[80]

- Just as in Medicare, opportunistic private insurers seek out healthier enrollees by cherry picking the market, shifting the care of sick people to the public sector, and perpetuating inefficiencies and inequities of care.

- The uninsured and underinsured delay or avoid necessary care and treatments, thereby experiencing worse clinical outcomes and higher death rates than their insured counterparts.[81]

- In the face of spiraling costs of health care, almost one-half of Americans find it difficult to afford care, and a "medical divide" now disadvantages those earning less than $50,000 per year.[82]

- Medical bills are a leading cause of personal bankruptcy; the extent of underinsurance is revealed by the recent finding that 75 percent of those filing for bankruptcy had health insurance.[83]

- The for-profit sector has been found to have worse quality of care and poorer clinical outcomes than the not-for-profit sector.[84-87]

- The employer-based insurance system, an accident of history, provides less coverage at more cost and less value to only two-thirds of the U.S. workforce; it does not cover part-time workers, and today's trend toward consumer-directed health care involves increased cost-sharing and high deductible policies which will further exacerbate financial barriers to care.[88,89]

- All market-based incremental "reforms" over the last 30 years have failed to resolve cost, access and quality problems of the U.S. health care system, despite the continued promises of market advocates.

- With employers facing escalating costs of employee health benefits, many are becoming less competitive in a global economy as they compete with other countries with public universal coverage.[90]

- Independent projections by several government agencies and private sector analysts have shown that single-payer universal coverage would <u>not</u> increase total health care costs while covering entire populations of states or the country as a whole.[91-96]

Since NHI, as Medicare for all, would abolish duplicative private health insurance, it has been strongly opposed over the years by the insurance industry and allied advocates of the market-based system. Nevertheless, as pointed out by Donald Bartlett and James Steele, two-time Pulitzer prize winning investigative journalists at *Time* magazine, in their new book *Critical Condition: How Health Care in America Became Big Business and Bad Medicine*, universal coverage in this country will inevitably be forced into existence by two forces—"working Americans who are disenchanted with ever rising costs and shrinking care, and U.S. corporations, which are increasingly refusing to pick up the added costs."[97]

Returning to the urgent need for Medicare reform, it is important to assess the merits of each proposal against the National Academy of Social Insurance's seven values and public policy concerns—<u>financial security</u>, <u>equity</u>, <u>efficiency</u>, <u>affordability</u> <u>over time</u>, <u>political accountability</u>, <u>political sustainability</u>, and <u>maximizing individual liberty</u> (Chapter 2, pp). As NASI's Study Panel on Medicare's Larger Social Role concluded in its 1999 report:[98]

> *"The Panel sees some of the current debate to be counterproductive, diverting attention from the value of Medicare past and present. We believe that the American people have accomplished a great deal by solving problems of health care for the elderly through social insurance— including universal coverage, objective standards of qualification, no application of means tests, avoidance of financial destitution, creation of a sense of security and belonging, and acceptance of mutual obligations by the working population. Medicare has dignified the elder generation. It serves families of all ages: it is a promise to workers for their own retirement or disability, and a safeguard for young and middle-aged family members with sick or disabled grandparents, parents, or other relatives or friends who may depend on them. There is no doubt that Medicare's delivery system and benefit structure need modernizing, to*

*take better account of the elderly population's health care needs, to
create efficiencies, and to reflect changes in the organization of the health
care delivery system. But as we evaluate options for restructuring the
Medicare program, we should remember what we have accomplished,
and what we stand to lose, as well as gain, by change."*

Based on the track record of private market-based "reforms" over the
past 20 years, as documented in earlier chapters of this book, any satisfactory
approach to meet the health care needs of the nation's elderly and disabled
will necessarily require maintenance of universality, a reasonable set of
defined benefits, and a broad risk pool.

A VALUE AND PROBLEM-BASED APPROACH TO MEDICARE REFORM

Most reform proposals for Medicare deal with one or another changes
to its financing, neglecting content issues and broader social impacts of such
changes. Many reform proposals are also driven by ideology, and may thereby
be disconnected from evidence or social impacts. After 40 years' experience
with Medicare in this country, as well as over 20 years' experience with
reform attempts, there is ample evidence available to assess the program's
problems and the effects of previous reform efforts. Reform of Medicare
should be a bipartisan issue. Both major parties should be concerned with
best meeting the needs of the elderly and disabled as resources permit, while
eliminating waste and unnecessary services.

As a nonprofit, nonpartisan institution founded in 1919, the Twentieth
Century Fund (now renamed as The Century Foundation) has committed
itself to a mission of "calling attention to facts and analyses that correct
widespread misconceptions and provide policymakers with new ideas for
addressing the challenges facing the nation."[99]After two years of study of
the Medicare program, its 2001 report *Medicare Tomorrow: The Report
of the Century Foundation Task Force on Medicare Reform* recommended
these seven principles:[100]

1. "Medicare should remain a social insurance program that protects
    older and disabled Americans from the financial burden of health
    care, that shares the financial risk of serious illness and disability
    among the millions of Americans who are covered and who will

be covered, and that requires contributions from workers and employers.

2. Medicare should continue to be financed in part through general revenues and in part by contributions from workers, employers, and the covered population, but as Medicare's financial needs grow, older and disabled Americans should not shoulder a significantly higher proportion of program expenditures or medical costs.

3. The scope of health care benefits covered under Medicare should be expanded to include elements that are critical to preventing or detecting disease and managing chronic conditions, as well as treating acute illness.

4. Proposals to reform Medicare should reduce and eliminate rather than maintain or exacerbate, the disadvantages faced by vulnerable populations within the program.

5. Medicare should be a responsible steward that works to promote and encourage high quality care and the efficient delivery of medical services.

6. The process by which people with Medicare choose among alternative health insurance options and products should be made easier: it should clarify important distinctions among different types of health insurance and provide useful and unbiased education, information, and decision support to beneficiaries and those who help them make choices.

7. Medicare's management and administrative capacities should be adequately funded so that the goals implied by these principles can be carried out effectively in the context of a growing Medicare population."

Together with other recent studies, the 2004 report of the Community Tracking Study, after 9 years of study in 12 major metropolitan markets, casts serious doubt on the claims by market advocates that competition in the private marketplace can bring efficiency and value to health care.[101]

As earlier chapters document, markets are failing the elderly and disabled more today than they were in 1965. The problem list shown in Table 15.2 for the Medicare program is, in my view, a recipe for a perfect storm for this vulnerable part of our population. Based upon these problems and the values presented by NASI's criteria and the Century Foundation's principles, these five directions for Medicare reform are needed.

1. <u>Reduce corporate profiteering and waste</u>

Useful steps in this direction include:

- repeal of objectionable provisions in MMA 2003 in order to allow the government's use of its purchasing clout for prescription drugs

- permit drug reimportation from Canada and other countries

- eliminate overpayments to private plans

- eliminate the penalty for delayed signup for the prescription drug benefit starting in 2006

- cancel provisions for HSAs and the "competition demonstration projects" starting in 2010. Since risk adjusters remain ineffective safeguards against cream skimming by private plans[102] and private plans still claim to save money, competition between traditional Medicare and private plans needs a level playing field

- return to 95% payment levels of the mid-1990s seems in order.

- Other useful steps include the addition of a cost-effectiveness criterion to coverage and reimbursement decisions, adding resources to an empowered and more accountable FDA to apply that criterion, and establishing CMS (or a successor Medicare agency) as an evidence-based and more independent agency better protected from political influences by industry and legislators. In his recent book *Redesigning the Medicare Contract: Politics, Markets, and Agency,* Edward Lawlor proposes that a new Medicare Agency be created with increased analytic capability and overall responsibility for Medicare's costs, quality, accessibility, and outcomes.[103]

2. Reduce barriers to access

- In order to increase the numbers of physicians willing to accept new Medicare patients, provider reimbursement levels must be increased to reasonable levels. MMA 2003 contains provisions to cut physicians' Medicare fees by about 5% a year starting in 2006.[104] Such cuts would further exacerbate the existing problem which many Medicare beneficiaries have in finding a physician. House Democrats have suggested that unnecessary overpayments to private plans could be re-directed to physician reimbursement.[105]

- Establishing parity of mental health services with other Medicare services at an 80% reimbursement level would go a long way in improving Medicare beneficiaries' access to these essential services.

- Other useful directions to improve access for Medicare patients include extension of Medigap guaranteed issue protections, prohibition against discrimination by private plans against Medicare patients with major illnesses, and elimination of Medicare's lock-in rules and 24-month waiting period for the disabled.[106,107] Consideration should also be given to elimination of means or affluence testing in view of its threat to universality and the minimal cost savings involved.[108, 109]

3. Fill gaps in coverage for essential services

Gaps in coverage which need to be addressed include:

- interventions which help to prevent or delay functional decline;

- interventions to reduce or correct sensory impairment;

- essential long-term care and rehabilitation services;

- home health coverage including better integration of care for chronic illness;

- reversal of Medicare's current incentives to hospitalization of terminally ill patients toward care in less acute settings and increased utilization of hospice.[110]

4. Improve quality of care

- Overuse of ineffective care in higher-reimbursed areas of the country is an obvious target to reduce waste and improve quality of care at the same time. Wennberg and his colleagues have recommended that Comprehensive Centers for Medical Excellence (CCMEs) be established to improve quality of care and to allow Medicare to reward both quality and efficiency.[111]

- Organizational and administrative problems in the Medicare program need to be corrected in order to make coverage and reimbursement decisions more evidence-based and reduce geographic variations in care.

- The NCQA should be empowered to require all Medicare plans to report quality of care data

- information technology should be used to monitor longitudinal care and health status.[112]

5. Reduce complexity and administrative redundancy

- Shifting coverage and reimbursement decision making for NT and TE from local jurisdictions to a national agency would decrease duplicative functions, save money, and provide more expertise centrally for this important process.

- Increased use of information technology for oversight and management functions could likewise increase efficiency.

- Medicare has been responsible for two other areas as "add-ons" to its basic mission—graduate medical education (GME) and disproportionate share payments (DSH) to hospitals that care for a higher proportion of patients without health insurance or resources to pay for their own care. GME and DSH expenditures accounted for about 5% of Medicare's total spending in 1997. Although both payment streams are critically important to the ongoing needs of graduate medical education and the costs of

Table 15-5

A VALUE AND PROBLEM-BASED ACTION PLAN FOR MEDICARE REFORM

PROBLEM	DIRECTIONS FOR REFORM
1. Corporate profiteering and waste	Repeal provisions of MMA 2003 in order to: —allow government to use its purchasing power to discount prescription drugs, medical devices, and supplies —reimport prescription drugs from Canada and other countries —eliminate overpayments to private plans —eliminate penalties for beneficiaries who don't sign up at start of prescription drug benefit —eliminate means/affluence testing Return to 95% reimbursement of private plans with required risk adjustment Add cost-effectiveness criterion to NT and TE assessment Reform FDA approval processes to include cost-effectiveness, with added resources, accountability, and protection from political influence
2. Barriers to access	Cancel projected cuts in provider reimbursement Establish parity for mental health services Extend Medigap guaranteed access Eliminate lock-in rules Eliminate 24-month wait for disability coverage
3. Gaps in coverage for essential services	Improve coverage to prevent or delay functional decline Cover interventions to correct sensory impairment Improve coverage for rehabilitative services and long-term care Expand coverage for home health care Provide new incentives for expanded use of hospice for terminally ill patients
4. Improve quality of care	Address geographic variations in reimbursement and outcomes of care Require NCQA reports from all participating plans Expand use of information technology for monitoring of longitudinal care and health status

Table 15.5 Continued

5. Reduce complexity and administrative redundancy	Simplify administration by centralizing coverage and reimbursement decision making process for NT and TE Empower CMS (or a successor national agency) for expanded management responsibilities and authority with more protection from political influence Expanded use of IT for program oversight and management Remove GME and DSH from Medicare budget and address separately in terms of public policy

hospitalization of acutely ill lower-income patients, the Study Panel on Medicare's Larger Social Role has recommended that these two areas be addressed as generic public policy issues separately from the debate over the future of Medicare.[113]

These directions for Medicare reform are by no means all inclusive or encyclopedic, but could open new opportunities to resolve Medicare's major problems. Some would save money, such as through wider use of CEA, bulk purchasing power, reduction of unnecessary services, and elimination of administrative duplication. Savings from these and related areas could offset the costs of providing essential new benefits, and the program could be strengthened as long as its broad risk pool is preserved. Table 15.5 summarizes these directions as an action plan for strengthening Medicare and bringing more value to its beneficiaries.

WHERE FROM HERE?

We are at a crossroads for the Medicare program today. It is under attack from the right and even the center with a shove toward further privatization of the program. The program needs to be redesigned and reformed to better meet the needs of an expanding population in this new century. Its problems can be fixed, but only if we have the political will to confront efforts to swamp Medicare with a private marketplace which places its own interests above the public interest. As the public debate continues over the future shape and role of Medicare, we need to weigh all reform alternatives against the values and principles advanced earlier by NASI's Study Panel on Medicare's Larger Social Role and the Century Foundation's Task Force on Medicare Reform. Because whatever new directions Medicare takes depends so much on its political environment, that must necessarily be the focus of our next and last chapter.

CHAPTER 16

MEDICARE AS A POLITICAL FOOTBALL

"The new (health care) system also must be responsive primarily to individual consumers rather than to third-party payers, such as the government, insurers, and employers. A consumer-driven system will empower all people—if they choose—to make decisions that will directly affect the most fundamental and intimate aspect of their life—their own health. This empowerment gives people a greater stake in and more responsibility for their own health care. Health care will not improve in a sustained and substantial way until consumers drive it."

Senate Majority Leader Bill Frist, 2004,[1]

"Markets are designed to facilitate the free exchange of goods and services among willing participants, but are not capable, on their own, of taking care of collective needs. Nor are they competent to ensure social justice. These "pubic goods" can only be provided by a political process."

George Soros, 2004[2]

Earlier chapters have attempted to comprehensively review and describe the evolution of Medicare over the last 40 years, to assess its current strengths and weaknesses, and to consider options for needed reforms of the program. We have found a coalescence of trends that threaten its future, including increasing costs, decreasing access, suboptimal quality, and insufficient accountability in a largely for-profit and wasteful delivery system. With the imminent arrival of the age wave of retiring baby boomers, to begin around 2010, and the country beset by serious budget deficits at federal and state levels, there is an urgent need to rein in unnecessary services, eliminate waste, and improve the value and reliability of services for a vulnerable population of elderly and disabled Americans. As the public debate over Medicare reform continues, the democratic process is challenged on two counts (1) the clout of economic self-interests as they lobby and reward legislators for votes favoring their interests, and (2) not only do lobbying and campaign dollars offset many votes of individuals, but many lower-income individuals most affected by changes in Medicare do not vote and are politically voiceless. In the 1998 elections, for example, more than two-thirds of eligible voters with incomes above $75,000 per year voted, compared with less than one-third of eligible voters earning less than $75,000 a year.[3]

This chapter has four objectives: (1) to briefly describe the ideologic gulf between the right and left over Medicare; (2) to examine the potential role of the political center to mediate and shape public policy concerning Medicare; (3) to consider what can be learned from the 2004 elections; and (4) to project how the current post-election political landscape may impact the future of Medicare and its beneficiaries.

A BATTLE OF IDEOLOGIES

As we saw in Chapter 2, the first 30 years of Medicare was characterized by broad bipartisan consensus. This support collapsed 10 years ago with the Republican sweep of both the House and Senate in the 1994 elections.[4] Since then conservatives and many moderates have promoted market-based strategies to resolve problems of the health care system, including Medicare. Unfortunately, the debate over Medicare has been driven more by ideology and political rhetoric than by an informed and value-based evaluation of options for change. On the right, and even among many moderates, the view is that health care should be more of a personal responsibility, for which people save and make more prudent decisions for their own care, that the open marketplace will provide more choice and value, and that the responsibility of government for a growing "entitlement program" should be reduced. Proponents for this view include diverse and powerful economic interests within the medical-industrial complex, which benefit from the rewards of the current market-based system. On the left, the opposing view holds that health care is too important to be left to the market, that Medicare services are an earned right for its beneficiaries, that the integrity of Medicare depends on its universality and a broad social insurance risk pool, and that patient care takes precedence over profits. Advocates for this view include such non-profit, non-partisan groups as Public Citizen, Families USA, and the Medicare Rights Center, as well as a growing number of health professionals and others concerned about social justice in health care.

It is interesting to find that this wide ideologic gulf crosses national borders as an international pattern. In a recent book *The Public—Private Mix for Health*, health care systems are examined for many countries, including Canada, the U.S., Scandinavia, France, Germany, Australia and New Zealand. Alan Maynard, Professor of Health Economics at the University of York in the U.K., found common themes and similarities in these countries, with polar opposites in two camps—the Libertarian-Conservative-Republican camp stressing freedom as the supreme goal for society vs. the Egalitarian-Socialist-Democrat camp, with its highest priority on creating and sustaining equality of opportunity. Table 16.1 illustrates this ideologic gap in terms of attitudes, which rings true in the U.S. today.[5]

It is often argued by proponents of the status quo in this country that American society and its politics are exceptional, and that political views and policy approaches in other industrialized countries are not relevant to the U.S. This is another claim that doesn't hold water, as shown by these attitudinal similarities from one country to another. Table 16.1 goes a long way to debunk the theory of American exceptionalism. Indeed, when one considers how it is that these other industrialized countries have better performing health care systems at a fraction of the costs spent in the U.S., as is well documented,[6-11] the obvious question is why. The major difference, of course, is that this country's health care system is by far the most privatized and the least regulated by government.

While polarized ideologies typically fuel political debates on health care in many countries around the world, they are not effective in setting health policy. Don McCanne, Senior Health Policy Fellow for Physicians for a National Health Program, makes this important point:[12]

> *"The problem is that the debate over ideology is the wrong debate. Instead the dialogue should be over the best mechanisms to provide efficiency, control of expenditures, and ensuring equity in funding and access. No system will be purely public or private, so decisions should be made on changes that will improve the functioning of the system based on understanding of the impact of various well-described policies. Effective solutions would invariably have the support or opposition of ideologues, but the ideology should not control the process. Health policy science has advanced dramatically in the past couple of decades, and we have the knowledge on how to make the systems work."*

With respect to Medicare, the Republican and Democratic presidential candidates in the 2004 election campaigns were sharply opposed concerning substantive issues. Table 16.2 compares the intentions of Kerry and Bush, if elected, with regard to nine policy issues for Medicare, as found by a survey

Attitudes Typically Associated with Viewpoints A and B

Table 16.1

	Viewpoint A (Libertarian)	Viewpoint B (Egalitarian)
Personal responsibility	Personal responsibility for achievement is very important, and this is weakened if people are offered unearned rewards. Moreover, such unearned rewards weaken the motive force that assures economic well-being and in so doing they also undermine moral well-being, because of the intimate connection between moral well-being and the personal effort to achieve	Personal incentives to achieve are desirable, but economic failure is not equated with moral depravity or social worthlessness
Social concern	Social Darwinism dictates a seemingly cruel indifference to the fate of those who cannot make the grade. A less extreme position is that charity, expressed and effected preferably under private auspices, is the proper vehicle, but it needs to be exercised under carefully prescribed conditions, for example, such that the potential recipient must first mobilise all his own resources and, when helped, must not be in as favourable a position as those who are self-supporting (the principle of 'lesser eligibility')	Private charitable action is not rejected but is seen as potentially dangerous morally (because it is often demeaning to the recipient and corrupting to the donor) and usually inequitable. It seems preferable to establish social mechanisms that create and sustain self-sufficiency and that are accessible according to precise rules concerning entitlement that are applied equitably and explicitly sanctioned by society at large
Freedom	Freedom is to be sought as a supreme good in itself. Compulsion attenuates both personal responsibility and individualistic and voluntary expressions of social concern. Centralised health planning and a large governmental role in healthcare financing are seen as an unwarranted abridgement of the freedom of clients as well as of health professionals and private medicine is thereby viewed as a bulwark against totalitarianism	Freedom is seen as the presence of real opportunities of choice; although economic constraints are less openly coercive than political constraints, they are nonetheless real and often the effective limits on choice. Freedom is not indivisible but may be sacrificed in one respect in order to obtain greater freedom in some other. Government is not an external threat to individuals in the society but is the means by which individuals achieve greater scope for action (that is, greater real freedom)
Equality	Equality before the law is the key concept, with clear precedence being given to freedom over equality wherever the two conflict	Since the only moral justification for using personal achievement as the basis for distributing rewards is that everyone has equal opportunities for such achievement, then the main emphasis is on equality of opportunity; where this cannot be assured, the moral worth of achievement is thereby undermined. Equality is seen as an extension to the many, of the freedom actually enjoyed by only the few

Source: Reprinted with permission from Maynard, A. *Enduring Problems in Healthcare Delivery*. In Maynard, A. (Editor) *The Public Trust - Private Mix for Health*. The Nuffield Trust, Oxford, Seattle. Radcliffe Publishers 2005: p. 300

Table 16.2

Questionnaire for 2004 Presidential Candidates

As President, will you:	Kerry	Bush
1. Support legislation to **eliminate the 24-month waiting period** for Americans with disabilities to gain Medicare coverage?	YES	NO
2. Support legislation to make Medicare **cover outpatient mental health care at 80% of its approved rate**, as Medicare does for all other outpatient medical services?	YES	NO
3. Support administrative initiatives to **expand Medicare's coverage of durable medical equipment** (e.g., wheelchairs) to include devices needed to function outside the home?	YES	NO
4. Support legislation to **extend Medicare home care services** to individuals who are not homebound?	YES	NO
5. Support legislation to **guarantee people who have Medicare because of disability the same right to access Medigap policies** as people who have Medicare because of age?	YES	NO
6. Support legislation to **federalize administration and financing of the Medicare Savings Programs**?	YES	NO
7. Support legislation to **permit adults ages 55-64 to purchase health care coverage through Medicare**?	YES	NO
8. Support legislation or administrative initiatives to **increase overall annual funding for State Health Insurance Assistance Programs** (SHIPs) to at least $3 per person with Medicare?	YES	NO
9. Support legislation or administrative initiatives to **ensure that Americans pay no more for prescription drugs** than the median price paid by Canadians?	YES	NO

A copy of this survey is available at www.medicarerights.org/QuestResults01142004.pdf
The Democrat candidates' responses can be found at:
 www.medicarerights.org/MRC Candidate Questionnaire.pdf

Repeated efforts were made to elicit a response from the Bush-Cheney campaign. The campaign
 finally refused to respond, advising MRC staff to deduce the President's position from his campaign
web site, www.georgebush.com, which it did.

Reprinted with permission from Medicare Rights Center.

by the Medical Rights Center, a national, not-for-profit consumer service organization.

MMA 2003 is for the most part a Republican bill (the final vote included 25 Republicans against it with 16 Democrats supporting it). As we have seen earlier, the Republican agenda for many years has been to privatize Medicare, dismantle it as an entitlement program, and limit the obligation of the federal government to the nation's elderly and disabled population. Despite all evidence to the contrary with privatized Medicare plans to date, Representative Bill Thomas (R-Calif), chairman of the House Ways and Means Committee and a principal player in the passage of MMA 2003, still maintains that "The new law does more to cut drug prices than any other action ever taken by Congress....Congress believes that private plans and competition will help to drive down the explosive growth of Medicare spending....The new law will markedly improve the health care of 40 million seniors and begin making Medicare more efficient and responsible to the beneficiaries, providers, and taxpayers it serves."[13]

Ideology blinded to the facts successfully influences health policy through money as the "milk of politics" in lobbying and political contributions. As pointed out recently by Senator Ted Kennedy, ranking member of the Senate Health, Education, Labor, and Pensions Committee, MMA 2003 "practically bribes health insurers to enter the health insurance market for seniors."[14] A 2004 staff report of this Senate committee estimates that private insurers will see $189 billion more per year by entering the Medicare market.[15] Implementation of ideologic-based health policy is further facilitated by a revolving door of appointed staff leadership positions. There are many examples of revolving door connections with obvious conflicts of interest. The career trajectory of Tom Scully, until recently the head of CMS, is but one of many examples. As the former president of the American Federation of Hospitals and Health Systems (a for-profit health industry trade group), he was a strong proponent of increasing privatization of Medicare,[16] asked for and received a special conflict of interest waiver from the head of the Health and Human Services Department, then negotiated a high-paying job with a legal firm serving drug industry clients while still heading CMS and helping to shape the 2003 Medicare bill.[17]

Meanwhile, as the ideologic debate continues between these polarized ends of the political spectrum, the practical details which largely determine policy are hammered out by staff with participation of special interest groups, behind the scenes, usually well beyond any public awareness. Here are just four important examples relating to implementation of MMA 2003, which together give little basis to be optimistic about their ultimate impact on access and costs for Medicare beneficiaries.

* The federal government released in July 2004 nearly 2,000 pages of proposed rules to implement the drug benefit, requesting public comment before they are finalized. Reacting to critics' concerns that employers may be able to gain subsidies as windfalls even when reducing drug benefits to their retirees, new rules were developed to address that potential loophole. Under the final rules, however, employers will receive subsidies up to $1,330 per retiree from the government for 28% of the cost of drug benefits provided to each retiree between $250 and $5,000, even if the employers had shifted more of their own costs onto their retirees.[18] Critics are still concerned that employers can reduce their present level of drug benefits and qualify for the subsidy, and the rules also raise the possibility of waivers to provide employers with "additional flexibility."[19]

* The question of how many classes of drugs should be covered by the prescription drug benefit has also been a hot issue. Drug manufacturers have wanted more than 200 classes to be covered in order to increase their chances of having their drugs listed on formularies covered by insurers. Health insurers and pharmacy-benefits managers (PBMs) have favored as few as 50. Congressional negotiators of MMA 2003 could not decide on who should make that decision. The non-profit United States Pharmacopeial Convention Inc (USP) was tasked to settle this dispute, and is in the process of developing voluntary guidelines for insurers.[20] USP released draft model guidelines in August, 2004, calling for 146 unique therapeutic categories and pharmacologic classes. The president of the Pharmaceutical Care Management Association promptly responded with a warning that these guidelines "could have the unintended consequence of increasing costs and jeopardizing a workable prescription drug benefit for seniors."[21]

- According to the final rules adopted by CMS in January 2005, insurers are allowed to use formularies and cover only one drug in a therapeutic category or class if only two drugs are available and one is clearly better; however, insurers must cover any drug not on the formulary if the prescribing physician judges it to be medically necessary. Beneficiaries are locked into a private drug plan for a year, during which insurers can end coverage of a particular drug or raise co-payments with 60 days' notice to patients and the government.[22]

- Another contentious issue has been how many health insurance coverage areas should be established for the Medicare Advantage program. About 10 large, multistate regions were preferred by the Administration, partly to force insurers to serve rural areas which they have tended to avoid and in an effort to discourage insurers from discriminating against sicker patients. The Administration hopes to reverse the decline in private Medicare plans, is promoting PPOs which need at least 200,000 enrollees, and 11 states do not have such populations—Alaska, Delaware, Hawaii, Idaho, Montana, New Hampshire, North Dakota, Rhode Island, South Dakota, Vermont, and Wyoming. The insurance industry has forcibly resisted such multistate regions, calling for 50 regions, one for each state, warning that their financial risk will be too great in a smaller number of larger regions and that they will not be ready to provide coverage by 2006 if that is the case.[23] The Administration recently compromised with a decision by CMS to divide the country into 26 health insurance areas for private Medicare plans.[24]

IS THERE A CENTER?

The stereotypes of the ideologic extremes of the political spectrum in the U.S., inaccurate as they may be, portray the fundamental wings of the two parties as the "religious right" and the "lifestyle left," each side attempting to impose its beliefs on American society. In an important new book *Independent Nation*: How *the Vital Center is Changing American*

Politics, John Avlon points out that the electorate in this country has steadily grown more centrist despite the intense partisanship and polarization among legislators in Congress.[25] Concerning Medicare, the question becomes whether, and to what extent, centrist views will prevail in determining its future. As Dwight Eisenhower observed in 1965: "It is only common sense to recognize that the great bulk of Americans, whether Republican or Democrat, face many common problems and agree on a number of basic objectives.[26]

Five lines of reasoning suggest to me that the political center will play a determining role in preserving and strengthening Medicare for future generations, if the electorate is provided with accurate information as to its present problems and alternatives for reform.

First, a growing number of American voters are defining themselves as moderates. Their numbers increased from 36% to 50% between 1980 and 2000, when only 20% of voters called themselves liberal and 29% conservative.[27] According to a 2002 national poll, Independents now outnumber Republicans and Democrats nationwide.[28] with 44% of voters under 30 listing themselves as Independent.[29] A 1994 report found that only 14% of the electorate always supported candidates from a single party.[30]

Second, with regard to health care, we saw in Chapter 8 how recurrent studies over the last 30 years have documented high levels of public support (typically about two-thirds) favoring replacement of the market-based system by a government-financed national health plan. A large 2005 study by the Pew Research Center of the People and the Press is the most recent addition to this well-established pattern. Figure 16-1 shows its findings based on two national surveys involving 2,000 interviews and over 1,000 re-interviews across the political spectrum. Strong majorities of every group, with the sole exception of Enterprisers, favor a government guarantee of health insurance for all Americans, even if taxes increase. This study shows that Republicans are deeply divided over health care, with both social conservatives and pro-government conservatives supporting health care as a public good over the current market-based business ethic.[31]

Third, there is increasing evidence that fiscal conservatives on the right are finding common ground, though perhaps for different reasons, with progressives, consumer groups, and their allies on the left. We saw this in the votes in Congress for and against MMA 2003. Recall from Chapter 3 that members of Congress were given a false low estimate by the Administration

Figure 16.1

Government Health Insurance For All, Even if Taxes Increase

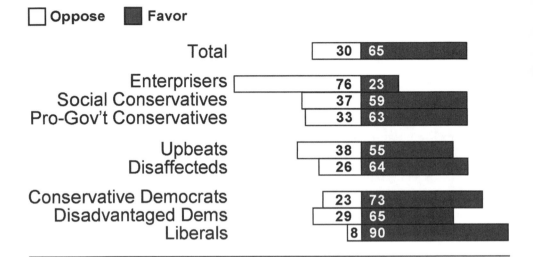

□ Oppose   ■ Favor

	Oppose	Favor
Total	30	65
Enterprisers	76	23
Social Conservatives	37	59
Pro-Gov't Conservatives	33	63
Upbeats	38	55
Disaffecteds	26	64
Conservative Democrats	23	73
Disadvantaged Dems	29	65
Liberals	8	90

Reprinted with permission from Beyond Red vs. Blue. *Report of The Pew Research Center of the People and the Press*, Washington, D.C., May 10, 2005

of the 10-year cost of the bill ($395 billion vs. what is now estimated to be $724 billion).[32,33] Some Republicans voted against the bill on the basis of fiscal discipline (e.g., 9 Republican Senators voted against the bill when it passed the Senate 54-44).[34] More recently, a non-partisan coalition of employers, unions, consumer groups and political leaders are calling for an independent board, to be overseen by Congress, with the authority to set limits on reimbursement rates paid providers and hospitals for a set of core medical benefits and to restrict increases in health insurance premiums. With almost 100 members, this coalition has three honorary co-chairmen—former Presidents Gerald Ford, Jimmy Carter, and George H.W. Bush—and views escalating health care costs as not just a health care issue, but also an economic problem for the country. Not surprisingly, Karen Ignagni, president of American Health Insurance Plans, quickly reacted to this recommendation with concerns over placing limits to premium increases.[35]

A fourth reason that we can anticipate broad support among moderates for the strengthening of Medicare is a growing backlash to shrinking of the middle class which impacts Americans across generations. In their excellent 2003 book *The Two Income Trap: Why Middle-Class Mothers and Fathers are Going Broke*, Elizabeth Warren and Amelia Warren Tyagi report that the average middle-class family today, despite having dual incomes, has less discretionary income than an average middle-class single-income family of a generation ago. Although an average combined income is now about $67,800, 75% higher than an average fully employed single-income family income of $38,700 in 1973, today's dual-income family has less discretionary income (about $17,000) after basic fixed costs are met (mortgage, child care, health insurance, car, taxes).[36,37] Wages for middle-class working families are stagnant, and their median income even dropped by $1,500 a year between 2000 and 2003.[38] About 2.5 million jobs have been lost over the last three years as U.S. corporations continue to downsize and outsource more jobs to cheaper labor markets in other countries. A recent study by the Progressive Policy Institute found that the number of middle-class jobs has plummeted since 2000, and that most of the new jobs are in low-income jobs.[39] As the squeeze on the middle-class grows tighter, debt, defaults and foreclosures for typical middle-class families have increased markedly, with four such families now falling into bankruptcy every minute.[40] Meanwhile, many middle-class working Americans find themselves caught between the needs of their children and parents, often having to assist their elders with health care and living expenses and finding it increasingly difficult to save for their own retirement. As a result, middle-class Americans in their working years need to know that Medicare provides good coverage for their parents and will also be there for them in future years.

A fifth reason to expect that moderates will play a major role in shaping Medicare's future is the considerable political power of seniors themselves, especially when informed and energized. Recall from Chapter 2 their ability to force Congress to repeal the 1988 Medicare Catastrophic Care Act a year later. Both AARP and Congress were surprised then by the intensity of this backlash, as they were again by the resignation of 60,000 AARP members in the immediate aftermath of MMA's passage in 2003. So far the response of seniors has been less than united, owing most likely to minimal knowledge and experience with some of the bill's provisions. But a March 2004 *USA Today*/CNN/Gallup poll showed a majority of both enrollees and the general public opposing the bill. Since the legislation does nothing about the main problem—soaring drug prices—more united opposition by seniors can be anticipated as they better understand its provisions, which include a meager and confusing drug benefit, reimbursement cuts to physicians and home health agencies, means testing, a voucher program, and pressure to enroll in private plans being subsidized by wasteful government overpayments under the guise of increased "choice" and "competition." AARP is once again caught in a crossfire over the bill which it helped to pass in 2003. Its conflicts of interest and cozy relationship over the years with advocates of Medicare privatization are detailed in a recent article by Barbara Dreyfuss.[41] In recent months, AARP has attempted to regain some of its credibility as an advocacy organization by supporting efforts to repeal some of MMA's provisions, such as its endorsement of a Senate bill to allow imports of lower-priced drugs from Canada and other foreign countries, as well as taking a strong position against privatization of Social Security.[42,43]

WHAT CAN BE LEARNED FROM THE 2004 ELECTIONS?

Republicans touted the benefits of MMA 2003 as a major advance in modernizing Medicare. They promoted its provisions for HSAs as a way for individuals to take more control over their own health care spending. Senate Majority Leader Bill Frist (R-Tenn.) described the issue in these words:[44]

> "We believe true compassion encourages and empowers Americans to be responsible and take control of their own lives. That's what President Bush and the Republican Congress did when we made Health Savings Accounts—HSAs—the law of the land. With an HSA you can invest tax-free in a personal savings account. You can roll it over year to year or withdraw funds if you get sick...without paying a penny of tax. YOU own it. YOU invest it. YOU grow it. YOU control it. It is YOURS.
>
> So here's the choice: do we grow the bureaucracy and gouge you with higher taxes, as Mr. Kerry will do? Or, do we let the American people grow their own HSAs and own their health care, as George Bush wants to do? We've made our choice."

Meanwhile, Frist in his Senate leadership role blocked all efforts to repeal any of MMA's provisions while claiming that private plans are better equipped than the federal government in negotiating prices with drug manufacturers.

Democrats called for repeal of several of MMA's provisions, including those that prevent reimportation of prescription drugs from Canada and that prevent the government from negotiating drug prices. They also opposed HSAs as a threat to sick beneficiaries with greater health needs and as a device allowing government to reduce its responsibility for the care of the elderly and disabled.

There was little question where the electorate stood concerning Medicare during the 2004 election cycle. An August 2004 report of a Kaiser Family Foundation/Harvard School of Public Health national survey found that 47% of over 1,200 Medicare enrollees polled had an unfavorable impression of the new Medicare law; the three main reasons given were that the law does not provide enough help with drug costs, that it's too complicated to understand, and that it benefits private health plans and drug companies too much. Only 20% of seniors and disabled enrollees were enthusiastic about the law. One in five said they would not enroll in the Medicare drug plan when it becomes available in 2006, while six in ten had not yet heard enough about it to decide. Eight in ten respondents favored changing the law to permit imports of drugs from Canada and to allow the government to use its buying power to negotiate lower drug prices. Despite high levels of dissatisfaction with the law, two-thirds of respondents felt that Congress should work to fix problems in the law rather than repeal it entirely.[45] (Figure 16.2).

Other public opinion polls were similarly distrustful of both the Republican Administration and industry. A March 2004 *Washington Post—ABC News* poll found that two-thirds of respondents believe that the Bush administration cares more about protecting the interests of large corporations than those of ordinary people.[46] The 2004 annual Harris Poll found that only 44% of respondents viewed drug companies favorably (down from 79% in 1997), with insurance companies rated favorably by only 36% (down from 55% in 1997).[47]

After a hotly contested election campaign, President Bush won re-election by a 51-48% majority in the popular vote, while Republicans added to their majorities in both the Senate and the House. Among the lessons that can be learned from the 2004 elections, these three are of special interest:

•   Health care did not turn out to be the main or decisive issue. A study of 22 national opinion surveys found that health care ranked fourth

Figure 16.2

What Should Lawmakers Do?

Which of the following comes closest to your view of what lawmakers in Washington should do with the new Medicare law?

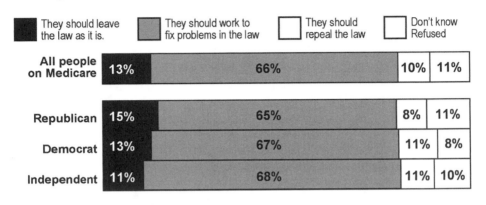

Source: Views of the New Medicare Drug Law: A Survey of People on Medicare, (#7145), The Kaiser Family Foundation/Harvard School of Public Health, August 2004.

This information was reprinted with permission of the Henry J. Kaiser Family Foundation. The Kaiser Family Foundation, based in Menlo Park, California, is a nonprofit, independent national health care philanthropy and is not associated with Kaiser Permanente or Kaiser Industries.

among issues in deciding votes for president, after the economy, the war in Iraq, and the campaign against terrorism. The leading health care issues for voters were found to be the affordability of health care and prescription drugs, the uninsured, and Medicare, especially prescription drug benefits for the elderly[48]

• Campaign rhetoric was often focused on side issues (e.g., the Swift boat controversy), thereby distracting attention from more fundamental issues. Meanwhile, media coverage of the issues tended to be right of center; for example, mainstream media citations of the top 25 think tanks in the U.S. (a majority of which are right of center) increased by 13% from 2002 to 2003 while right-leaning institutions accounted for 47% of citations in 2003[49]

• Campaign finance reform again failed. Although the McCain-Feingold legislation banned national political parties from raising unlimited soft money campaign contributions in 2002, the Republican and Democratic parties had raised more than $1 billion in contributions by mid-October 2004, more than their total for the same period during the 2000 election. A new category of groups, "527 organizations" (named for a section in the IRS tax code) are allied but formally separate from the political parties, and have been able to pour large sums of unregulated contributions into elections.[50] Public Citizen has found that PhRMA, the drug industry's trade group, funneled money into some non-profit senior groups as stealth PAC front groups (egs, United Seniors Association, Seniors Coalition) to influence the 2004 elections, as it had in some closely contested Congressional races in 2002.[51] By the summer of 2005, even in the midst of money scandals in government and corporate management, a disingenuously titled bill was brought forward in the House, the 527 Fairness Act (H.R. 1316) in an effort to repeal Key provisions in the 2002 McCain-Feingold Act, as well as essential campaign contribution limits enacted after Watergate in 1974.[52]

MEDICARE AND THE NEW POLITICAL LANDSCAPE

In the aftermath of the divisive and polarized 2004 elections, all indications so far are that the Bush Administration in its second term will see the election results as a mandate to pursue its agenda. That agenda will be to make permanent tax cuts favoring the wealthy, advance corporate-friendly policies, privatize such programs as Social Security and Medicare, and address its growing deficit by cutting domestic programs and shifting responsibility for safety net programs such as Medicaid to the states.[53] To the extent that this agenda is implemented, much of the social contract established by the government with Americans in the 1930s and 1960s will be dismantled as citizens are expected to shoulder more personal risks in an "ownership society."[54]

With regard to Medicare, this will mean energetic efforts to increase the private sector's role through Medicare Advantage plans, HSAs, and the new prescription drug benefit starting in 2006. With majorities in both houses of Congress, the Republicans can be expected to block all attempts to repeal objectionable provisions of the MMA of 2003. President Bush has reiterated his promise to veto any bill which reaches his desk repealing any provisions of MMA 2003.[55] Strong attempts to further privatize Medicare, as well as Social Security, can be anticipated, with increased cost sharing all along the line for Medicare beneficiaries.

The insurance and pharmaceutical industries especially welcomed the 2004 election results, and stand to gain handsomely from implementation of the 2003 Medicare legislation. A securities analyst at Smith Barney stated in a research report that "Medicare is a profitable new growth driver"..."A managed care organization can receive an average of $10,000 per customer per year for each Medicare enrollee they sign on, and marginal profit of about $300 to $400 per member per year." The chairman of Aetna, which offers managed care plans to Medicare beneficiaries as well as high-deductible plans with HSAs to employers acknowledged that the election "does brighten the outlook for us."[56] A conference was held for health care executives in New York City in June 2005 entitled *The Medicare Drug Gold Rush.*[57]

Projected increases in the costs of Medicare, together with massive budget and trade deficits, are certain to lead the Bush Administration to vigorous attempts to cut Medicare spending, and convert the program from a defined-benefit to a defined-contribution program. The CBO has estimated that the federal budget deficit for fiscal 2004 was about $415 billion, 3.6% of the nation's GDP[58] The federal debt has grown by about 40% since 2001, or $2.1 trillion, and Congress has been forced to raise the debt ceiling on three occasions. The centrist Brookings Institution estimates that the Republican agenda for privatization of Social Security and permanent tax cuts will cost about $4 trillion over the next 10 years.[59] All of this leads Bruce Vladeck, former administrator of the Health Care Financing Administration during the Clinton administration, to this observation.[60]

> "This means that future Medicare beneficiaries will receive the equivalent of a fixed-price voucher with which they can purchase whatever combination of utilization controls, deductibles and co-payments private insurance plans choose to offer. By controlling the price of the voucher, future governments would also be able to shift the risk of increasing health care costs from the community as a whole to

individual beneficiaries—thus sidling away, without visible fingerprints,
from Medicare's basic commitment to provide access to health care."

Medicare spending for fiscal year 2005 is projected to be about $325 billion and account for 13% of federal spending.[61] That share will grow as the prescription drug benefit enacted by the MMA in 2003 takes full effect. The GAO describes this benefit as "one of the largest unfunded liabilities ever undertaken by the federal government," and estimates that it will cost over $6.3 trillion over 75 years for current workers and retirees.[62] In early 2005, major Medicare budget cuts are already being considered. MEDPAC has recently recommended that projected payment increases of 3.2% to hospitals be cut to 2.8%, while freezing Medicare payments to nursing homes and home care services at their present levels.[63]

As is clear from the above, the political struggle over Medicare continues even as the stakes become higher, both for the nation's treasury and the growing numbers of elderly and disabled. Few observers see reconciliation across party lines after the polarized and divisive 2004 election campaigns.[64] Political gridlock can be expected over the next two years as positions are taken for the 2008 election year. Meanwhile, public opinion appears to be increasingly opposed to the current Administration's priorities. A May 2005 Wall Street Journal/NBC News poll of 1,005 adults found that only 17% of respondents felt that Congress shares their priorities, while the number of respondents feeling that the economy has gotten worse in the last year more than doubled from 20% to over 40% in just 4 months.[65]

CONCLUSION

In 1986, the Institute of Medicine issued this warning about the for-profit health care enterprise evolving in the United States[66]

"Ordinarily in our predominantly capitalist society, it would be deemed odd to inquire into the implications of making a business of providing services or of making money from such a business. However, the services discussed here help people to keep or regain their health and can affect at minimum, whether they are able to pursue their life goals, and, at maximum, whether they live or die. Many people see health care as the sort of public good that should be the right of all citizens, but this view has never prevailed in public policy."

Despite this admonition 20 years ago, a Darwinian marketplace has taken over in the U.S. whereby health care has become just another commodity for sale. More than two-third's of the nation's HMOs are for-profit, mostly investor-owned and accountable more to Wall Street than the public interest.[67] As we have seen, private Medicare plans seek out the most profitable markets and have little reluctance in leaving unprofitable ones. These comments by three long-term close observers of U.S. health care are especially relevant to where we now find ourselves:

> *"U.S. health policies have failed to meet national needs during the past four decades because they have been heavily influenced by the delusion that medical care is essentially a business"... "The current rate of inflation in health care costs is unsustainable, and it is likely that any market-based solutions will fail to address the problem, "... "A real solution to our crisis will not be found until the public, the medical profession and the government reject the prevailing delusion that health care is best left to market forces. "*
>
> Arnold S. Relman[68] Former Editor,
> *The New England Journal of Medicine*

> *"For the past quarter-century, America has been deregulating capitalism in expectation of a more dynamic and efficient economy. In fact, average economic growth since 1976 has slightly lagged that of the previous quarter-century, when capitalism was more highly regulated. But there has been a much more serious set of consequences...widening inequality, the dismantling of public remedy, and the neutering of the Democratic Party as a medium of progressive politics"... "Nothing about the new economy changes time-tested truths about capitalism: It is a dynamic system of innovation and creative destruction. Either we harness it for general benefit, using the instruments of political democracy, or the destruction overwhelms the creativity. "*
>
> Robert Kuttner[69]
> Co-Editor, *The American Prospect*

> *(Concerning past health reform efforts in the U.S.), "the political and ideological clout of leading health interests stood in stark contrast to the organizational struggles of health reformers. Although reformers always commanded a clear and substantial majority of public support, they only rarely made themselves heard above the cacophony of the corporate compromise and were quickly silenced when they did. In part this reflected a political system characterized by routine deference to*

economic interests, weak ties between reform interests and party politics, and non-programmatic electoral competition. And in part it reflected the peculiar politics of health care, in which private interests are well entrenched, the organization of public interests proved extraordinarily difficult, and fragmented provision fragmented reform energies as well.[70]

Colin Gordon, Associate Professor of History
at the University of Iowa and author of *Dead on Arrival*:
The Politics of Health Care in Twentieth-Century America

Two fundamental questions remain unanswered concerning Medicare and indeed the entire U.S. health care system at this writing: (1) is health care a basic human need and right or just another commodity for sale in a deregulated market; and (2) should the delivery system be designed to give highest priority to the needs of patients or to the interests of providers and suppliers of services? Further privatization of Medicare, if allowed to proceed, answers both questions in ways which fail to meet any of NASI's criteria.

From the beginning, this book has been an honest attempt to describe Medicare as it really is, with its various strengths and shortcomings, and assess ways to improve it. As we have seen, this is challenging given the extent to which Medicare is tossed about as a political football amidst conflicting ideologies, distortions, and disinformation. Although Medicare remains a complex subject, these basic conclusions appear inescapable:

- What has been a largely successful, popular and essential program over 40 years is now threatened by a continued trend toward privatization

- Access, continuity, affordability, and quality of care are all being eroded by present trends

- An enormous for-profit industry has enveloped Medicare over the years siphoning off large sums from patient care to bureaucratic waste and corporate profits, and trumping the public interest

- Despite the claims of the private marketplace for more efficiency, choice and value, the track record of private Medicare plans is one of less efficiency, less choice, increased costs, higher overhead, and less reliability compared to traditional Medicare

- Cost containment and sustainability of Medicare cannot be achieved unless enormous waste and profiteering can be reined in and cost-effectiveness added to its coverage policies

- The program was designed around an acute care model of the 1960s and is long overdue for redesign around a chronic care model in a new century

- Major reform is now required in order to assure long-term sustainability of a vital social insurance program for a growing and vulnerable part of the population

- All reform alternatives should be measured against NASIs seven criteria—financial security, equity, efficiency, affordability over time, political accountability, political sustainability, and maximizing individual liberty[71]

- In view of polarization and political gridlock in Congress over the last 10 years, still in place after the 2004 elections, a broad inter-generational centrist movement will be required to sustain Medicare's social contract for future generations

There are rays of hope which indicate that privatization, as the principal threat to Medicare, can be arrested before it decimates the program. Demographics are on the public interest side. A growing population of seniors, united and energized over Medicare reform, can be politically powerful, as was demonstrated in 1989 by the repeal of the Medicare Catastrophic Care Act. Shrinking of the middle class will further empower a backlash to current trends threatening Medicare and Social Security. A broad public backlash to NAFTA and global trade policies is growing, as shown by the recent bipartisan opposition in Congress to the Central America Free Trade Agreement (CAFTA).[72] And the public is not fooled as much as market advocates would like to think, as reflected by negative opinions among Medicare beneficiaries to MMA 2003, their disinterest in private Medicare plans, and cautious reaction to HSAs.

How public policy for Medicare is debated and decided over coming years will test our democracy and real values to their core. Do we believe in a Darwinian jungle or a society where our often-evoked values of equal opportunity, fair play, and compassion for the less fortunate are actually practiced? As the debate proceeds, we need to be vigilant to separate evidence from rhetoric and distinguish whose interests will be served by any particular proposal for reform. Returning to our football analogy, we (the public interest) are on the 50-yard line and have the ball. It seems fitting to close with this observation by Bill Moyers concerning the task at hand:[73]

> *"The first order of business is to understand the real interests and deep opinion of the American people. What are these?*
>
> *—That a Social Security card is not a private portfolio statement but a membership ticket in a society where we all contribute to a common treasury so that none need face the indignities of poverty in old age*
>
> *—That tax evasion is not a form of conserving investment capital but a brazen abandonment of responsibility to the country*
>
> *—That income inequality is not a sign of freedom of opportunity at work, because if it persists and grows, then unless you believe that some people are naturally born to ride and some to wear saddles, it's a sign that opportunity is less than equal*
>
> *—That self-interest is a great motivator for production and progress but is amoral unless contained within the framework of social justice*
>
> *—That the rich have the right to buy more cars than anyone else, more homes, vacations, gadgets, and gizmos, but they do not have the right to buy more democracy than anyone else*
>
> *—That public services, when privatized, serve only those who can afford them and weaken the sense that we all rise and fall together as "one nation, indivisible"*
>
> *—That concentration in the production of goods may sometimes be useful and efficient, but monopoly over the dissemination of ideas is tyranny*
>
> *—That prosperity requires good wages and benefits for workers*
>
> *—That our nation can no more survive as half democracy and half oligarchy than it could survive half slave and half free, and that keeping it from becoming all oligarchy is steady work—our work"*

APPENDIX 1

Glossary

Adverse Selection:

This occurs when lower-risk individuals are split off by insurers from a larger risk pool in order to minimize their financial risk and increase these profits. The smaller risk pool of higher-risk individuals that results requires higher costs of treatment. Adverse selection is the Achilles' heel of capitation, since for-profit HMOs and some physicians are often tempted to selectively care for healthier patients.

Agency for Healthcare Policy and Research (AHCPR):

This federal agency was established by Congress in 1989 to promote better quality of patient care. Since then, its name has been changed to the *Agency for Healthcare Research and Quality* (AHRQ). Its activities include development of clinical practice guidelines, promotion of evidence-based medicine, reduction of medical errors, and expansion of research on the cost, utilization, and outcomes of health care.

Capitation:

A method of payment for patient care services used by managed care organizations, such as health maintenance organizations (HMOs), to reimburse providers under contractual agreements. Payment rates are set in advance, and are paid monthly or annually regardless of what services are actually provided to covered patients.

Carrier:

Private insurers which contract with Medicare to administer supplementary health insurance under Part B of Medicare. In the earlier years, Blue Shield held most of these contracts for physician services. Today's decentralized market has many commercial insurers involved as carriers.

Center for Medicare and Medicaid Services (CMS):

The federal agency which administers the Medicare program and works with the States to administer Medicaid, the State Children's Health Insurance Program (SCHIP), and health insurance portability standards.

CMS accounts for 20% of the federal government's budget. In FY 2005, this amounted to about $519 billion, with nearly two-thirds of that spent on Medicare.

Co-Insurance:

This refers to the percentage of health care costs which are not covered by insurance and which the individual must pay. Many health insurance plans cover 80% of the costs of hospital and physician care, leaving 20% to be "self insured" by patients receiving these services.

Community Rating:

A method for setting premiums for health insurance which is based on the average cost of health care for the covered population in a geographic area. This method shares risk across all covered individuals, whether sick or well, so that the healthy help to subsidize the care of the sick who otherwise may not be able to afford coverage on their own. As a then not-for-profit insurer, Blue Cross pioneered this method in the 1930s, but it was abandoned by most commercial insurers after the 1960s, as *experience rating* spread throughout the industry.

Competitive Bidding:

A process authorized by Medicare legislation in the late 1990s whereby private Medicare plans could submit sealed bid proposals to cover Medicare beneficiaries. Although intended as a strategy to infuse greater competition into the marketplace, it has been blocked by health plans through both political and legal means.

Competitive Pricing:

The Health Care Financing Administration (HCFA) attempted demonstration projects during the 1990s as part of the competitive bidding process. Due to opposition from health plans and their successful lobbying efforts targeting their legislators in Congress, this strategy has never been successful.

Consumer-Directed Health Care (CDHC):

A strategy to contain health care costs by shifting more responsibility to consumers in choosing and paying for their own health care. Currently popular with conservatives and many moderates in government, the consumer-choice theory of cost containment assumes that there is a free market in health care, that consumers can be well informed about their choices, and that they will be more prudent in their health care decisions by taking more responsibility for their costs.

Cost Effectiveness:

When applied to health care, this concept attempts to estimate the value for expenditures of procedures or services that is returned to patients. Value may include longer life, better quality of life, or both. This is a complex but important area of study if affordable care of good quality is to be made available to broad populations. *Cost-effectiveness analysis* (CEA) is the technique used to measure costs and efficacy of alternative treatments in order to estimate their economic value, which then are typically measured in quality-adjusted life years (QALYs).

Co-Payment:

Flat fee charged directly to patients whenever they seek health care services or drug prescriptions regardless of their insurance coverage. As today's trend toward consumer-directed health care gains momentum, co-payments are increasing across the health care marketplace to the point of becoming a financial barrier to care for many lower-income people.

Cost-Sharing:

This term refers to requirements that patients pay directly out-of-pocket for some portion of their health care costs. The level of cost-sharing varies from one health plan to another. Although intended by insurers and many policy makers to help control the costs of health care, cost-sharing has a serious downside of discouraging many people from gaining access to necessary health care.

Death Spiral:

This term is used to describe the progressive effects of adverse selection in shrinking a risk pool into a smaller population of high-risk individuals requiring expensive care. For example, as a result of "cream-skimming" by for-profit private health plans, public programs such as Medicare are placed at risk because of reduced cross subsidies from the healthy to the sick.

Deductible:

Out-of-pocket costs which patients must pay before their insurance coverage kicks in for subsequent costs. This amount is required to be met each year. As policy-makers and health plans pursue the model of consumer-directed health care, deductibles and co-payment requirements of cost-sharing are increasing each year.

Defined Benefits:

This term is applied when an insurance program offers a pre-determined set of benefits to all enrollees. The Medicare program is such an example, with covered benefits authorized by law.

Defined Contribution:

This is the polar opposite of defined benefits. In this instance, a fixed set of benefits is not provided by the insurer, whether public or private. Instead, a defined contribution is made toward the costs of coverage (egs., by an employer or perhaps by Medicare if further privatization "reforms" are enacted) (see also Premium Support).

Diagnosis-Related Groups (DRGs):

A system for payment of hospital costs for Medicare patients started in 1983 with the intent to limit spiraling costs of hospitalization. Instead of paying hospitals on a fee-for-service basis, predetermined lump sum payments are made based on a diagnosis for each episode of hospitalization. This change has put hospitals at financial risk for the lengths of hospital stays and the amount of services provided in the hospital.

Distributive Justice:

When used in health care, this term connotes a principle of fairness whereby health care is considered a right that should be shared within a society on the basis of need. The countervailing view held by proponents of an open market is that health care is a privilege that should be allocated by ability to pay. With an emphasis on markets, the U.S. is atypical from almost all other industrialized countries around the world where distributive justice is the dominant ethic underlying various systems of social health insurance.

Dual Eligible:

A term describing the more than 6 million Americans who meet eligibility requirements for both Medicare and Medicaid and are simultaneously enrolled in both programs. Dual eligibles tend to be sicker and poorer than most of the Medicare population. More than 60% live below the federal poverty level and more than one-third are disabled.

Employer-Based Insurance:

A voluntary system established during the wartime economy of the 1940s whereby many employers have provided health insurance coverage to their employees. Today, that system is unraveling steadily, now covering only about two-thirds of the non-elderly workforce and with many employers shifting to a defined contribution approach toward their employees' insurance costs.

Employer-Mandate:

A policy considered in some states whereby all employers would be required to provide health insurance for their employees. Such a policy is usually opposed by small business, fearing costs that could put them out of business.

Experience Rating:

This is the current norm in U.S. health insurance markets, as opposed to the community rating tradition originally established by Blue Cross in the 1930s. Under experience rating, insurers avoid high-risk groups and increase premiums based upon illnesses experienced by enrollees. Experience rating weakens the ability of health insurance to share risk across a large risk pool of healthy and sick individuals.

Favorable Risk Selection:

This is the process by which insurers screen potential enrollees according to health status, avoiding higher-risk sick individuals and groups in favor of healthier enrollees requiring less costly care (i.e., the opposite of adverse selection).

Fee-for-Service (FFS):

A common method of reimbursement for health services provided, such as by visit, procedure, laboratory test or imaging study. Fees are often based on a fixed fee schedule or on more complex relative value scales.

Fiscal Intermediary:

Private insurers which contract with Medicare to administer hospitalization insurance under Part A of Medicare. Blue Cross has held most of these contracts over the years. In this capacity, insurers are empowered to make coverage and reimbursement decisions and to provide related administrative services.

Formulary:

Lists of drugs updated at regular intervals, which can be prescribed by physicians for enrollees in specific programs. Formularies have been developed by health plans in recent years as a means of containing escalating drug spending. Formulary development is a contentious area, with the pharmaceutical industry arguing for wider coverage lists while health plans strive to balance cost, efficacy and safety issues against patients' access to medically necessary medications.

Geographic variation:

This term is used to describe wide variations from one part of the country to another in practice patterns and services provided to Medicare beneficiaries. Regional and small area variations date back to the origins of the program, including marked differences in utilization of services as well as coverage and reimbursement policies.

Generic Drugs:

Drugs which are essentially the same as their brand-name counterparts, but whose patents have expired. They are generally considerably less expensive than their brand-name equivalents.

Health Care Financing Administration (HCFA):

As part of the Department of Health and Human Services (DHHS), HCFA was created in 1977. It administered Medicare and Medicaid for many years until reconstituted in 2001 as the Center for Medicare and

Medicaid Services (CMS).

Health Maintenance Organization (HMO)

HMOs are organizations which provide a broad range of services, coordinated by primary care physicians on a prepaid basis for enrollees. First authorized by federal legislation in 1973, HMOs have developed since the 1980s to now cover about 80 million Americans. About two-thirds of HMOs are for-profit, such as Humana, while the rest are not-for-profit, such as Kaiser Permanente and Group Health of Puget Sound. HMOs vary organizationally from staff models, where physicians are salaried and work only with that HMO (egs., Kaiser and Group Health) to looser structures, such as independent practice associations (IPAs), where physicians in independent practices contract with an HMO to provide care for enrollees and are reimbursed on a capitation basis. Though it has become an imprecise term over the years, "managed care" encompasses these variations within an overall pattern of prepaid medical care.

Health Savings Account (HSA)

As part of the current trend toward consumer-directed health care, health savings accounts shift more financial responsibility to consumers for the costs of their health care decisions. HSAs were authorized under the Medicare Prescription Drug, Improvement, and Modernization Act of 2003 (MMA). Employer and employee contributions are tax-free when accompanied by high deductible insurance policies. While providing new investment opportunities for healthy individuals, HSAs provide little financial protection against the costs of serious illness.

Local Medical Review Policy (LMRP):

These are Medicare coverage policies made by almost 50 private contractors to define covered benefits for Medicare beneficiaries. About 90% of Medicare coverage decisions are made locally, and there is wide variation in covered benefits and reimbursement policies from one part of the country to another. These variations persist since this local system of Medicare governance through private contractors was established in 1965.

Managed Care:

Although this term has often become ambiguous and unclear in common usage, it expresses a new relationship between purchasers, insurers and providers of care. To a variable extent, organizations that pay for patient care have also taken on the role of making decisions about patient care management. In practice, however, ""managed care" is often more managed *reimbursement* than care. Three common types of managed care organizations are preferred provider organizations (PPOs), group and staff model HMOs, and independent practice association (IPA) HMOs.

Medicaid:

A federal-state health insurance program, also enacted in 1965 with Medicare, which covers low-income people who meet variable and changing state eligibility requirements. Most elderly, disabled, and blind individuals who receive assistance through the federal Supplemental Security Income (SSI) program are covered under Medicaid, which is also the main payer of nursing home costs. Federal matching funds to the state range from about 50 to almost 80 percent. Current budget deficits in federal and state budgets threaten this vital safety net program, which provides last-resort coverage for about one in six Americans, including one-fifth of all children in the U.S.

Medigap:

Private supplementary insurance which covers medical expenses not covered by Medicare, which may include co-payments, deductibles and other related costs. The rising costs of Medigap policies have led to serious underinsurance for many elderly people, with increasing out-of-pocket expenses and difficulties in affording necessary medical care. The annual costs of Medigap policies now run as high as $11,000 per year, and only one in four elderly Americans carry such coverage.

Medical Necessity:

An elusive but important term which is applied to treatments and healthcare services which can be judged on the basis of clinical evidence to be effective and indicated as essential medical care. It is an ongoing challenge for insurers, payers and policymakers to define medical necessity as part of coverage policy, made more difficult as costs are considered and as new treatments are brought into use.

Medicare:

A federal insurance program for the elderly and disabled enacted in 1965 which now covers 41 million Americans with benefits including hospital care, physician and other provider services, and limited coverage of the costs of prescription drugs. Medicare beneficiaries include seniors 65 years of age and older, as well as the disabled and those with chronic kidney failure. Traditional (Original) Medicare, as the major source of coverage for one in seven Americans, pays for about one-half of beneficiaries' health care expenses, and accounts for about one-fifth of the personal national health expenditures. There are four components of Medicare today:

Part A   Hospitalization insurance

Part B   Supplementary medical insurance

Part C   Medicare + Choice private plans, now

Medicare Advantage

Part D   Prescription drug coverage, starting in 2006

Medicare Advantage (MA):

Private health plans authorized by Medicare legislation in 2003 as the sequel to Medicare + Choice programs. Most are HMOs, though recent years have seen an increasing number of preferred provider organizations (PPOs).

Medicare + Choice (M + C):

Private health plans authorized by the Balanced Budget Act of 1997 (BBA) intended by their supporters to increase choices available to Medicare beneficiaries. Most were HMOs, with other alternatives including PPOs, provider sponsored organizations (PSOs) and private fee-for-service plans (PFFS).

Medicare Prescription Drug, Improvement and Modernization Act of 2003 (MMA):

Controversial legislation enacted in 2003 as the most important change in the 40-year life of Medicare. This is a very complex bill, which offers a limited prescription drug benefit while including many other elements which would further privatize the program and shift more of its costs from the government to consumers. The pharmaceutical and insurance industries will see far more benefits from this bill than Medicare beneficiaries themselves, and future cost projections for Medicare are already surging way beyond initial estimates.

Moral Hazard:

A theory gaining favor in the 1960s which is applied by advocates of consumer-directed health care (CDHC) with an assumption that insured people use more health care services than they need. Moral hazard is seen as the change of behavior of people when they become insured, leading to overuse of health services. Based on this theory, cost sharing with consumers is increasing. There is abundant evidence, however, which discredits moral hazard as a major cause of health care inflation and recognizes the adverse effects of cost sharing in restricting access to necessary health care for many lower-income people.

National Health Insurance (NHI)

A national health insurance program which would provide universal coverage to the entire U.S. population for necessary health care. As with Medicare, NHI would be a single-payer system, government-financed with a private delivery system. Through simplified administration, such a system would provide more efficiency and cost containment than the current market-based system while offering new opportunities to improve accountability and quality assurance within the system.

Overpayment:

Administratively set payments to private Medicare plans in excess of payments to traditional FFS Medicare. These are provided as incentives to bring in and retain more private plans in the Medicare program. Overpayments belie the notion that private plans save money. Overpayments vary widely around the country, averaging 107% for Medicare Advantage in 2004 and ranging up to 132% of FFS Medicare in some high-cost counties.

Pharmacy-Benefit Manager (PBM):

Private companies that contract with health plans to process pharmaceutical claims, negotiate prices with retail pharmacies and drug manufacturers, and manage prescription drug use of enrollees. Merck Medco (now Express Scripts) is one leading example.

Point of Service (POS):

Hybrid health plans developed by insurers to give enrollees more choice of providers than provided in conventional HMO plans. Under a POS plan, enrollees are permitted to seek out-of-network care by paying the additional costs out-of-pocket.

Preferred Provider Organization (PPO):

An increasingly popular health plan developed in reaction to many patients' resistance to being locked-in to limited panels of providers. Providers in a PPO panel agree to accept set discounted fees in exchange for the practice-building opportunity of being listed as a "preferred provider."

Premium Support:

This is a strategy being promoted by some in an effort to limit the government's financial responsibility to Medicare beneficiaries by shifting from a *defined benefit* program to a *defined contribution* approach. Under premium support, the government would pay a set amount toward the cost of a plan, whether FFS, HMO or PPO, with enrollees responsible for any price differences. First proposed in the mid-1990s, the premium support concept remains controversial, including the extent to which it could save the government money.

Provider Sponsored Organization (PSO):

Another kind of managed care organization which can contract with Medicare as a Part C participating private plan under federal legislation passed in 1997. PSOs are organizations of hospitals, physician groups, or combinations thereof, which bear some financial risk for providing covered services.

Resource-Based Relative Value Scale (RBRVS):

Under this system, fees for physicians are set for each service by estimating such factors as time, mental effort and judgment, and technical skill involved in each service. RBRVS was adopted by Medicare in the early 1990s in an effort to reduce the wide disparities in reimbursement of procedure-oriented specialists and primary care physicians.

Risk Adjustment:

A complex technical process intended to estimate the difference in health status and risk in populations enrolled in Medicare private plans compared to FFS Medicare. It is well documented that private plans attract healthier patients requiring less costly care than Original Medicare through favorable risk selection. Risk adjustment techniques so far have been too crude to deal effectively with this problem and have been strongly resisted by private plans.

Risk Pool:

A group of people considered together in order to price their insurance coverage. The larger and more diverse the group in terms of health status, the more effective insurance can be in having healthier individuals share the higher costs of care of sicker individuals while assuring the most affordable insurance premiums for the entire group.

Quality Assurance:

A broad field which has developed in recent years with the goal to improve the quality of clinical practice, reduce the rate of medical errors, and improve patient care outcomes. This is an ongoing and difficult challenge, with evidence-based clinical practice guidelines an integral part of the process.

Quality-Adjusted Life Year (QALY):

A commonly used measure of the cost-effectiveness of a medical treatment or procedure which takes into account both the length of life after treatment and the quality of life during extended life. Interventions which extend a reasonable quality of life for one year are generally seen by our society as appropriate up to about $50,000 a year. Interventions costing $50,000 to $120,000 per QALY are usually questioned, while those above that level are not considered cost-effective.

State Children's Health Insurance Program (SCHIP):

A federal health insurance program enacted in 1997 as a companion program to Medicaid. SCHIP is intended to cover uninsured children in families with incomes at or below 200% of the federal poverty level ($36,800 for a family of four in 2003) but above the traditional income eligibility level for Medicaid. There is wide variation from state to state in these eligibility levels.

Selective Contracting:

A change during the 1980s when many purchasers and insurers chose to contract selectively with physicians and hospitals, deciding which providers they would pay and which they would not pay. This was intended to hold costs down, and has significantly changed the power relationships among these parties.

Single-payer:

One health care financing system covering an entire population on the basis of social insurance and replacing a multipayer system of private insurance. The Medicare program in the U.S. is one such program for the elderly and disabled. Other industrialized countries around the world have their whole populations covered under one or another form of universal health insurance. The U.S. has had such bills put forward in Congress on a number of occasions, including H.R. 676 in the House today, but so far there has not been the political will to overcome the resistance of private stakeholders in our current market-based system.

Social Insurance:

Social insurance is compulsory, usually provided by a public agency, and spreads the financial risk of illness across an entire population, making its costs affordable to a large population. This is in marked contrast to private insurance, which is voluntary, provided by private insurers (usually for-profit) which selectively enroll better risks, thereby rendering coverage unaffordable or otherwise unavailable to higher-risk individuals. Medicare over the last 40 years has been a social insurance program, but it is threatened by further privatization.

Tiered Cost Sharing:

Tiered cost sharing refers to multiple levels of cost sharing for some services, such as certain kinds of hospitals or some kinds of prescription drugs. For more expensive services or drugs, enrollees are required to pay more, either in higher co-payments and/or higher out-of-pocket costs. As an example, drug formularies for some health plans may encourage enrollees to use generic and formulary drugs by setting higher levels of cost-sharing for brand-name and non-formulary drugs.

Universal Coverage:

This term is used to describe countries which provide health insurance to all citizens regardless of age, income, or health status. The U.S. is atypical in not having universal coverage, as illustrated by one in seven Americans being uninsured and tens of millions underinsured.

Utilization Management (UM):

A cost containment strategy used by Medicare and Medicaid for many years, and more recently adopted by private health plans. Under utilization management, the clinical activities of physicians are monitored and payment for some services are denied if considered by the payer to be unnecessary. Critics of this approach contend that UM is an unwarranted intrusion into the physician-patient relationship, involves burdensome administrative hassle for caregivers, and doesn't save much money anyway.

Voucher:

A grant of money for a specific purpose, such as for meals. The idea of vouchers has been raised by supporters of premium support for Medicare, which would change the program from one of defined benefits guaranteed by the government to one of defined contributions by the government to Medicare beneficiaries. Critics see this approach as a threat to the integrity and viability of the Medicare program, by also opening the door to step-wise future reductions in the level of government contributions.

APPENDIX 2

SOME USEFUL RESOURCES

The following sources are recommended as especially useful in providing up-to-date authoritative and unbiased information on Medicare. This information is readily available on each source's Web site, with target audiences ranging from health professionals, administrators, health policy analysts, and others interested in Medicare as an evolving program, including elderly and disabled patients, their families and caregivers.

1. Henry J. Kaiser Family Foundation

The Medicare Policy Project conducts research and analysis on current Medicare policy issues, monitors key trends, and produces fact sheets, resource books and reports to inform policy discussions.

Publications include:

Medicare Chartbook for 2005
Fact Sheet for Medicare Advantage
Navigating Medicare and Medicaid: Resource Guide for
People with Disabilities, their Families and their Advocates

Headquarters: 2400 Sand Hill Road
Menlo Park, CA 94025
Phone: 650-854-9400
Washington, D.C. office/Public Affairs Center
1330 G Street NW
Washington, D.C. 20005
Phone: 202-347-5270

Web sites:

www.kff.org
www.kaiserEDU.org (includes narrated slide tutorials, background reference libraries, and issue modules on current topics and policy debates)

2. National Academy of Social Insurance

A nonprofit, nonpartisan organization with a mission to promote understanding and informed policymaking on social insurance and related programs through research, public education, training, and the open exchange of ideas.

Publications include:

> *The Role of Private Health Plans in Medicare: Lessons From the Past, Looking to the Future* (November, 2003)
> *Reporters' Social Security and Medicare Sourcebook*
> Fact sheets, Working Papers, Briefs, and Press releases

Headquarters: 1776 Massachusetts Avenue, NW, Suite 615
Washington, D.C. 20006
Phone: 202-452-8097
Web site:www.nasi.org

3. Families USA

A national non-profit non-partisan organization dedicated to the achievement of high quality affordable health care for all Americans.

Its Medicare Central provides these helpful resources:

> —gearing up for the new Medicare drug benefit, including impacts on Medicaid in the States
> —bills introduced in Congress to change the law
> —history behind passage of MMA 2003
> —what's new in the new Medicare law

Headquarters: 1201 New York Avenue, Suite 1100
Washington, D.C. 20005
Phone: 202-628-3050
Web site:www.familiesusa.org

4. Medicare Rights Center

Founded in 1989, the Medicare Rights Center is the nation's largest independent source of health care information and assistance for people on Medicare.

Its resources include:

> —Materials on the new Medicare law (English and Spanish)
> —How to compare Medicare plan options

—List of discount drug prescription programs, including state prescription drug assistance programs, drug discount cards, and Internet and mail-order discount pharmacies

—Assistance in finding a Hotline counselor in all states through the State Health Insurance Assistance Program (SHIP). This program offers Medicare beneficiaries and their families help with their health insurance choices, Medicare rights and protections, dealing with payment denials or appeals, complaints about care or treatment, and Medicare bills.

Publications include:
Asclepios (Weekly Medicare consumer advocacy update)
Dear Marci (free weekly newsletter for Medicare beneficiaries)
Medicare Rights Center News

Headquarters: 1460 Broadway, 17th Floor
New York, NY 10036
Phone: 212-869-3850
Washington, D.C. office:
1030 15th Street NW, Suite 250
Washington, D.C. 20005
Fax: 202-589-1310
Web site: www.medicarerights.org

5. Medicare Payment Advisory Commission (MedPAC)

An independent federal body of 17 members established by the Balanced Budget Act of 1997 to advise the U.S. Congress on issues affecting the Medicare program

MedPAC releases two comprehensive and updated reports each year

Headquarters: 601 New Jersey Avenue, NW, Suite 9000
Washington, D.C. 20001
Phone: 202-220-3700
Questions or comments to webmaster@medpac.gov

6. Public Citizen

A national non-profit public interest organization which was founded in 1971 to represent consumer interests in Congress, the executive branch, and the courts. It is an independent organization which accepts no funds from corporations, professional associations, or government agencies.

Its resources include:
>   Health Letter (regular publication of the Health Research Group)
>   Worst Pills Best Pills (a Newsletter also available as a searchable online drug database for over 500 drugs including warnings about unsafe or ineffective drugs)
>   Public Citizen News
>   Other articles, reports and press releases

Headquarters: 1600 20th Street NW
                  Washington, D. C. 20009
                  Phone: 202-588-1000
                  Web sites: www.citizen.org/hrg
                  www.worstpills.org

7. The Commonwealth Fund

Dedicated to promotion of a high performing health care system that achieves better access, improved quality, and greater efficiency, particularly for society's most vulnerable, including low-income people, the uninsured, minority Americans, young children, and elderly adults.

Publications include:
>   —Donut Holes and Price Controls
>   —How Beneficiaries Fare Under the New Medicare Drug Law
>   —The Cost of Privatization: Extra Payments to Medicare
>   —How Asset Tests Block Low-Income Medicare Beneficiaries from needed Benefits
>   —Other reports and Issue Briefs

Headquarters: One East 75th Street
New York, NY 10021
Phone: 212-606-3800
Web site:www.cmwf.org

REFERENCES

References—Preface

1 Oberlander J. *The Political Life of Medicare*. Chicago: University of Chicago Press, 2003:157-60.
2 As quoted in: *Congressional Quarterly Almanac*, 1995, p 7-3 and Smith D.G. *Entitlement Politics: Medicare and Medicaid, 1995-2001*. New York: Aldine de Gruyter, 2002:71.
3 Halberstam D. as quoted from C-Span Booknotes, interview with Brian Lamb, November 4, 1993.

References—Chapter 1

1. Interview on C-span Books. December 3, 2001.
2. Derber C. Corporation Nation: How Corporations Are Taking Over Our Lives and What We Can Do About It. New York: St. Martin's Press. Front Matter, 1998:64-6.
3. Josephson M, as cited in Wasserman H. America Born and Reborn. New York: Collier Books, 1983:92-3.
4. Grossman RL, Adams FT. Taking Care of Business: Citizenship and the Charter of Incorporation. Cambridge, Mass: Charter Ink. 1993:18-20.
5. Ibid #3, p 110.
6. Ibid #2, pp 4-5.
7. Hartmann T. Unequal Protection: The Rise of Corporate Dominance and the Theft of Human Rights. Emmaus, Pa: Rodale Press, 2002:131.
8. Ibid #7, pp 131-2.
9. Korten DC. When Corporations Rule the World. San Francisco: Berrett-Koehler Publishers, Inc. 2001:68-71.
10. Ibid #9
11. Ibid #9
12. Ibid #9
13. Phillips K. Wealth and Democracy. Rich-poor gap, corruption are harbingers of economic decline. Public Citizen News. November/December 2002:22(6) 7.
14. Ibid #9
15. Forbes 400: Record 313 U.S. billionaires. *CNN Money*. September 23, 2004.
16. Zinn H. A People's History of the United States: 1492—Present. New York: Harper & Row Publishers, 1980.
17. Bryce R. Pipe Dreams: Greed, Ego and the Death of ENRON. New York: Public Affairs 2002:8-12.
18. Ibid #17
19. Solomon D. Enron cut tax bill by $2 billion in working around IRS rules. *Wall Street Journal*. February 14, 2003:A2.
20. Sapsford J. Enron ties may haunt J. P. Morgan anew. *Wall Street Journal*

February 21, 2003:C1.

21. Johnston DC. Tax moves by Enron said to mystify the IRS. *New York Times* February 13, 2003:C1.

22. The politics of Enron. Four committees in search of a scandal. *The Economist* January 19, 2002:25.

23. Ibid #17, xv-xviii.

24. Ibid #17, pp 270-1.

25. Beckett P, Sapsford J, Barrionuevo A. Power outage. How energy traders turned bonanza into an epic bust. *Wall Street Journal* December 31, 2002:A1.

26. Henriques DB, Fabrikant G. Deciding on executive pay: lack of independence seen. *New York Times* December 18, 2002:A1.

27. Ibid #9, p 73.

28. Greider W. Who Will Tell the People: The Betrayal of American Democracy. New York: Simon & Schuster 1992:401.

29. Ibid #2, p 18.

30. Ibid #28, p 390.

31. Ibid #28, p 35.

32. Ibid #9, p148.

33. Ibid #2, p 154.

34. Ibid #9, p 105.

35 Wallach L, Sforza M. Whose Trade Organizations? Corporate Globalization and the Erosion of Democracy. Washington, DC: Public Citizen, 1999;XI.

36. Dobbs L. Exporting America: Why Corporate Greed Is Shipping American Jobs Overseas. New York: Warner Business Books, 2004:156-7.

37. Wallach L. Facts cloud attempt to "celebrate" NAFTA anniversary signing ceremony. Public Citizen press release. December 10, 2002.

38. Ibid #9, p 131.

39. Solomon J, Kranhold K. In India's outsourcing boom, GE played a starring role. *Wall Street Journal* March 23, 2005:A1.

40. Farrington M. Outsourcing your privacy: protections are lost when records are sent overseas. *Public Citizen News* 24(6), November/December 2004:12.

41. Moffett M. Working children: underage laborers fill Mexican factories. *Wall Street Journal* April 8, 1991.

42. Ibid #28, p 393.

43. Ibid #35, p4.

44. Ibid #37.

45. Ibid #9, pp 18-9.

46. Slevin C. Trade negotiators push agreement on health care, education and other services. *Public Citizen News.* January/February 2003:23(1): 1.

47. Consumer group warns California AG-New trade agreement could accelerate

acquisition of California public water works by foreign firms. Public Citizen press release. February 6, 2003.

48. Ibid #7, p 246.
49. Phillips K. Wealth and Democracy: A Political History of the American Rich. New York: Broadway Books, 2002:412-3.
50. Krugman P. The good guys. *New York Times* Op-ed. December 24, 2992:A25.
51. Eichenwald K. Policy leaves most players exposed to suits on Enron. *New York Times*, December 21, 2002:B3.
52. Ibid #37.
53. Greider W. The real Cancun: WTO heads nowhere. *The Nation* 277 (8), September 22, 2003:11.
54. Murray A. Political Capital. No longer business as usual for forces of U.S. capitalism. *Wall Street Journal* October 1, 2002:A4.
55. Ibid #2, p 224.
56. Kuttner R. Taking care of business. *The American Prospect* July/August 1996 (28-34): 29.
57. Ibid #46.
58. Ibid #49, front matter.
59. Eichenwald K. After a boom, there will be a scandal. Count on it. *New York Times* December 16, 2002:C3.
60. Durant W, Durant A. The Lessons of History. New York: Simon & Schuster 1968.
61. Ibid #7, p 216.
62. Ibid #13, p 297.
63. Ibid #28, p 349.
64. Hawken P. The Ecology of Commerce: Doing Good Business. New York: Harper Business, 1993:108.
65. Ibid #37.
66. Ibid #28, p 349.
67. Nader R, Green M, Seligman J. Taming the Giant Corporation. New York: W.W. Norton 1976:51.
68. The global giants: amid market pain, U.S. companies hold greater sway. *Wall Street Journal* October 14, 2002:R10.
69. Ibid #9, p 207.
70. Democratic U.S. Senator Fritz Hollings. Unto the breach. *Harpers* May 2000:20.
71. Ibid #13.
72. Ibid #7, pp 175-6.
73. www.taxfoundation.org
74. 1995 GAP study commissioned by Senator Byron Dorgan (D-North Dakota).

75. Ibid #7, pp 177-8.
76. Ibid #13, p 166.
77. Ibid #7, p327.

References—Chapter two

1. *Study Panel on Medicare's Larger Social Role*, Final Report. Washington, D.C.: National Academy of Social Insurance, 1999, pp 1-2.

2 Blumenthal D, et al. *Renewing the Promise: Medicare & Its Reform*. New York: Oxford University Press, 1988.

3 U.S. Congress, House of Representatives, Committee on Ways and Means. *Medical Care for the Aged*, material submitted for the published record of the hearing, hearings on H.R. 3920, Washington, D.C., 1964.

4 Ball M. The American Social Security Program. *New England Journal of Medicine,* 270, 232-36, 1964.

5. Marmor T. R. *The Politics of Medicare*. New York: Aldine Publishing Company, 1970, 119-20.

6. Friedman L. Social Welfare Legislation. *Stanford Law Review*, 21, 247, Jan. 1969.

7. Ibid #1, pp 31-5.

8. Ibid #5, p 24.

9. Oberlander J. *The Political Life of Medicare*. Chicago: University of Chicago Press, 2003:34.

10. Ibid #5, pp 27-31.

11. Andrews C. *Profit Fever: The Drive to Corporatize Health Care and How to Stop It*. Monroe, Me: Common Courage Press, 1995:3-8.

12. Gordon C. *Dead on Arrival: The Politics of Health Care in Twentieth Century America.* Princeton: Princeton University Press, 2003:238.

13. Ibid #5, p 74.

14. Ibid #9, pp 108-11.

15. Foote S.B. Focus on locus: evolution of Medicare's local coverage policy. *Health Affairs (Millwood)* 22, 137, 2003.

16. MedPac. Medicare Payment Advisory Commission. Reducing Medicare Complexity and Regulatory Burden. Washington: MedPac, 29, December, 2001.

17. Himmelstein D.U. & Woolhandler S. The Corporate Compromise: A Marxist View of Health Policy. *Monthly Review* (May 14): 20-22, 1990.

18. Ibid #11.

19. Ibid #5, p 86.

20. Ginsberg E. Ten encounters with the U.S. health sector, 1930-1999. *Journal of the American Medical Association*, 282,1665, 1999.

21. Ibid #9, pp 32-3.
22. Foote S.M. & Hogan C. Disability levels and health care costs of Medicare beneficiaries under age sixty-six. *Health Affairs (Millwood)* 20,242-53, 2001.
23. Rettig R. Origins of the Medicare Kidney Disease Entitlement. In: *Biomedical Politics*, Hanna K, editor, pp 176-208, Washington, D.C.: National Academy Press, 1991.
24. Rice T. An Economic Assessment of Health Care Coverage for the Elderly. *Millbank Quarterly* 65, 491, 1987.
25. Cafferata G.L. Private Health Insurance of the Medicare Population and the Baucus Legislation. *Medical Care* 23, 1087, 1985.
26. Rice T. Supplemental Insurance and Its Role in Medicare Reform. In: *Medicare Tomorrow: The Report of the Century Foundation Task Force on Medicare Reform*. New York: Century Foundation Press, 195-96, 2002.
27. Vladeck B.C. *Unloving Care: The Nursing Home Tragedy*. New York: Basic Books, 50, 1980.
28. Weiner I., Tilley J., Goldenson S. Federal and State Initiatives to Jump-Start the Market for Private Long-Term Care Insurance. *Elder Law Journal* 8, 57-102, 2000.
29. Ibid #9, pp 120-5.
30. Epstein A. & Blumenthal D. Physician Payment Reform: Past and Future. *Milbank Quarterly* 71 (2), 193-215, 1993.
31. Rovner J. Doctor Bills are Next Target for Cost-Control Efforts. *Congressional Quarterly*, February 25, 386, 1989.
32. Moon M. Will the care be there? Vulnerable beneficiaries and Medicare reform. *Health Affairs (Millwood)*, 18, 107-17, 1999.
33. Boccuti C. & Moon M. Comparing Medicare and private insurers: growth rates in spending over three decades. *Health Affairs (Millwood)*, 22(2), 232, 2003.
34. Health Care Financing Administration, 1999 HCFA Statistics: Providers/ Suppliers, 1999. All numbers are rounded to the nearest 100. Available at www. hcfa.gov/stats
35. Pear R. Cut in Medicare payments to hospitals is advised. *New York Times* January 18, 2005:A13.
36. Kaiser Family Foundation. Medicare at a Glance. Fact Sheet. Menlo Park, Calif: March 2004.
37. Levit K., Smith C., Cowan C., et al. Health spending rebound continues in 2002. *Health Affairs (Millwood)* 23(1):147-59, 2004.
38. Graetz M.J. & Mashaw J.L. *True Security: Rethinking American Social Insurance*. New Haven, Conn, Yale University Press, 16-17, 26, 1999.
39. Lubove R. *The Struggle for Social Security, 1900-1935*, pp 1-24, Cambridge, Mass: Harvard University Press, 1968.

40. Ibid #1, pp 35-6.
41. Ibid #9, p 58.
42. Himmelfarb R. *Catastrophic Politics: The Rise and Fall of the Medicare Catastrophic Coverage Act of 1988*, p 80. University Park: Pennsylvania State University Press, 1995.
43. Pear R. Medicare costs are expected to soar in coming years. *New York Times*, March 24, 2004:A1a.
44. Kirchoff S. Greenspan urges: Fix Social Security. *USA Today*, February 26, 2004:1A.
45. Andrews E.L. Medicare and Social Security challenges. *New York Times*, March 2, 2004:C1.
46. Maxwell S, et al. Growth in Medicare and out-of-pocket spending: Impact on vulnerable beneficiaries. New York: The Commonwealth Fund, 2000.
47. Ibid #2, p 26.
48. Ibid #32
49. Hakim D & Peters J.W. G.M. retirees fearing cuts in health benefits. *New York Times* June 30, 2005:C1.
50. Starr P. End of the private New Deal. *The American Prospect* 16(7): 3,2005.
51. Pear R. Social security payment will increase, as will Medicare bite. *New York Times* October 20, 2004:A17.
52. Connolly C. Up, up, up. An OMB chart shows the cost of Medicare rising to $42 billion in 10 years. *Washington Post* September 27-October 3, 2004:21.
53. King K.M. & Schlesinger, M. (eds). *Final Report of the Study Panel on Medicare and Markets—The Role of Private Health Plans in Medicare: Lessons from the Past, Looking to the Future*. Washington, D.C.: National Academy of Social Insurance, September 2003:163-5.
54. Moffett S. Senior moment. Fast-aging Japan keeps its elders on the job longer. *Wall Street Journal* OnLine. June 15, 2005:A1.
55. Institute of the Future. *Health & Health Care 2010: The Forecast, The Challenge*. San Francisco: Jossey-Bass, January 2003: pp 17-23.
56. Ibid #45.
57. Ibid #9, p 196.
58. Ibid #33.
59. Dalleck G, Biles, Nicholas LH. Lessons from Medicare + Choice for Medicare reform. New York: The Commonwealth Fund. Policy Brief. June 26, 2003.
60. New York Times Editorial. Entitlements "crisis." *New York Times*, March 26, 2004:A18.
61. Ibid #1, pp 69-72.

References—Chapter Three

1. Gordon C. *Dead on Arrival: The Politics of Health Care in Twentieth Century America*. Princeton: Princeton University Press, 2003, 25-28.
2. Oberlander J. *The Political Life of Medicare*. Chicago: University of Chicago Press, 2003,108-12.
3. Starr P. *The Social Transformation of American Medicine*. New York: Basic Books, 1982 p 375.
4. Law S.A. *Blue Cross: What Went Wrong?* New Haven, Conn: Yale University Press, 1974, p 6-30.
5. Ibid # 1, p 234.
6. Ibid #1, p 243
7. Brodie R. *Virus of the Mind: The New Science of the Meme*. Seattle: Integral Press, 1996.
8. Oberlander J.B. Managed care and Medicare reform. *Journal of Health Politics, Policy, and Law* 22 595,598, 1997.
9. King K. M. & Schlesinger M. (eds). *Final Report of the Study Panel on Medicare and Markets—The Role of Private Health Plans in Medicare: Lessons from the Past, Looking to the Future*. Washington, D.C.: National Academy of Social Insurance, September 2003: 8, 41.
10. Ibid #9, pp 607-8.
11. Ibid #2
12. *ProPAC, Medicare and the American Health Care System, Report to Congress* Washington, D.C.: ProPAC, June 1997.
13. Cherney A. Payment Methodology, in: *Risk Contracting and Medicare + Choice*, edited by Towles W. & Collins C. New York: McGraw-Hill, 2000, p 84.
14. General Accounting Office (GAO). *Medicare: Reasonableness of Health Maintenance Organization Payments Not Assured*. GAO/HRD-89-41. Washington, D.C.: Government Printing Office, 1989.
15. Ibid #9, p 11.
16. Smith D.G. *Entitlement Politics: Medicare and Medicaid 1995-2001*. New York: Aldine de Gruyter, 2002:71, citing *Congressional Quarterly Almanac*, 1995, p 7-3.
17. Johnson H. & Broder D.S. *The System: The American Way of Politics at the Breaking Point*. Boston: Little Brown and Company, 1996, 591-2.
18. Ibid #9, pp 5-16.
19. The Heritage Foundation Media Campaign. Washington,D.C.: Medicare Rights Center. http://www.medicarerights.org/maincontentheritage.html. Accessed December 1, 2003.

20. Iglehart J.K. The American health system—Medicare. *New England Journal of Medicine*, 340, 327-32, 1999.
21. Ibid #9, pp 16-21.
22. Christensen S. Medicare + Choice provisions in the Balanced Budget Act of 1997. *Health Affairs (Millwood)* 17(4): 224-31, 1998.
23. Berenson R.A. Medicare + Choice: doubling or disappearing? Health Affairs Web Exclusive, November 28, 2001.
24. Lake T. & Brown R. Medicare + Choice Withdrawals: Understanding Key Factors. Kaiser Family Foundation, June 2002.
25. Bodenheimer T.S. The dismal failure of Medicare privatization. Senior Action Network. San Francisco, June 2003, p 18.
26. Ibid #9, pp 22-3.
27. General Accounting Office (GAO). *Medicare + Choice, Plan Withdrawals Indicate Difficulty of Providing Choice while Achieving Savings*. GAO/HEHS-00-183, Washington, D.C.: Government Printing Office, 2000a.
28. Ibid #9, pp 23-5.
29. Medicare + Choice Withdrawals: Experiences in Major Metropolitan Areas. Monitoring Medicare + Choice Operational Insights, Number 8, Mathematica Policy Research, September 2003.
30. Goozner M. *The $800 Million Pill: The Truth Behind the Cost of New Drugs*. Berkeley, Calif: University of California Press, 2004.
31. Angell M. *The Truth About the Drug Companies: How They Deceive Us and What We Can Do About It*. New York: Random House, 2004.
32. Lueck S. Drug industry exaggerates R & D costs to justify pricing, consumer group says. *The Wall Street Journal*, July 24, 2002, B6.
33. Mintz M. Still hard to swallow. *The Washington Post* Outlook Section, February 2001.
34. Reinhardt U. E. Perspectives on the pharmaceutical industry. *Health Affairs (Millwood)* 20(5), 136, 2001.
35. Angell M. & Relman A.S. Prescription for profit. Available at www. washingtonpost.com. June 21,2001.
36. Public Citizen Press Release. Drug industry employs 675 Washington lobbyists, many with a revolving door connection, new report finds. Washington, D.C. June 23, 2003a.
37. Lewis C. & the Center for Public Integrity. *The Buying of the Congress: How Special Interest Have Stolen Your Right to Life, Liberty and the Pursuit of Happiness*. New York: Avon Books, 1998, p 60.
38. Gerber M. S. Insurance trade groups okay merger: AAHP and HIAA consolidates Hill lobbying efforts. *The Hill*, September 23, 2003.
39. McGinley L. & Lueck S. Medicare bill: Prescription for politics. *Wall Street*

Journal, July 14, 2003, pA4.

40. Schlesinger J. M. & Hamburger T. Democrats take on business as campaign weapon; Medicare will be a double-edged sword. *Wall Street Journal*, November 25, 2003, p A4.

41. NOW with Bill Moyers. PBS, April 30, 2004.

42. Welch W. M. Back scratching and arm-twisting win Medicare fight. *USA Today*, November 28, 2003:5A.

43. Pear R. Sweeping Medicare change wins approval in Congress: President claims a victory. *New York Times*, pA1, November 26, 2003.

44. Center for Responsive Politics, as cited Universal Health Care Action Network (UHCAN) Health-e-Action #4, August 23, 2004 from http://rs6.net/tn.jsp?t=j5sy c7n6.0osfkd7n6.z8580yn6.809&p=http:%2f%2Fwww.publiccampaign.org%2Fhealth carepaybacks%2Findex.htm]report using data from the [http://rs6.net/tn.jsp?t=j5sy c7n6.0.qsfkd7n6.z8oyn6.809&p=http:%2F%2Fwww.opensecrets.org]

45. Baker C. Would prescription drug reimportation reduce U.S. drug spending? Economic and budget issue brief. Washington, D.C.: Congressional Budget Office, April 29, 2004.

46. Shearer G. Medicare prescription drugs: Conference Committee agreement asks beneficiaries to pay too high a price for a modest benefit. *Consumers Union*, Washington, D.C., November 25, 2003.

47. Martinez B. Drug price surge may erode savings from Medicare card. *Wall Street Journal*, March 24, 2004:B1.

48. Welch W. M. AARP: Drug prices soaring. *USA Today* May 26, 2004:A1.

49. Ibid #39

50. Pear R. & Hulse C. Senate removes two roadblocks to drug benefit. *New York Times*, November 25, 2003, pA1

51. MEDPAC Report to the Congress. New Approaches in Medicare: Medicare Payment Advisory Commission, Washington, D.C., June 2004:p210.

52. Rogers D. Medicare actuary reveals e-mail warning. *Wall Street Journal*, March 18, 2004a:A4.

53. Rogers D. Memo raps Bush on drug-bill cost. *Wall Street Journal*, May 4, 2004b:A2.

54. Medicine & Health. Medicare cost estimates, GAO says Scully should return pay over Foster flap. Medicine & Health, 58(33): 4, 2004.

55. Pear R. Medicare actuary gives wanted data to Congress. *New York Times*, March 20, 2004:A8.

56. Toner R. Political Memo. Seems the last word on Medicare wasn't. *New York Times*, March 17, 2004:A12.

57. Drinkard J. AARP accused of conflict of interest. *USA Today*, November 21, 2003, p11A.

58. Brown S. & Doyle S. Op-Chart. The Medicare Index. *New York Times*, January 28, 2004:A25.
59. Pear R. Estimate revises fight on Medicare costs. *New York Times*, February 10, 2005:A16.
60. MRC. Act now: The first step to improving prescription drug coverage. Asclepios 5(26): 1, June 30, 2005.

References—Chapter Four

1. Pellegrino E. Remarks to the Annual Meeting of the Association of Academic Health Centers. Tucson, Arizona: October 7, 2000.
2. CMS Medicare Fact Sheet. Centers for Medicare and Medicaid Services, September 2002.
3. Medicare + Choice Withdrawals: Experiences in Major Metropolitan Areas. Monitoring Medicare + Choice Operational Insights, Number 8, Mathematica Policy Research, September 2002.
4. Waldholz M. Prescriptions. Medicare seniors face confusion as HMOs bail out of program. *Wall Street Journal*, D4, October 3, 2002.
5. King M. & Schlesinger M. (editors). *Final Report of the Study Panel on Medicare and Markets—The Role of Private Health Plans in Medicare: Lessons from the Past, Looking to the Future*, p 28. Washington, D.C.: National Academy of Social Insurance, September 2003.
6. Kronick R., Goodman D.C., Wennberg J. & Wagner E. The marketplace in health care reform. The demographic limitations of managed competition. *New England Journal of Medicine*, 328, 148, 1993.
7. Armstrong J. Washington Watch. Medicare + Choice not an option for rural seniors. *Physicians' Financial News* July 15, 21(9), 13, 2003.
8. Gold M. Medicare + Choice: An interim report card. *Health Affairs (Millwood)* 20(4), 131, 2001.
9. Ibid #8, p 121.
10. Bierman A.S., Bubolz T.A., Fisher E.S.& Wasson, J.H. How well does a single question about health predict the financial health of Medicare managed care plans? *Effective Clinical Practice* 2(2), 56, 1999.
11. Department of Health and Human Services, Office of the Inspector General. Beneficiary perspectives on Medicare risk HMOs. Washington, D.C.: DHHS, 1995.
12. Eichner J. & Blumenthal D, editors. Medicare in the 21st Century: Building a Better Chronic Care System. Washington, D.C.: National Academy of Social Insurance, 2003.
13. Neuman P., Maibach E., Dusenbury K., Kitchman M., & Zupp R. Marketing HMOs to Medicare beneficiaries. *Health Affairs (Millwood)*17(4): 132-9,

1998.

14. Moon M. & Storeygard M. One-Third at Risk: The Special Circumstances of Medicare Beneficiaries with Health Problems, New York, *The Commonwealth Fund*, September 2001.

15. Public Citizen's Congress Watch. Medicare Privatization: The Case Against Relying on HMOs and Private Insurers to Offer Prescription Drug Coverage. Washington, D.C., September 2002, p 11-12.

16. Lee D. Health Net earnings up 32% over year ago. *Los Angeles Times*, October 25, 2002:C2.

17. *Los Angeles Times*, California. PacifiCare reports $37 million in fourth-quarter earnings. *Los Angeles Times*, February 13, 2003:C2.

18. Inspector General, Department of Health and Human Services. *Adequacy of Medicare's Managed Care Payments After the Balanced Budget Act of 1997*. September, 2000.

19. Bodenheimer T. *The Dismal Failure of Medicare Privatization*. San Francisco: Senior Action Network, June 2003a, p 15.

20. *Achman L. & Gold M.K. Medicare + Choice Plans Continue to Shift More Costs to Enrollees*. New York: The Commonwealth Fund, 2003.

21. Maxwell S., Moon M, & Segal M. *Growth in Medicare and Out-of-Pocket Spending: Impact on Vulnerable Beneficiaries*. New York: The Commonwealth Fund, 2001.

22. Neuman P. Testimony to the Subcommittee on Health, Committee on Ways and Means, House of Representatives. Washington, D.C. May 1, 2003. Available on Web at http://waysandmeans.house.gov/hearings.asp?formmode=view&id+338.

23. Henry J. Kaiser Family Foundation and Health Research and Educational Trust, Employer Health Benefits: 2003 Annual Survey. Washington: Kaiser Family Foundation, 2003.

24. Kim J.J. Retiree costs are far higher than expected. *Wall Street Journal*, May 13, 2004:D2.

25. Medicare Rights Center. Ensuring choice of doctors. Medicare Facts and Faces. January 2002,p1-2.

26. Ibid #5, p 60.

27. Bodenheimer T. *The Human Faces of Medicare Privatization*. San Francisco: Senior Action Network, September 2003b:p7.

28. Ibid #5, p 71.

29. MRC. Case stories concerning pre-existing condition waiting period. New York: Medicare Rights Center, 2003.

30. Lake T. & Brown R. Medicare + Choice Withdrawals: Understanding Key Factors. Menlo Park, Calif: Kaiser Family Foundation, June 2002.

31. Ibid #29.

32. Hibbard J.H., Jewett J.J., Englemann S., & Tusler, M. Can Medicare beneficiaries make informed choices? *Health Affairs (Millwood)* 17(6):181-93, 1998.

33. Mathematica Policy Research. *Educating New Members of Medicare + Choice Plans About Their Health Insurance Options: Does the National Medicare Education Program Make a Difference.* Washington, D.C.: Mathematica Policy Research, Inc., 2001.

34. Ibid #14.

35. Vastag B. Low health literacy called a major problem. *Journal of the American Medical Association* 291 (18):2182, 2004.

References—Chapter Five

1. Public Citizen. Medicare Privatization: The Case Against Relying on HMOs and Private Insurers to Offer Prescription Drug Coverage. Washington, D.C. Public Citizen Congress Watch. September 2002, pp 6-7.

2. Armstrong J. Washington Watch. Medicare + Choice not an option for rural seniors. *Physicians' Financial News* July 15, 21(9), 13, 2003.

3. GAO. Medicare + Choice Plan Withdrawals Indicate Difficulty of Providing Choice While Achieving Savings. U.S. General Accounting Office, September 2000.

4. Ibid #1, p 2.

5. Lake T. & Brown R. Medicare + Choice Withdrawals: Understanding Key Factors. Kaiser Family Foundation, June 2002.

6. GAO. U.S. General Accounting Office. Federal Employees Health Program: Reasons Why HMOs withdrew in 1999 and 2000. May, 2000.

7. MRC. Case stories on HMO termination. New York: Medicare Rights Center, 2003.

8. Bodenheimer T. *The Dismal Failure of Medicare Privatization.* San Francisco: Senior Action Network, June 2003a, p 14.

9. Dallek G. & Dennington A. *Physician Withdrawals: A Major Source of Instability in the Medicare + Choice Program.* New York: The Commonwealth Fund, 2002.

10. King M. & Schlesinger M. (editors*). Final Report of the Study Panel on Medicare and Markets—The Role of Private Health Plans in Medicare: Lessons from the Past, Looking to the Future,* p 36. Washington, D.C.: National Academy of Social Insurance, September 2003.

11. Chernew M.E. Wodchis W.P., Scanlon D.P., & McLaughlin C.G. Overlap in HMO physician networks. *Health Affairs (Millwood)* 23(2):91-101, 2004.

12. Wagner L. Citing national losses of $2.2 billion, physicians closing doors to seniors. *Physicians Financial News,* May 15, 2002, 20(7): 1,24.

13. Booske B., Lynch J., & Riley G. Impact of Managed Care Marker Withdrawal

on Beneficiaries. *Health Care Financing Review* 24(1):95-115, 2002.

14. Forced Exit: Beneficiaries in Plans Terminating in 2000. Monitoring Medicare + Choice, Fast Facts, Number 3, Mathematica Policy Research, September 2000.

15. California Seniors and Prescription Drugs. Menlo Park, Calif: Kaiser Family Foundation, November 2002.

16. Wasson J.H., Sauvigne A.E. & Mogielnicki, R.P., et al. Continuity of outpatient medical care in elderly men. A randomized trial. *Journal of the American Medical Association,* 252:2413-2417, 1984.

17. Franks P., Cameron C., Bertakis K.D. On being new to an insurance plan: Health care use associated with the first years in a health insurance plan. *Annals of Family Medicine*, 1:156-61, 2003.

18. Flocke S.A., Stange K.C., & Zyzanski S.J. The impact of insurance type and forced discontinuity on the delivery of primary care. *Journal of Family Practice*, 45(2): 129-35, 1997.

19. Fuhrmans V. Cut off twice, retiree distrusts Medicare HMOs. *Wall Street Journal*, December 5, 2003:B1.

20. Ibid #1, p 8.

References—Chapter Six

1. Bartlett D.L. & Steele J.B. *Critical Condition: How Health Care in America Became Big Business and Bad Medicine.* New York: Doubleday, 2004, p 7.

2. Cooper B.S. & Vladeck B.C. Bringing competitive pricing to Medicare. *Health Affairs (Millwood)* 19(5), 48-9, 2000.

3. Public Citizen's Congress Watch. Medicare Privatization: The Case Against Relying on HMOs and Private Insurers to Offer Prescription Drug Coverage. Washington, D.C., September 2002, p 9.

4. Reinhardt U.E. Interview. The Medicare world from both sides: conversations with Tom Scully. *Health Affairs (Millwood)* 22(6), 173-4, 2003.

5. CMS. Centers for Medicare & Medicaid Services. Medicare + Choice in 2004. October 9, 2003 (transcript). Accessed January 27, 2004 at http://www.medpac.gov/public_meetings/transcripts/100903_M%20C_SH_transc.pdf

6. King K. & Schlesinger M, (eds). *Final Report of the Study Panel on Medicare and Markets—The Role of Private Health Plans in Medicare: Lessons from the Past, Looking to the Future.* Washington, D.C.: National Academy of Social Insurance, September 2003, p 94.

7. Boccuti C. & Moon M. Comparing Medicare and private insurers: growth rates in spending over three decades. *Health Affairs (Millwood)* 22(2), 232, 2003.

8. General Accounting Office. *Medicare + Choice: Payments Exceed Costs of Fee for Service Benefits, Adding Billions to Spending.* GAO/HEHS-00-161.

Washington, D.C.: Government Printing Office, 2000.

9. Jost T.S. *Disentitlement? The Threats Facing Our Public Health-Care Programs and a Rights-Based Response*. New York: Oxford University Press, 2003, p 113, citing multiple reports from the Office of Inspector General (OIG) for 1997 to 2000 and related documents.

10. MRC. Overpayments for private plans in Medicare, $4.7 billion in 2005; $80 billion 2002-2014. New York: Medicare Rights Center. *F.A.I.R. Medicare* May 13, 2004.

11. Ibid #9, pp 17-8.

12. Ibid #4, pp 169-70, 174.

13. Evans R.G. Going for the gold: The redistributive agenda behind market-based health care reform. *Journal of Health Politics, Policy and Law*, 22(2): 427-65, 1997.

14. Nichols L. M., Ginsberg P.E., Berenson R.A., Christianson I., & Hurley R.E. Are market forces strong enough to deliver efficient health care systems? Confidence is waning. *Health Affairs (Millwood)*, 23(2): 8-21, 2004.

15. Freudenheim M. Companies trim health benefits for many retirees as costs surge. *New York Times* On the Web, May 10, 2002.

16. Appleby J. Patients drop treatment due to costs. Copayments too steep for some Medicare HMO clients. *USA Today*. com January 28, 2002.

17. Federman A.D., Vladeck B.C. & Sin A.L. Avoidance of health care services because of cost: Impact of the Medicare Savings Program. *Health Affairs (Millwood)* 24(1):263-276, 2005.

18. MRC, Press Release. Barriers to enrolling in Medicare Assistance Programs identified in Medicare Rights Center study. New York: Medicare Rights Center. November 6, 2000a.

19. MRC. Making health care available to people with low incomes. Facts and Faces. New York: Medicare Rights Center, fall, 2000b.

20. Kleinke J.D. *Oxymorons: The myths of the U.S. health care system*. p 192 San Francisco: Jossey-Bass, 2001

21. Geyman J.P. *The Corporate Transformation of Health Care: Can the Public Interest Still Be Served?* Springer Publishing Co, New York, 2004.

22. Woolhandler S., Campbell T. & Himmelstein, D. U. Costs of health care administration in the United States and Canada. *New England Journal of Medicine* 349:768-75, 2003.

23. Ibid # 14.

24. MRC. Case stories on HMOs. New York: Medicare Rights Center, 2003.

25. Bodenheimer T. *The Human Faces of Medicare Privatization*. San Francisco: Senior Action Network, September 2003b:p21.

References—Chapter Seven

1. King M. & Schlesinger M. (eds). *Final Report of the Study Panel on Medicare and Markets—The Role of Private Health Plans in Medicare: Lessons from the Past, Looking to the Future.* Washington, D.C.: National Academy of Social Insurance, November 2003: pp 31-34, 55.
2. Pear R. Medicare will foot the bill for an initial exam at 65. *New York Times,* July 28, 2004:A14a.
3. Pear R. Medicare to all help for smokers. *New York Times,* December 24, 2004: A14b.
4. Achman L. & Gold M. *Trends in Medicare + Choice Benefits and Premiums, 1999-2002.* New York: The Commonwealth Fund, 2002.
5. Ibid #1.
6. Court J. & Smith F. *Making a Killing: HMOs and the Threat to Your Health.* Monroe, Me: Common Courage Press, 1999, p 65.
7. Frank R.G., Koyanagi C. & McGuire T.G. The politics and economics of mental health "parity" laws. *Health Affairs (Millwood)* 16 (4):108-119, 1997.
8. Munoz R. How health care insurers avoid treating mental illness? *San Diego Tribune,* May 22, 2002.
9. Bartels J. *Prevention, Treatment and Intervention for Mental Disorders in Older Persons: Priorities for Health Policy and Research,* comments from a Congressional briefing: Addressing *the Unmet Needs of America's Elderly*—A briefing on Mental Health and Aging, June 5, 2001.
10. Bodenheimer T. *The Human Faces of Medicare Privatization.* San Francisco: Senior Action Network, September 2003: p 6.
11. Ibid #10, p 7.
12. Ibid #10, p 11.
13. MRC. Overpayments to private plans in Medicare $4.7 billion in 2005; $80 billion 2004-2014. New York: Medicare Rights Center. *F.A.I.R. Medicare* May 13, 2004.
14. Guglielmo W.U. Update. Boom times for Medicare plans. *Medical Economics,* April 9, 2004: p 17.
15. Pear R. Insurers plan broader coverage. *New York Times* February 4, 2004: A17c.
16. Waldhoz M. Prescription. Medicare seniors face confusion as HMOs bail out of program. *Wall Street Journal,* October 3, 2004:D4.
17. Pear R. Inquiry on Medicare finds improper limits on choices. *New York Times,* September 28, 2004:A17d.

References—Chapter Eight

1. Hellander I. Quality of care lower in for-profit HMOs than in non-profits. PNHP news release, July 12, 1999.
2. U.S. House of Representatives 45th Report by the Committee on Government Operations, April 14, 1988. Medicare Health Maintenance Organizations: The International Medical Centers Experience. U.S. Government Printing Office, 1988.
3. Ware J, E., Bayliss M.S. & Rogers W.H., et al. Differences in 4-year health outcomes for elderly and poor, chronically ill patients treated in HMO and fee-for-service systems. *Journal of the American Medical Association* 276:1039-47, 1996.
4. Morgan R. O., Virnig B.A., De Vito C.A.& Persily N.A. The Medicare-HMO revolving door—the healthy go in and the sick go out. New England Journal of *Medicine* 337(3): 169-75, 1997.
5. Retchin S.M., Brown R.S., Yeh S.J., Chu D. & Moreno L. Outcomes of stroke patients in Medicare fee-for-service and managed care. *Journal of the American Medical Association* 278(2): 119-24, 1997.
6. Himmelstein D.U., Woolhandler S., Hellander I. & Wolfe S.M. Quality of care in investor-owned vs. not-for-profit HMOs. *Journal of the American Medical Association* 282(2): 159-63, 1999.
7. Landon B.E., Zaslavsky A.M., Beaulieu N.D., Shaul J.A.& Cleary P.D. Health plan characteristics and consumers' assessments of quality. *Health Affairs (Millwood)* 20(2): 274-86, 2001.
8. Safran D.G., Wilson I.B., Rogers W.H., Montgomery J.E. & Chang H. Primary care quality in the Medicare program; comparing the performance of Medicare health maintenance organizations and traditional fee-for-service Medicare. *Archives of Internal Medicine* 162:757-65, 2002.
9. Schneider E.C., Zaslavsky A.M. & Epstein A.M. Use of high-cost operative procedures by Medicare beneficiaries enrolled in for-profit and not for-profit plans. *New England Journal of Medicine* 350:143-50, 2004.
10. McCormick D., Himmelstein D.U., & Woolhandler S, et al. Relationship between low quality-of-care scores and HMOs subsequent public disclosure of quality-of-care scores. *Journal of the American Medical Association* 288(12): 1484-90, 2002.
11. King M. & Schlesinger M. (eds). *Final Report of the Study Panel on Medicare and Markets—The Role of Private Health Plans in Medicare: Lessons from the Past, Looking to the Future.* Washington, D.C.: National Academy of Social Insurance, September 2003, p 128.
12. Geyman J.P. The corporate transformation of medicine and its impact on costs

and access to care. *Journal of the American Board of Family Practice* 16(5):449, 2003.

13. Chen J., et al. Do "America's Best Hospitals" perform better for acute myocardial infarction? *New England Journal of Medicine* 340:286, 1999.

14. Hartz A. J., et al. Hospital characteristics and mortality rates. *New England Journal of Medicine* 321:1720, 1989.

15. Kover C. & Gergen P.J. Nurse staffing levels and adverse events following surgery in U.S. hospitals. *Image: Journal of Nursing Scholarship* 30:315, 1998.

16. Silverman E. M., et al. The association between for-profit hospital ownership and increased Medicare spending. *New England Journal of Medicine* 341:420, 1999.

17. Woolhandler S. & Himmelstein D.U. Costs of care and administration at for-profit and other hospitals in the United States. *New England Journal of Medicine* 336:769, 1997.

18. Yuan Z. The association between hospital type and mortality and length of stay: a study of 16.9 million hospitalized Medicare beneficiaries. *Medical Care* 38:231, 2000.

19. Devereaux P.J., Heels-Arsdell D., Lacchetti C., Haines T. & Burns K.A., et al. Payments for care at private for-profit and private not-for-profit hospitals: a systematic review and meta-analysis. *Canadian Medical Association Journal* 170(12):187-24, 2004.

20. Harrington C, et al. Does investor-ownership of nursing homes compromise the quality of care? *American Journal of Public Health* 91(9): 1, 2001.

21. Devereaux P.J., et al. Comparison of mortality between private for-profit and private not-for-profit hemodialysis centers: a systematic review and meta-analysis. *Journal of the American Medical Association* 288:2449, 2002.

22. Garg R.P., et al. Effect of the ownership of dialysis facilities on patients' survival and referral for transplantation. *New England Journal of Medicine* 341:1653, 1999.

23. Wrich J. Brief summary of audit findings of managed behavioral health services. J. Wrich & Associates, Chicago, 1998.

24. Munoz R. How health care insurers avoid treating mental illness. *San Diego Union Tribune*, May 22, 2002.

25. Peeno L. A physician answers questions about denial of care in managed care corporations. *Citizen Action*, 1996.

26. Bodenheimer T. *The Human Faces of Medicare Privatization*. San Francisco: Senior Action Network, September 2003:p 5.

27. Ibid #3.

28. Ibid #4.

29. Moon M. Medicare and Private Plans: Separating Fact from Fiction, Testimony for the Senate Committee on Aging, May 6, 2003.
30. Dallek G. & Dennington A. *Physician Withdrawals: A Major Source of Instability in the Medicare + Choice Program.* New York: The Commonwealth Fund, 2002.
31. Ibid #26, p 8.
32. CMS Medicare Fact Sheet. Centers for Medicare and Medicaid Services, September 2002.
33. Chernew M.E., Wodchis W.P., Scanlon D.P. & McLaughlin C.G. Overlap in HMO physician networks. *Health Affairs (Millwood)* 23(2): 91-101, 2004.
34. Eichner J. & Blumenthal D, editors. Medicare in the 21st Century: Building a Better Chronic Care System. Washington, D.C.: National Academy of Social Insurance, 2003.
35. Ibid #6.
36. Kuttner R. The American health care system: Wall Street and health care. *New England Journal of Medicine* 340:664, 1999.
37. HMO honor roll. *U.S. News & World Report* 1997, Oct 23, p 62.
38. Born P. & Geckler C. HMO quality and financial performance: is there a connection? *Journal of Health Care Finance* 24(2): 65-77, 1998.
39. Kuttner R. Must good HMOs go bad? Second of two parts. The search for checks and balances. *New England Journal of Medicine* 338, 1635, 1998.
40. Lee D. Rising costs put pressure on Kaiser. *Los Angeles Times*, September 29, 2002.
41. Ornstein C. Kaiser clerks paid more for helping less. *Los Angeles Times*, May 19, 2002.

References—Chapter Nine

1. Avlon J.P. *Independent Nation: How the Vital Center Is Changing American Politics.* New York: Harmony Books, 2004, p 336.
2. Princeton Survey Research Associates, September 1997.
3. Directions for Medicare: Perspectives of older and disabled Americans. Medicare Facts and Faces. Medicare Rights Center, Washington, D.C.: October 2002.
4. Gold M., Sinclair M., Cahill M., Justh N., & Mittler J. Monitoring Medicare + Choice: Medicare Beneficiaries and Health Plan Choice, 2000. Washington, D.C.: Mathematica Policy Research, Inc., January, 2001.
5. Kertesz L. Complaints against Medicare HMOs show large variations nationwide. *Modern Healthcare* February 13, 1995, p 17.
6. King K. M. & Schlesinger M. (eds). *Final Report of the Study Panel on Medicare and Markets—The Role of Private Health Plans in Medicare: Lessons from the*

Past, Looking to the Future. Washington, D.C.: National Academy of Social Insurance, September 2003, p142.

7. Davis K. Medicare versus private insurance: rhetoric and reality. Health Aff Web exclusive. October 9, 2003, W311-23.

8. Steinmo S. & Watts J. It's the institutions, stupid? Why comprehensive national health insurance always fails in America. *Journal of Health Politics, Policy and Law* 20:329, 1995.

9. Blendon R. J. & Benson J. M. Americans' views on health policy: a fifty-year historical perspective. *Health Affairs (Millwood)* 20(2): 33, 2001.

10. Congress Daily. American Hospital Association poll. Washington D.C., *Congress Daily* January 14, 2003.

11. Commonwealth Fund. Press release. March 29, 2004 as cited in Hellander I. A review of data on the U.S. health sector. *International Journal of Health Services* 35(2): 285,2005.

12. *Health Management Quarterly* 3:2, 1991, cited in Chernomas R. & Sepehri A. (Eds). *How to Choose? A Comparison of the U.S. and Canadian Health Care Systems.* Amityville, New York: Baywood Publishing Company, 1998, p 277.

13. Himmelstein D. U. & Woolhandler S. Public opinion and health care reform. In: Chernomas R. & Sepehri A. (eds). *How to Choose? A Comparison of the U.S. and Canadian Health Care Systems.* Amityville, New York: Baywood Publishing Company, 1998, pp 275-284.

14. Ibid #13.

15. Harris Interactive. Should health care be a public good (entitlement) or a private economic good? Harris Interactive. *Health Care News* 3(16): October 27, 2003.

16. Lester W. Public supports health care for all. *Washington Post*, October 19, 2003.

17. AFL-CIO News Release Poll: Seniors oppose Medicare bill in Congress. November 19, 2003.

18. Kaiser Family Foundation. Health Poll Report Surveys. Menlo Park, Calif: March/April 2004 and April 2005.

19. Center for American Progress. Washington, D.C.: March 16, 2004.

20. Toner R. Political Memo. Seems the last word on Medicare wasn't. *New York Times*, March 17, 2004:A12.

21. Medicare Rights Center. Asclepius.. Weekly Medicare Advocacy Update, November 18, 2004a.

22. Kaiser Family Foundation, February 2005.

23. Canadian Patented Medicine Prices Review Board, 2003, as cited in Asclepios, Weekly Medicare Consumer Advocacy Update. New York: Medicare Rights Center 4 (23): June 11, 2004, p 3.

24. Hensley S. Drug makers cry "danger" over imports. *Wall Street Journal*, September 22, 2003, pB1.
25. 60 Minutes, March 14, 2004, as cited in Prescriptions for profit. *Health Letter*. Public Citizen Health Research Group 20(4): 1-3, 2004.
26. Belluck P. Maine and one of its tribes look to buy Canadian drugs. *New York Times*, October 1, 2004:A9.
27. Ibid #24.
28. Manchester Union Leader, March 25, 2004, as cited in Hellander I. Data on the U.S. health sector. *International Journal of Health Services* 35(2):281, 2005.
29. Lueck S. & Mathews A.W. Drug makers not out of the woods. *Wall Street Journal* April 13, 2004: A4.
30. Japsen B. Few use Medicare free-drug benefit. *Chicago Tribune*. As reported in *Seattle Times* March 26, 2005:A1.
31. Medicare Rights Center. Asclepios, *Weekly Medicare Consumer Advocacy. Update* June 11, 2004, p 4.
32. Families USA. Sticker shock: rising prescription drug prices for seniors. Publication No. 04-103. Washington, D.C., June 2004.
33. AARP. http://www.aarp.org/legislative/prescriptiondrugs/rxprices/Articles/a2004-05-24-drug prices.html. Accessed June 11, 2004.

References—Chapter Ten

1. Friedman M. *Capitalism and Freedom*. Chicago: University of Chicago Press, 1967.
2. Angell M. Sweeping health care reform proposed by nation's top physicians. Press Release. Physicians for a National Health Program. Chicago: May 1, 2001.
3. Brodie R. *Virus of the Mind: The New Science of the Meme*. Integral Press, Seattle, WA, 1996.
4. Hurley R.E., Strunk B.C., & Grossman J. M. Preferred provider organizations and Medicare: is there an advantage? Washington, D.C. Issue Brief No. 81, Center for Studying Health System Change, April, 2004.
5. Achman L. & Gold M. New analysis describes 2004 payment increases to Medicare Advantage plans. Washington, D.C.: Mathematica Policy Research, Inc., April, 2004.
6. Pear R. Private plans costing more for Medicare. *New York Times*, September 17, 2004:A12a.
7. AARP. What happens next—The drug benefit rollout. *AARP Bulletin* 46(6): June 2005, p 18.
8. Szabo J. Managed-care survival guide. Sweetening the pot. *Physicians Financial News* 22(2), S11, February 15, 2004.

9. Lueck S. Health plans boast benefits for seniors. Wall Street Journal, February 24, 2004:D1a.
10. Berenson R.A. Medicare disadvantaged and the search for the elusive 'level playing field.' *Health Affairs* Web Exclusive W4-572, December 15, 2004.
11. Medco announcement. Medco: Few private Rx-only insurers will play in original Medicare. June 16, 2004. As cited in PNHP Newsletter, Fall 2004, p 13.
12. Kaiser Family Foundation. Fact Sheet. Medicare + Choice. Menlo Park, CA: April, 2003.
13. Kaiser Family Foundation. Fact Sheet. Medicare Advantage. Menlo Park, CA: March 2004.
14. Kaiser Family Foundation, April 2005, as reported in *Medicare Watch* 8(11), May 24, 2005.
15. HSC. News Release. Preferred provider organizations and Medicare: no panacea for cost, quality issues. Washington, D.C.: Center for Studying Health System Change, April 29, 2004.
16. Hurley R.E., Strunk B.C. & White J.S. The puzzling popularity of the PPO. *Health Affairs (Millwood)* 23(2), 67, 2004.
17. Robinson J.C. From managed care to consumer health insurance: the fall and rise of Aetna. *Health Affairs (Millwood)* 23(2):43-55, 2004.
18. Decision Maker News. How to successfully implement the Medicare prescription drug benefit. Supplement to *American Journal of Managed Care*, June 2004, p 3.
19. Gold M., Sinclair M., Cahill M., Justh N., & Mittler J. Monitoring Medicare + Choice: Medicare Beneficiaries and Health Plan Choice, 2000. Washington, D.C.: Mathematica Policy Research, Inc., January, 2001.
20. *GAO. Medicare Demonstration PPOs. Financial and Other Advantages for Plans. Few Advantages for Beneficiaries.* Pub. No. GAO 04-960. Washington, D.C.: GAO, September 2004.
21. Ibid #13.
22. Aaron C, et al. *The Medicare Drug War: An Army of Nearly 1,000 Lobbyists Pushes a Medicare Law that Puts Drug Company and HMO Profits Ahead of Patients and Taxpayers.* Washington, D.C.: Congress Watch, Public Citizen, June 2004.
23. Clemente F. Deception, bribery—securing Medicare law made for good theatre but bad policy. *Public Citizen News* 24(3), May/June 2004: 1-5.
24. Public Citizen. Press release. House Majority Leader Tom DeLay should resign leadership post over ethical lapses. Washington, D.C.: October 7, 2004.
25. Ibid #22, p 9.
26. Hart Research Associates, Inc. Reactions to the new Medicare law. Kaiser

Family Foundation, Menlo Park, Calif, June 2004, p 19.

27. Schultz E.E., Francis T. U.S. drug subsidy benefits employers. *Wall Street Journal*, January 8, 2004:A3.

28. MRC, Asclepios. MRC Advocacy Update. New York. Medicare Rights Center 4(1): January 9, 2004a.

29. Hellander I. A review of data on the U.S. health sector. Fall 2004. *International Journal of Health Services* 35(2): 281, 2005.

30. Medicare Watch 7 (12), AARP backs importation. January 24, 2004. New York: Medicare Rights Center.

31. Kaiser Family Foundation. Health Poll Report Survey, April, 2004.

32. MRC, Asclepios. MRC Advocacy Update. New York: Medicare Rights Center 4(25): June 25, 2004b.

33. Pear R. & Toner R. Partisanship and the fine print seen as hindering Medicare law. *New York Times*, October 11, 2004:A1.

34. Song K. M. Medicare discount cards: what seniors need to know. *Seattle Times* April 27, 2004:A1.

35. MRC, Asclepios. MRC Advocacy Update. New York: Medicare Rights Center 4(14): May 27, 2004c.

36. Kaiser Family Foundation, April 2005, as reported in *Medicare Watch* 8(10), May 10, 2005.

37. GAO Medicare workers need help with help line. *USA Today*, December 9, 2004:5A.

38. Pear R. Inaccuracies reported in new Medicare Web site comparing drug prices. *New York Times*, May 1, 2004.

39. Lueck S. Prices keep shifting as seniors evaluate Medicare drug card. *Wall Street Journal*, May 19, 2004:D3b.

40. Kaiser Family Foundation. Selected findings on the new Medicare prescription drug law. Presentation Chartpack, Menlo Park, Calif, June 3, 2004.

41. Houtz J. Beware: swindlers see opportunity knocking. *Seattle Times* April 29, 2004:A14.

42. Pear R. Low-income non-applicants to get Medicare drug cards. *New York Times*, September 23, 2004:A18c.

43. Kaufman M. & Brubaker B. A discount with little relief. *Washington Post-National Weekly Edition*, May 31-June 6, 2004:29.

44. Claybrook J. Greedy Rx drug companies raise prices to discount savings from cards. *Public Citizen News* 24(3): May/June 2004:2.

45. Tesoriero H.W., & Hensley S. Prices increase on popular drugs. *Wall Street Journal*, January 25, 2005:D1.

46. Medicare Watch 7(2). Report on 2006 drug premiums shows wide variations. October 20, 2004. New York: Medicare Rights Center.

47. Kaiser Family Foundation. Estimates of Medicare beneficiaries' out-of-pocket spending in 2006. Menlo Park, CA: November 2004.
48. Anderson G.F., Shea D.G., Hussey P.S., Keyhani S. & Zephyrin L. Market Watch. Doughnut holes and price controls. *Health Affairs* (*Millwood*) July 21, 2004.
49. CBO. "A detailed description of CBO's cost estimate for the Medicare Prescription Drug Benefit." Congressional Budget Office, July 2004.
50. Draper D.A., Cook A.E., & Gold M. R. How do M + C plans manage pharmacy benefits? Implications for Medicare reform. Kaiser Family Foundation. Menlo Park, CA, March 2003.
51. Hellander I. & Young Q. Voice of the people. Medicare prices. *Chicago Tribune*, May 8, 2004.
52. Woolhandler S. & Himmelstein D. U. The high costs of for-profit care. *Canadian Medical Association Journal*, June 8, 170(12): 1814-5, 2004.

References—Chapter Eleven

1. U.S. General Accounting Office, *Medicare + Choice: Payments Exceed Costs of Fee—for-Service Benefits, Adding Billions to Spending*. GAO/HEHS-00-161. Washington, D.C.: Government Printing Office, 2000.
2. Thomas W. as cited in Guglielmo W.U. Update. Boom times for Medicare plans. *Medical Economics*, April 9, 2004: p 17.
3. GAO. *Medicare: Reasonableness of Health Maintenance Organization Payments Not Assured.* GAO/HRD-89-41. Washington, D.C.: General Accounting Office, Government Printing Office, 1989.
4. King K.M. & Schlesinger M. (Eds*). Final Report of the Study Panel on Medicare and Markets—The Role of Private Health Plans in Medicare: Lessons from the Past, Looking to the Future.* Washington, D.C.: National Academy of Social Insurance, September 2003, p 11.
5. Moon M. & Storeygard M. One-Third at Risk: The Special Circumstances of Medicare Beneficiaries with Health Problems, The Commonwealth Fund, September 2001.
6. Mutti A. A Context for Medicare Spending. MedPAC September 11, 2003.
7. Public Citizen's Congress Watch. Medicare Privatization: The Case Against Relying on HMOs and Private Insurers to Offer Prescription Drug Coverage. Washington, D.C., September 2002, p 9.
8. OIG. Inspector General, Department of Health and Human Services. Adequacy of Medicare's Managed Payments After the Balanced Budget Act of 1997, September, 2000.
9. Ibid #4, pp 17-8.
10. Achman L. & Gold M. New analysis describes 2004 payment increases to

Medicare Advantage plans. Press release. Washington, D.C.: Mathematica Policy Research, Inc., June 24, 2004.

11. MedPac. M + C payment rates compared with county Medicare per-capita fee-for-service spending (revised). Medicare Payment Advisory Commission, April 8, 2004.

12. Berenson RA. Medicare disadvantaged and the search for the elusive 'level playing field.' *Health Affairs* Web Exclusive. W4-572, December 15, 2004.

13. Kaiser Family Foundation. Fact Sheet. Medicare Advantage. Menlo Park, CA: March, 2004.

14. Ibid #12.

15. MRC. Overpayments for private plans in Medicare, $4.7 billion in 2005; $80 billion 2002-2014. New York: Medicare Rights Center. *F.A.I.R. Medicare* May 13, 2004.

16. Dowd B., Coulan R., Feldman R. A tale of four cities: Medicare reform and competitive pricing. *Health Affairs (Millwood)* 19(5): 9-29, 2000.

17. DeParle N.A. & Berenson R. The need for demonstrations to test new ideas. Health *Affairs (Millwood)* 19(5): 57-59, 2000.

18. Ibid #4, pp 83-5.

19. Ibid #4, p84.

20. Nichols L. & Reischauer R. Who really wants price competition in Medicare managed care? *Health Affairs (Millwood)* 19(5): 38, 42, 2000.

21. Cooper B. & Vladeck B. Bringing competitive pricing to Medicare. *Health Affairs* (Millwood) 19(5): 53, 2000.

22. Ibid #21, p 51.

23. NASI. Press release. Expert panel examines role of private health plans in Medicare, makes policy recommendations for improving both traditional and private health plans in Medicare. Washington, D.C.: November 3, 2003.

24. Relman A.S. The new medical-industrial complex. *N. Engl. J. Med.* 303:963-70, 1980.

25. Nichols L. M., et al. Are market forces strong enough to deliver efficient health care systems? Confidence is waning. *Health Affairs (Millwood)* 23(2):8-21, 2004.

26. General Accounting Office. *Medicare + Choice: Payments Exceed Costs of Fee For Service Benefits, Adding Billions to Spending.* GAO/HEHS-00-161. Washington, D.C.: Government Printing Office, 2000.

27. Jost T.S. *Disentitlement? The Threats Facing Our Public Health Care Programs and a Rights-Based Response.* New York: Oxford University Press, 2003, p 113, citing multiple reports from the Office of Inspector General (OIG) for 1997 to 2000 and related documents.

28. The Heritage Foundation Media Campaign. Washington, D.C.: Medicare Rights

Center. http://www.medicarerights. org/maincontentheritage.html. Accessed December 1, 2003.

29. Carey A. *Taking the Risk Out of Democracy: Corporate Propaganda versus Freedom and Liberty.* University of Illinois Press, Chicago: 1995:91-3.

30. Greider W. *Who Will Tell the People? The Betrayal of American Democracy.* New York: Simon & Schuster, 1992:300-1.

31. Ibid #4, pp 5-16.

32. Hacker J.S. *The Divided Welfare State: The Battle Over Public and Private Social Benefits in the United States.* Cambridge: Cambridge University Press, 2002, p 329.

33. Smith D.G. Entitlement Politics: Medicare and Medicaid 1995-2001. New York: Aldine de Gruyter, 2002:71, citing *Congressional Quarterly Almanac*, 1995, p 7-13.

34. McCanne D. Quote of the Day. Comment on the Medicare Prescription Drug, Improvement, and Modernization Act of 2003. Don@mccanne.org, accessed November 26, 2003.

35. Hurley R.E., Strunk B.C., & Grossman J.M. Preferred provider organizations and Medicare: is there an advantage? Washington, D.C. Issue Brief No. 81, Center for Studying Health System Change, April, 2004.

References—Chapter Twelve

1. Eddy D. M. A manual for assessing health practices and designing practice policies: the explicit approach. Philadelphia: American College of Physicians, 1992.

2. Anderson G.F., Reinhardt, U.E., Hassey P.S., Petroyan V. It's the prices, stupid: Why the United States is so different from other countries. *Health Affairs* (*Millwood*) 22(3), 89, 2003.

3. Towers Perrin. 2003 Health Care Cost Survey. Available at www.towersperrin. com.

4. Schuster M.A., McGlynn E.A. & Brook R. H. How good is the quality of health care in the United States? *Milbank Quarterly*, 76(4), 517, 509, 1998.

5. Commonwealth Fund. *Quality of care in the U.S. chartbook.* New York, 2002.

6. Tunis S. R. Why Medicare has not established criteria for coverage decisions. *N. Engl. J. Med* 350(21):2196-98, 2004.

7. *Federal Register* 63 no. 239 (14 December 1998): Notices, 68780.

8. Strongin R. J. Medicare coverage: lessons from the past, questions for the future. Washington, D.C.: National Health Policy Forum, 2001.

9. Ibid #8, p 7.

10. Tunis S.R., & Kang J. L. Improvements in Medicare coverage of new technology. *Health Affairs (Millwood)* 20(5): 83-5, 2001.

11. Ibid #8, p 8.

12. CLC comments on proposed coverage criteria. Cancer Leadership Council. July 17, 2000. Accessed at http://www.cancerleadership.org/policy/medicare_payment/ 000717.html. on June 21, 2004.

13. Ibid #6, p 2196.

14. McGinley L. & Lueck S. Harsh medicine. As Medicare chief reins in costs, opposition grows. *Wall Street Journal*, July 16, 2003:A1.

15. Ramsey S.D. & Sullivan S.D. Weighing the economic evidence: Guidelines for critical assessment of cost-effectiveness analysis. In: Geyman J.P., Deyo R.A. & Ramsey S.D. *Evidence-Based Clinical Practice: Concepts and Approaches.* Woburn, Mass: Butterworth-Heinemann, 2000, pp 103-10.

16. Gold M.R., Russell L.B., Siegal J.E. & Weinstein M.C. *Cost-Effectiveness in Health and Medicare.* New York: Oxford University Press, 1996, pp 12-13.

17. Ibid #15.

18. Ibid #16, xvii-xviii.

19. Neuhauser D. & Lewicki A.M. What do we gain from the sixth stool guaiac? *N. Engl. J. Med.* 293:226-28, 1975.

20. Tengs T. O., Adams M.E. & Pliskin J.S. Five hundred life-saving interventions and their cost-effectiveness. *Risk Anal* 15:369-90, 1995.

21. Eddy D. M. *Clinical Decision Making From Theory to Practice: A Collection of Essays from the Journal of the American Medical Association*, Boston: Jones & Bartlett Publishers, Inc., 1996:pp 163-4.

22. Deyo R.A. Cost-effectiveness in primary care. In: Geyman J. P., Deyo R.A. & Ramsey S.D. *Evidence-Based Clinical Practice: Concepts and Approaches.* Woburn, Mass: Butterworth-Heinemann, 2000:pp 111-18.

23. Ibid #22.

24. Gillick M. R. Medicare coverage for technological innovations—time for new criteria? *N. Engl. J. Med* 350(21): 2199-2203, 2004.

25. Rose E.A. Gelijns A.C., Moskowitz A.J., et al. Long-term use of a left ventricular assist for end-stage heart failure. N. Engl. J. Med 345:1435-43, 2001.

26. Thoratec Press release. Medicare expands coverage of left ventricular assist devices for destination therapy. Thoratec, Pleasanton, Calif., October 2, 2003. (Accessed April 10, 2004, at http://ir.thomsonfin.)

27. Samson D. Special Report. Cost-effectiveness of left ventricular assist devices as destination therapy for end-stage heart failure. TEC Assessments, 19(2): 1-36, 2004. (Accessed at www.bcbs.com/tec.).

28. Agovino T. Expensive heart device expected to be rationed. *Boston Globe*, September 2, 2003:A10.

29. National Emphysema Treatment Trial Research Group. A randomized trial comparing lung-volume-reduction surgery with medical therapy in severe

emphysema. *N. Engl J. Med.* 348:2059-73, 2003a.

30. National Emphysema Treatment Trial Research Group. Cost-effectiveness of lung-volume-reduction surgery for patients with severe emphysema. *N. Engl J. Med.* 348:2092-102, 2003b.

31. Grady D. Medicare to pay for major lung operation. *New York Times,* August 21, 2003:A22.

32. Woodward K. Cost analysis of lung-volume-reduction surgery suggests 'cautious optimism' over long-term value of procedure. Fred Hutchinson Cancer Research Center News. May 2003. (Accessed April 12, 2004, at http:// www.fhcre.org/news/science/2003/05/20/lung_volume.html.)

33. AHRQ Agency for Healthcare Research and Quality. Healthcare Cost and Utilization Project, HCUPnet. (Accessed January 22, 2004, at http://www.ahrq. gov/data/hcup/.)

34. Grob D., Humke T. & Dvorak J. Degenerative lumbar spinal stenosis: decompression with and without arthrodesis. *J. Bone Joint Surg Am* 77:1036-41, 1995.

35. Katz J.N., Lipson S.J., Lew R.A., et al. Lumbar laminectomy alone or with instrumented or noninstrumented arthrodesis in degenerative lumbar spinal stenosis: patient selection, costs, and surgical outcomes. *Spine* 22 (10): 1123-31, 1997.

36. Gibson J. N.A., Grant I.C., & Waddell G. The Cochrane review of surgery for lumbar disc prolapse and degenerative lumbar spondylosis. *Spine* 24:1820-32, 1999.

37. Deyo R.A., Ciol M.A., Cherkin D.C, et al. Lumbar spinal fusion: A cohort study of complications, reoperations, and resource use in the Medicare population. *Spine* 18:463-70, 1993.

38. Mendenhall Associates, Inc. 2002 Spinal industry update. Orthopedic Network News, 13(4):7-8, 2002.

39. Deyo R.A., Nachemson A. & Mirza S.K. Spinal-fusion surgery—the case for restraint. N. Engl. J. Med 350:722-6, 2004.

40. Kuntz K. M., Snider R.J., Weinstein J.N., et al. Cost-effectiveness of fusion with and without instrumentation for patients with degenerative spondylolisthesis and spinal stenosis. *Spine* 25:1132-9, 2000.

41. Deyo R.A., Cherkin D.C., Loeser J.D., et al. Morbidity and mortality in association with operations on the lumbar spine: the influence of age, diagnosis, and procedure. *J. Bone Joint Surg Am.* 74:536-43, 1992.

42. Deyo R.A., Psaty B.M., Simon G., et al. The messenger under attack— Intimidation of researchers by special interest groups. *N. Engl J. Med* 336:1176-80, 1997.

43. Ibid #42.

44. AdvaMed Web. Site. http://www.advamed.org/aboutadvamed.shtml. Accessed June 22, 2004.
45. Moss A.J., Zareba W., Hall W.J., et al. Prophylactic implantation of a defibrillator in patients with myocardial infarction and reduced ejection fraction. *N. Engl. J. Med* 346:877-83, 2002.
46. Stecker E.C., Pollack H.A. Letter to the Editor. Implantable cardiac defibrillators. *N. Engl. J Med* 347(5):365, 2002.
47. Phurrough S., Farrell J., Chin J. Decision memorandum: implantable cardioverter defibrillators. June 6, 2003. (Accessed April 12, 2004, at http://www.cms.hhs.gov/coverage/download/id39-5.pdf.).
48. Lynd L.D. & O'Brien B.J. Cost-effectiveness of the implantable cardioverter defibrillator: a review of current evidence. *J. Cardiovasc Electrophysiol* 14: Suppl: S99-S103, 2003.
49. Hlathy M.A., Sanders G.D., Owens D.K. Evidence-based medicine and policy: The case of the implantable cardioverter defibrillator. *Health Affairs.* 241: 42-51, 2004.
50. Anderson G.F., Hussey P.S., Frogner B.K., & Waters H.R. Health spending in the United States and the rest of the industrialized world. *Health Affairs (Millwood)* 24(4):903.14, 2005.
51. Ibid #2
52. Ibid #6.
53. Redelmeier D.A. & Tversky A. Discrepancy between medical decisions for individual patients and for groups. *N. Engl. J Med* 322:1162-4, 1990.
54. Ethical Force Program. *Ensuring Fairness in Health Care Coverage Decisions.* Chicago: American Medical Association, 2004, p 8.
55. Sacramento Healthcare Decisions. Cost-effectiveness as a criterion for medical and coverage decisions: understanding and responding to community perspectives. October 2001, www.sachealthdecisions.org.vf.pdf (22 April 2004)
56. Neumann P. J. Why don't Americans use cost-effectiveness analysis? *Am. J Manag Care* 10:311, 2004.
57. Garber A. M. Cost-effectiveness and evidence evaluation as criteria for coverage policy. *Health Aff* Web exclusive. W4-294, May 19, 2004.
58. Lamm R.D. Marginal medicine. *JAMA* 280:931-33, 1998.

References—Chapter Thirteen

1. Cunningham R., III & Cunningham R.M, Jr. *The Blues: A History of the Blue Cross and Blue Shield System.* DeKalb, Ill: Northern Illinois University Press, 1997.
2. Myers R.J. *Medicare.* Homewood, Ill: Richard D. Irwin Inc., 1970, p 179.
3. Foote S.B. Focus on locus: evolution of Medicare's local coverage policy.

Health Affairs (Millwood) 22(4):137-46. 2003.

4. Foote S.B. Why Medicare cannot promulgate a national coverage rule: a case of <u>regula</u> mortis. *Journal of Health Politics, Policy and Law* 27(5): 707-30, 2002.

5. Benefits Improvement and Protection Act of 2000. Public Law Sections 521-22 December 21, 2000.

6. Ibid #4.

7. Ibid #3.

8. Foote S.B., Wholey D., Rockwood T. & Halpern R. Resolving the tug-of-war between Medicare's national and local coverage. *Health Affairs (Millwood)* 23(4): 108-23, 2004.

9. Ibid #8.

10. Testimony of Thomas A. Scully, administrator, CMS, before the House Energy and Commerce Subcommittees on Health and Oversight and Investigations. "Patients First: A Twenty-first Century Promise to Ensure Quality and Affordable Health Care," 28 June 2001, energycommerce. House.gov/107/ hearings/0628200/Hearing313/Scully509.htm (20 January 2003).

11. Ibid #8.

12. Frieden J. Local or national? Uniform Medicare decisions in dispute. *Family Practice News* 33(12):37, June 15, 2003.

13. Hawryluk M. Local commotion: the flip side of national Medicare policy-making. *AM News* August 5, 2002.

14. Hawryluk M. The waiting game: when will Medicare cover technology? *AM News* June 2/9, 2003, p 2.

15. Ibid #8.

16. King K. & Schlesinger M. (eds). *Final Report of the Study Panel on Medicare and Markets—The Role of Private Health Plans in Medicare: Lessons from the Past, Looking to the Future.* Washington, D.C.: National Academy of Social Insurance, September 2003, p 41.

17. Moon M. & Boccuti C. Location, location, location: geographic spending issues and Medicare policy. Health Policy Brief. Washington, D.C.: The Urban Institute, No. 2, June 2002.

18. Dartmouth Atlas of Healthcare Project Web site. (Accessed October 3, 2003) at http://www.dartmouthatlas.org/annals/fisher03.

19. Skinner J.S. & Fisher E. S. Regional disparities in Medicare expenditures: an opportunity for reform. *Nat Tax J* 50:413-25, 1997.

20. Wennberg J.B., Fisher E.S., & Skinner J.S. Geography and the debate over Medicare reform. Health Affairs Web Exclusive W96-114, February 13, 2002.

21. Ibid #17.

22. Ibid #19.

23. Fisher F.S. Wennberg D.E., Stukel T.A., et al. The implications of regional variations in Medicare spending. Part 1: The content, quality, and accessibility of care. *Ann Intern Med* 138:273-87, 2003a.

24. Fisher E.S., Wennberg D.E., Stukel T.A., et al. The implications of regional variations in Medicare spending. Part 2. Health outcomes and satisfaction with care. *Ann Intern Med* 138:288-98, 2003b.

25. Ibid #23

26. Fisher E. S. More medicine is not better medicine. *New York Times*, December 1, 2003:A25 Op Ed.

27. Baicker K. & Chandra A. Medicare spending, the physician workforce, and beneficiaries' quality of care. Health Affairs Web Exclusive. April 7, 2004.

28. Kolata G. Patients in Florida lining up for all that Medicare covers. *New York Times*, September 13, 2003: A1.

29. Wennberg D. E. Perspective. Practice variations and health care reform: Connecting the dots. *Health Affairs* Web Exclusive. October 7, 2004.

30. Ibid #8.

31. Ibid #8.

32. Medicare Payment Advisory Commission. *Reducing Medicare Complexity and Regulatory Burden.* Washington: MedPAC, 2001.

33. GAO. U.S. General Accounting Office. *Medicare: Divided Authority for Policies on Coverage of Procedures and Devices Results in Inequities.* Pub. No. GAO-03-175. Washington: GAO, 2003.

34. Ibid #8.

35. Aston G. Doctors urge national standards for Medicare carriers. *Am News*, April 10, 2000.

36. Foote S. B. & Neumann P. J. The impact of Medicare modernization on coverage policy: Recommendations for reform. *Am J Manage Care* 11(3):March 2005, 140-2.

37. Ibid #36.

38. Medical Device Amendments. 21 U.S. Code, sec. 321. See the 1976 *Medical Device Amendments to the Food, Drug, and Cosmetic Act.*

39. Geyman J. P. *The Corporate Transformation of Health Care: Can the Public Interest Still Be Served?* New York: Springer Publishing Co, 2004, p 132.

40. Boccuti C. & Moon M. Comparing Medicare and private insurers: growth rates in spending over three decades. *Health Affairs (Millwood)* 22(2), 232, 2003.

41. Bodenheimer T. The not-so-sad history of Medicare cost containment as told in one chart. *Health Affairs* Web Exclusive January 23, 2002:W88-90.

References—Chapter Fourteen

1. Hacker J.S. & Marmor T.R. Medicare reform: fact, fiction, and foolishness. Public Policy & Aging Report 13(4): 1, Fall 2003.
2. Oberlander J. *The Political Life of Medicare*. Chicago: University of Chicago Press, 2003:29-31.
3. Kaiser. Edgar Kaiser papers. Bancroft Library. Berkeley: University of California, 1964.
4. *Business Week* January 16, 1965, p 132.
5. Gordon C. *Dead on Arrival: The Politics of Health Care in Twentieth Century America*. Princeton, NJ: Princeton University Press, 2003:97-8.
6. Friedman L. Social Welfare Legislation. *Stanford Law Review*, 21, 247, January 1969.
7. Marmor T.R. *The Politics of Medicare*. New York: Aldine Publishing Company, 1970, 119-20.
8. Miller A., Hager M. & Roberts B. The elderly duke it out. *Newsweek*, September 11, 1989:42-3.
9. Himmelfarb R. *Catastrophic Politics: The Rise and Fall of the Medicare Catastrophic Coverage Act of 1988*, p 80. University Park: Pennsylvania State University Press, 1995.
10. Ibid #2, p 166.
11. King K. M. & Schlesinger M. (eds). *Final Report of the Study Panel on Medicare and Markets—The Role of Private Health Plans in Medicare: Lessons from the Past, Looking to the Future*. Washington, D.C.: National Academy of Social Insurance, September 2003:5-16.
12. Pianin E. & Baker P. Medicare means testing scrapped. *Washington Post* July 22, 1997:A1.
13. News Archive. The skyrocketing cost of health care: will seniors keep up? Washington, D.C., National Committee to Preserve Social Security and Medicare News Archive @1007: 11, May 2004. Accessed www.ncpssm.org/news/archive/vp_skyrocketing/ on June 21, 2004.
14. Broder D.S. AARP's tough selling job. *Washington Post National* Weekly Edition, March 22-28, 2004:4.
15. CBS News e-com. Hit rich for Medicare fix? October 6, 2003.
16. O'Neill P. Quoted in: Shlaes A. "Republicans Sample the Rhetoric of Confidence." *Financial Times*, May 22, 2001, p 23.
17. Reich R.B. *Reason: Why Liberals Will Win the Battle for America*. New York: Vintage Books, 2005, p 114.
18. Friedman M. *Free to Choose*. New York: Harcourt Brace Jovanovich, 1980, p 124.
19. Friedman S.T. High premiums for the rich won't help Medicare. Newsday. Com,

October 25, 2003, as cited in Campaign for America's Future. Washington, D.C. Accessed October 30, 2003 at http:www.ourfuture.org/issues_and campaigns/ medicare/national_news/newsday10_30_03.cfm.

20. Rice T. & Desmond K.A. Low-income subsidies for the Medicare prescription drug benefit: The impact of the asset test. Henry J. Kaiser Family Foundation, April, 2005.

21. Jost T.S. Disentitlement?: The Threats Facing Our Public Health-Care Programs and a Rights-Based Response. New York: Oxford University Press, 2003:153.

22. Ibid #19.

23. Health Cast. An interview of Mark Pauly and Marilyn Moon by Larry Levitt. Kaisernetwork.org, December 8, 2004.

24. Ibid #19.

25. The Kaiser Family Foundation/Harvard School of Public Health, *National Survey on Medicare: The Next Big Health Policy Debate*, reprint (Menlo Park, CA: The Henry J. Kaiser Family Foundation, October 20, 1998).

26. Arrow K. J. Uncertainty and the Welfare Economics of Medical Care. *American Economic Review* 53 (1963): 941-73.

27. Moon M. & Storeygard M. One-Third at Risk: The Special Circumstances of Medicare Beneficiaries with Health Problems, The Commonwealth Fund, September 2001.

28. Century Foundation, *Medicare Tomorrow: The Report of the Century Foundation Task Force on Medicare Reform*, New York: Century Foundation Press, 2002, 27.

29. Ibid #1.

30. Ibid #21, p 270.

31. Ibid #17, pp 105-6.

32. Hacker J.S. *The Divided Welfare State: The Battle Over Public and Private Social Benefits in the United States*. Cambridge: Cambridge University Press, 2002, p 329.

33. Reinhardt U.E. The mix of public and private payers in the U.S. health system. In: *The Public—Private Mix for Health.* Maynard A. (Ed). Oxford: Seattle: Radcliffe Publishing, The Nuffield Trust, 2005: pp 110-11.

References—Chapter Fifteen

1. Marmor T.R. *The Politics of Medicare.* New York: Aldine De Gruyter, 2000, p 191.

2. Cassel C.K., Besdine R.W. & Siegel L.C. Restructuring Medicare for the next century: what will beneficiaries really need? *Health Affairs (Millwood)* 18(1): 119, 1999.

3. Health Care Financing Administration, 1999 HCFA Statistics: Providers/

Suppliers, 1999. All numbers are rounded to the nearest 100. Available at www. hcfa.gov/stats

4. Pear R. Cut in Medicare payments to hospitals is advised. *New York Times* January 18, 2005:A13

5. Kaiser Family Foundation. Medicare at a Glance. Fact Sheet. Menlo Park, Calif: March 2004.

6. Levit K., Smith C., Cowan C., et al. Health spending rebound continues in 2002. *Health Affairs (Millwood)* 23(1):147-59, 2004.

7. Rundle R. L. Anthem, Wellpoint each report 34% rise in second quarter net. *Wall Street Journal*, July 28, 2004:A8.

8. Benko L. B. Managed care. Shakeup in California. *Modern Healthcare*, May 13, 2002. p 32.

9. PNHP (Physicians for a National Health Program), Chicago: Slide set; available from www.pnhp.org (sources Schramm, Blue Cross-conversion, Abell Foundation and CMS), 2002.

10. PNHP Press Release. Hellander I., Himmelstein D. U. & Wolfe S. M. Medicare drug bill will increase bureaucratic costs, reward insurers and the AARP. Chicago: January 15, 2004.

11. PNHP Slide Set, Physicians for a National Health Program, Chicago: 2004.

12. Walsh M. W. A mission to save money: a record of otherwise. *New York Times* on the Web June 7, 2002.

13. Meier B. & Walsh M.W. Medicine's middlemen. Questioning $1 million fee in a needle deal. *New York Times*, July 19, 2002.

14. Relman A. *For Profit Health Care: Expensive, Inefficient and Inequitable.* Presentation to the Standing Senate Committee on Social Affairs, Science and Technology. Ottawa: February 21, 2002

15. Boorstin J. Get real about your future. *Fortune* 152(1) July 11, 2005, p 45.

16. NASI. Study Panel on Medicare's Larger Social Role. Final Report. Washington, D.C.: National Academy of Social Insurance, 1999, pp 17-18.

17. Freudenheim M. Market Place. Higher Medicare charges may make beneficiaries turn to subsidized private insurance plans. *New York Times,* September 9, 2004: C10.

18. Pear R. Drug law is seen causing big drop in retiree plans. *New York Times* July 14, 2004: A1.

19. Pear R. Agency to allow insurance cuts for the retired. *New York Times* April 23, 2004:A1.

20. Rice T. Supplemental Insurance and Its Role in Medicare Reform, in: *Medicare Tomorrow: The Report of the Century Foundation Task Force on Medicare Reform.* New York: Century Foundation Press, 195-6, 2002.

21. Opdyke J.D. MediGap premiums vary greatly among insurers. *Wall Street*

Journal September 8, 2004:D4.

22. Ruffenach G. Nursing home costs jump 6.1%. *Wall Street Journal* September 28, 2004:D8.

23. Trustees Report. 2003 Annual Report of the Boards of Trustees of the Federal Hospital Insurance and Federal Supplementary Medical Insurance Trust Funds. Centers for Medicare and Medicaid Services, Baltimore.

24. Welch W. M. Medical costs eat at Social Security. *USA Today*. September 11, 2004:A1.

25. Kaiser Family Foundation, 2004.

26. MRC. Act now: 6.4 million reasons to support a Medicaid safety net. Medicare Rights Center. Asclepios 5(19), May 12, 2005.

27. AAFP. American Academy of Family Physicians FP Report, 2002, Leawood, Kan: September 8 (9).

28. Ostrom C. M. Seattle is losing Medicare doctors. *Seattle Times*, September 6, 2002:B1.

29. CMS Medicare Fact Sheet. Centers for Medicare and Medicaid Services, September 2002

30. CMS. Department of Health and Human Services issue Brief No. 10, May 2003.

31. Hogan C., Lunney J., Gable J., & Lynne J. Medicare beneficiaries cost of care in the last year of life. *Health Affairs (Millwood)* 20(4):188-95, 2001.

32. Shearer G. Medicare prescription drugs: Conference Committee agreement asks beneficiaries to pay too high a price for a modest benefit. *Consumers Union*, Washington, D.C., November 25, 2003.

33. Ibid #2.

34. Bartels S. J. Prevention, Treatment and Intervention for Mental Disorders in Older Persons. Priorities for Health Policy and Research, comments from a Congressional briefing: Addressing the Unmet Needs of America's Elderly—a Briefing on Mental Health and Aging, June 5, 2001.

35. Kaiser Family Foundation. The Faces of Medicare: Medicare and the Under-65 Disabled, July 1999.

36. Medicare Rights Center. Medicare: A Guide for 2004 Presidential Candidates. New York: 2003.

37. Ibid #36, pp 15-6.

38. Commonwealth Fund. Elimination of Medicare's waiting period for seriously disabled adults: Impact on coverage and costs. New York: Commonwealth Fund, July 2003.

39. Ibid #36, p 21.

40. Achman L. & Gold M. Trends in Medicare + Choice benefits and premiums, 1999-2002. New York: The *Commonwealth Fund*, 2002.

41. Wennberg J. B., Fisher E.S., & Skinner J.S. Geography and the debate over Medicare reform. Health Affairs Web Exclusive W96-114, February 13, 2002.

42. Field M. J. & Cassel C. K., Eds. *Approaching Death: Improving Care at the End of Life*. Washington, D.C.: National Academy Press, 1997.

43. Jencks S., et al. Quality of medical care delivered to Medicare beneficiaries: a profile at state and national levels. *Journal of the American Medical Association* 284 (13):1670-76, 2000.

44. Skinner J. S. & Fisher E.S. Regional disparities in Medicare expenditures: an opportunity for reform. *National Tax Journal,* 50:413-25, 1997.

45. Geyman J. P. The corporate transformation of medicine and its impact on costs and access to care. *Journal of the American Board of Family Practice* 16(5): 449, 2003.

46. Himmelstein D. U., Woolhandler S., Hellander I., & Wolfe S. M. Quality of care in investor-owned vs. not-for-profit HMOs. *Journal of the American Medical Association* 282(2):159-63, 1999.

47. McCormick D., Himmelstein D.U., Woolhandler S., et al. Relationship between low quality-of-care scores and HMOs subsequent public disclosure of quality-of-care scores. *Journal of the American Medical Association* 288(12):1484-90, 2002.

48. Ibid #9.

49. Ibid #41.

50. Commonwealth Fund. Quality of Health Care in the U.S. Chartbook. New York: 2002.

51. Samson D. Special Report. Cost-effectiveness of left ventricular assist devices as destination therapy for end-stage heart failure. TEC assessments, 19(2):1-36, 2004. (Accessed at www.bcbs.com/tec)

52. Agovino T. Expensive heart device expected to be rationed. *Boston Globe*, September 2, 2003:A10.

53. Public Citizen Health Research Group. Unsafe drugs: Congressional silence is deadly (Part 2). *Health Letter* 18(11):1, 2002.

54. Sigelman D. Unsafe drugs: Congressional silence is deadly. Public Citizen Research Group, *Health Letter* 18, 1, 2002.

55. Reich R. B. *Reason: Why Liberals Will Win the Battle for America*. New York: Vintage Books 2005, pp 105-6.

56. The Heritage Foundation Media Campaign. Washington, D.C.: Medicare Rights Center. http://www.medicareights.org/maincontentheritage.html.

57. Iglehart J. K. The American Health system—Medicare, *New England Journal of Medicine,* 340, 327-32, 1999.

58. King K.M. & Schlesinger M. (eds*). Final Report of the Study Panel on Medicare and Markets—the Role of Private Health Plans in Medicare: Lessons from the*

Past, Looking to the Future. Washington, D.C.: National Academy of Social Insurance, September 2003, pp 85-7.

59. GAO. *Federal Employees' Health Plans: Premium Growth and OPM's Role in Negotiating Benefits*. GAO-03-236. Washington, D.C.: Government Printing Office, 2002.

60. Merlis M. *Medicare Restructuring: The FEHBP Model*. Menlo Park, CA: Kaiser Family Foundation, 1999.

61. Ibid #6

62. Physicians for a National Health Program (PNHP) (2002, Fall). Data update PNHP Newsletter, 10.

63. Lee C. Health plan costs up 10.6%. *The Washington Post*, September 17, 2003.

64. Aaron H. & Reischauer R. The Medicare reform debate: what is the next step? *Health Affairs (Millwood)* 14(4):8-30, 1995.

65. Vladeck B. Plenty of nothing—a report from the Medicare Commission. *New England Journal of Medicine,* 340(19):1503-6, 1999.

66. Brock F. Weighing the risks in a health savings account. *New York Times* September 21, 2004:C3.

67. Economic Report of the President, 2004, p 200.

68. Shearer G. Testimony before the Joint Economic Committee on Impact of "Consumer—Driven" Health Care on Consumers. Washington, D.C.: February 25, 2004.

69. Scherer M. Medicare's hidden bonanza. Mother Jones, com, March/April 2004, accessed March 1, 2004.

70. Editorial. 'Ownership' isn't the cure. *Los Angeles Times* September 4, 2004.

71. Lueck S. Federal workers slow to sign up for health option. *Wall Street Journal,* May, 2005:D4.

72. Reinhardt U., as quoted in Freudenheim M. Bush health savings accounts slow to gain acceptance. *New York Times* October 13, 2004:C1.

73. Waidmann T. Potential effects of raising Medicare's eligibility age. *Health Affairs (Millwood)* 17(2):156-64, 1998.

74. Ibid #16, pp 79-88.

75. Woolhandler S., Himmelstein D.U., Angell M. & Young, Q.D. and the Physicians Working Group for Single-Payer National Health Insurance, 2003.

76. H.R. 676. The "United States National Health Insurance Act," (Expanded & Improved Medicare for All Bill.") Introduced by Cong. John Conyers, Jim McDermott, Dennis Kucinich, and Dona Christensen. House of Representatives. Washington, D.C.: 2004.

77. Himmelstein D.U., Woolhandler S., Wolfe S.M. Administrative waste in the U.S. health care system in 2003. The cost to the Nation, the States and

the District of Columbia, with state-specific estimates of potential savings. *International Journal of Health Services* 34(1), p 79, 2004.

78. National Coalition on Health Care. Press release. New projections from nation's largest healthcare coalition show health care reform would produce huge savings. Washington, D.C., May 23, 2005.

79. Heffler S., Smith S., Keehan S., et al. Health spending projections through 2013. *Health Aff* Web-Exclusive Abstract February 11, 2004.

80. Woolhandler S., Campbell T., & Himmelstein D.U. Costs of health care administration in the United States and Canada. *The New England Journal of Medicine*, 349: 768, 2003.

81. Institute of Medicine Committee on the Consequences of Uninsurance. *Coverage matters: Insurance and health care*. Washington, D.C.: National Academy Press, 2001.

82. Marlis M. Family out-of-pocket spending for health services. A continuing source of financial insecurity. *Commonwealth Fund*, June 2002.

83. Himmelstein D.U., Warren E., Thorne D., & Woolhandler S. Illness and injury as contributors to bankruptcy. *Health Affairs* Web Exclusive February 2, 2005.

84. Himmelstein D.U., Woolhandler S., Hellander I., & Wolfe S.M. Quality of care in investor-owned vs. not-for-profit HMOs. *JAMA* 282(2): 159-63, 1999.

85. Hartz A.J., Krakauer H., & Kuhn E.M., et al. Hospital characteristics and mortality. *New England Journal of Medicine* 321: 1720-5, 1989.

86. Harrington C., Woolhandler S., Mullan J., Carrillo H., & Himmelstein D.U. Does investor-ownership of nursing homes compromise the quality of care? *American Journal of Public Health* 91:1, 2001.

87. Garg P.P., Frick K.D., Diener-West M., & Powe N.R. Effect of the ownership status of dialysis facilities on patients' survival and referral for transplantation. *New England Journal of Medicine* 341: 1653-60, 1999.

88. Acs G. & Blumberg L.J. How a changing workforce affects employer-sponsored health insurance. *Health Aff (Millwood)* 20(1): 178-83, 2001.

89. Taylor H. How and why the health insurance system will collapse. *Health Aff (Millwood)* 21(6): 195, 2002.

90. Light D.W. A conservative call for universal access to health care. *Penn Bioethics* 9(4): 4-6, 2002.

91. U.S. Government Accounting Office. Canadian health insurance: lessons for the United States. Washington, D.C.: Government Accounting Office (GAO/HRD-91-90), 1991.

92. Congressional Budget Office. Single-payer and all-payer health insurance systems using Medicare's payment rates. Washington, D.C.: Congressional Budget Office, April, 1993.

93. California Health Care Options Project http://www.healthcareoptions.ca.gov/doclib.asp.

94. Brand R., Frod D., Sager A. & Socolar D. Universal comprehensive coverage: A report to the Massachusetts Medical Society. Waltham, Mass: The Massachusetts Medical Society, 1998.

95. Sheils J.F. & Haught R.A. Analysis of the costs and impact of universal health care models for the state of Maryland: the single-payer and multi-payer models. Fairfax, VA: The Lewin Group, 2000.

96. Smith R.F. Universal health insurance makes business sense. *Rutland Herald*, Novermber 2, 2001.

97. Bartlett DL & Steele J.B. Healthcare can be cured: Here's how. *Time* October 11, 2004:50-1.

98. Ibid #16, p 91.

99. Century Foundation. Home page. Accessed August 22, 2004 at http://www.tcf.org/AboutUS/AboutUShtml.

100.   Century Foundation. *Medicare Tomorrow: The Report of the Century Foundation Task Force on Medicare Reform*, 2002, p 6.

101.   Nichols L. M., Ginsberg P.E., Berenson R.A., et al. Are market forces strong enough to deliver efficient health care systems? Confidence is waning. *Health Affairs (Millwood)* 23(2):8-21, 2004.

102.   Rice T. Supplemental Insurance and Its Role in Medicare Reform in *Medicare Tomorrow*, 189-218, 2002.

103.   Lawlor E. *Redesigning the Medicare Contract: Politics, Markets, and Agency*. Chicago: University of Chicago Press, 2003:207-8

104.   Rose J. Focus on practice. Medicare fee cuts: postponed but not avoided? *Medical Economics* July 9, 2004, p 17.

105.   Silverman J. Overpayments could offset physician payment increases. *Medical Economics* July 9, 2004, p 17.

106.   MRC. Medicare Facts and Faces. Ensuring choice of doctors. New York: Medicare Rights Center, January 2002.

107.   MRC. Medicare Facts and Faces. Americans with disabilities: poor coverage, little choice. New York: Medicare Rights Center, April 2003.

108.   Friedman S.T. High premiums for the rich won't help Medicare. Newsday. Com, October 25, 2003, as cited in Campaign for America's Future. Washington, D.C.: Accessed October 30, 2003 at http:www/ourfuture.org/issues

109.   Hacker J.S. & Marmor J.R. Medicare reform: fact, fiction, and foolishness. Public Policy & Aging Report 13(4): 1, fall 2003.

110.   Ibid #2.

111 .   Ibid #41

112.   Whitelaw N.A. & Warden G.L. Re-examining the delivery system as part of Medicare reform. *Health Affairs (Millwood)* 18(1):141-2, 1999.

113.   Ibid #16, pp 23-4, 45.

References—Chapter Sixteen

1. Frist W. H. Health care in the 21ˢᵗ century. *N Engl J Med* 352(3):267-72, 2004.
2. Soros G. The bubble of American supremacy. *Public Affairs* December 2004.
3. Reinhardt U.E. Is there hope for the uninsured? Health Affairs Web Exclusive 2003: W3-387.
4. Oberlander J. *The Political Life of Medicare*. Chicago: University of Chicago Press, 2003: 1996
5. Maynard A. Enduring problems in healthcare delivery. In: Maynard A. (Ed). *The Public-Private Mix for Health*. The Nuffield Trust. Oxford, Seattle: Radcliffe Publishers 2005: pp 299-300.
6. Starfield B. *Primary Care: Balancing Health Needs, Services, and Technology*. New York: Oxford University Press, 1999.
7. Starfield B. Primary care and health. A cross-national comparison. *Journal of American Medical Association,* 266: 2268, 1991.
8. Institute of Medicine Committee on the Consequences of Uninsurance. *Coverage matters: Insurance and health care*. Washington, D.C.: National Academy Press, 2001.
9. Gray B.H., & Rowe C. Safety-net health plans: A status report. *Health Affairs (Millwood)* 19(1), 185, 2000.
10. Leape L. L. Unnecessary surgery. *Annual Review of Public Health* 13:363, 1992.
11. Anderson G.F., Hussey P.S., Frogner B.K. & Waters H.R. Health spending in the United States and the rest of the industrialized world. *Health Affairs (Millwood)* 24(4):903-14, 2005.
12. McCanne D. Comment on the *Public-Private Mix for Health*. In: Maynard A. (Ed): Nuffield Trust 2005. In: Quote of the Day (don@mccanne.org) July 8, 2005.
13. New England Journal of Medicine. Perspective. Dramatic improvement or death spiral: two Members of Congress assess the Medicare bill. *New England Journal of Medicine*, 350(8), 750-1,2004.
14. Ibid 13.
15. Senate Committee, 2004. The impact of Republican Medicare proposals on insurance industry revenues and profits. Report. Washington, D.C.: Senate Committee on Health, Education, Labor, and Pensions Minority Staff, January 16, 2004.
16. Reinhardt U.E. Interview. The Medicare world from both sides: conversation with Tom Scully. *Health Affairs (Millwood)* 22(6): 173-4, 2003.
17. PNHP Newsletter. Data Update. Government-corporate revolving door. Physicians for a National Health Program. Chicago: Spring, 2004, p 9, citing *Washington Post*, December 3, 2003.

18. Francis T. & Schultz E.E. Rules let firms get subsidy for retirees' drug cost. *Wall Street Journal* January 28, 2005:A4.

19. Lueck S. U.S. says firms with Medicare aid can't cut corners. *Wall Street Journal* July 27, 2004:A2 (a).

20. Lueck S. Obscure group gets star role in drug battle. *Wall Street Journal* July 27, 2004:B1 (b).

21. Medicine & Health Drug makers, PBMs argue over USP Medicare formulary guidelines. *Medicine & Health* 53(33), 2004:p6.

22. Pear R. New Medicare rules on drugs balance access against costs. *New York Times* January 22, 2005:A1a.

23. Pear R. Insurers object to new provision in Medicare law. *New York Times* August 22, 2004:A1.

24. Lueck S. Medicare creates structure to spur private insurance. *Wall Street Journal* December 7, 2004:A6c.

25. Avlon J. P. *Independent Nation: How the Vital Center is Changing American Politics*. New York: Harmony Books, 2004:1-13.

26. Eisenhower D.D. The future of the Republican Party. *Saturday Evening Post* January 30, 1965.

27. Poll conducted by the Voter News Service and the *Los Angeles Times*, as cited in Halstead T. & Lind M. *The Radical Center: The Future of American Politics*. New York: Doubleday, 2001, p 3.

28. *USA Today*/CNN/Gallup Poll. October 2002.

29. Halstead T. *A Politics for Generation X. Atlantic Online*, August 1999, p 3.

30. Black G.S. & Black B.D. *The Politics of American Discontent: How a New Party Can Make Democracy Work Again*. New York: John Wiley & Sons, 1994: p 150.

31. Beyond Red vs. Blue. Report of The Pew Research Center of the People and the Press, Washington, D.C.: May 10, 2005.

32. Rogers D. Medicare actuary reveals e-mail warning. *Wall Street Journal* March 18, 2004:A4.

33. Pear R. Estimate revives fight on Medicare costs. *New York Times* February 10, 2005:A16.

34. Pear R. Sweeping Medicare change wins approval in Congress; President claims a victory, as Senate backs bill. *New York Times* November 26, 2003: A1.

35. Lueck S. Coalition floats ideas to tame rocketing costs of health care. *Wall Street Journal* July 21, 2004d.

36. Warren E. & Tyagi A.W. *The Two-Income Trap: Why Middle-Class Mothers and Fathers Are Going Broke*. New York: Basic Books, 2003:50-57.

37. Bureau of the Census, *Historical Income Tables—People*, Current Population

Survey, various Annual Demographic Supplements. Available at http://www. census.gov/hhes/income/histinc/incperdet.html [15/2003], Table P36, Full-Time, Year-Round Workers (All Races) by Median Income and Sex, 1955 to 2000.

38. Lueck S & McKinnon J.D. Ranks of the poor, uninsured grew last year in U.S. *Wall Street Journal* August 27, 2004:A2.

39. Kuttner R. & Marshall W. Come together. *The American Prospect* 6(15):28, 2004.

40. Warren E. & Tyagi A.W. The vital middle: Redeeming and defending middle-class values. *The American Prospect* 6(15):45, 2004.

41. Dreyfuss B.T. The seduction. *The American Prospect* 6(15):18-23, 2004.

42. Wall Street Journal. AARP endorses Senate bill allowing drug imports. *Wall Street Journal* June 17, 2004:D2.

43. Calmes J. On Social Security, it's Bush vs. AARP. *Wall Street Journal* January 21, 2005:A4.

44. Frist B. Full text of the remarks of the Senate Majority Leader Bill Frist. *The New York Times* August 31, 2004.

45. Survey 2004, Summary and Chartpack. Views of the New Medicare Drug Law: A Survey of People on Medicare. The Kaiser Family Foundation/Harvard School of Public Health, August 2004.

46. Milbank D & Moria R. Compassionate no more: A poll shows that few think Bush serves the middle class. *Washington Post* National Weekly Edition April 12-18, 2004, p 12.

47. Wolfe S.M. The people have spoken: The drug industry doesn't serve us well. *Health Letter.* Public Citizen Health Research Group 20(8): 1, 2004.

48. Blendon R.J., Altman D.E., Benson M.K. & Brodie M. Health care in the 2004 presidential election. *New England Journal of Medicine* 351(13):1314-22, 2004.

49. Dolny M. Think tank coverage: more attention, but not more balances. Fairness and Accuracy in Reporting (FAIR). *Extra* 17(3):28, 2004.

50. Justice G. Fund raising. Under new law, parties collect $1 billion. *New York Times* October 26, 2004:A19.

51. Public Citizen Press Release. Challenge the drug makers' dirty money medicine. Washington, D.C. October 14, 2004, Fall report available at http://www.stealthpacs.org/documents/092004Phrma.pdf.

52. Roach D. Special interests try to roll back McCain-Feingold campaign reforms. *Public Citizen News* 25(4) July/August 2005:10.

53. Weisman J. Bush's wish list. His budget slashes farm subsidies, Medicaid, and other domestic programs. *Washington Post* National Weekly Edition, February 14-20, 2005:6.

54. Calmes J. New contract. In Bush's 'ownership society," citizens would take more risk. *Wall Street Journal* February 28, 2005:A1.

55. Pear R. Bush vows veto of any cutback of drug benefit. *New York Times* February 12, 2005:A1.

56. Pear R. Insurers and drug makers see gain in Bush victory. *New York Times* November 5, 2004:20b.

57. Pear R. Medicare pushes for wide choice in health benefits. *New York Times* June 15, 2005:A1.

58. *Wall Street Journal.* Government estimates deficit of $415 billion. October 7, 2004:A9.

59. Allen M. Bush's $3 trillion agenda: his pledges for permanent tax cuts and Social Security leave out the price tag. *Washington Post* September 20-26, 2004:11.

60. Vladeck B.C. Democrats and the struggle over Medicare. *Dissent* summer 2004:32-3.

61. Lueck S. U. S. health plans catch fiscal hawks' eyes. *Wall Street Journal* December 3, 2004:A43.

62. Wessel D. GAO says Medicare drug benefit will cost more than $6 trillion. *Wall Street Journal* December 20, 2004:A4.

63. Pear R. Cuts in Medicare payments to hospitals is advised. *New York Times* January 18, 2005:A12.

64. Hampson R. Few see conciliation on Bush agenda. *USA Today* November 4, 2004:3A.

65. Harwood J. Approval of Congress erodes in survey. *Wall Street Journal* May 19, 2005:A3.

66. Gray B. H. (Ed). *For-profit enterprise in health care. Supplementary statement on for-profit enterprise in health care.* Washington, D.C.: Institute of Medicine, National Academy Press, 1986, p 205.

67. Himmelstein D.U., Woolhandler S. & Hellander I. *Bleeding the Patient: The Consequences of Corporate Health Care.* Monroe, Me: Common Courage Press, 2001; 92.

68. Relman A.S. The health of nations. *The New Republic.* March 7, 2005.

69. Kuttner R. The road to Enron. *The American Prospect* March 25, 2002:1,3.

70. Gordon C. *Dead on Arrival: The Politics of Health Care in Twentieth Century America.* Princeton and Oxford: Princeton University Press, 2003:p 261.

71. NASI, Study Panel on Medicare's Larger Social Role. Final Report. Washington, D.C.: National Academy of Social Insurance, 1999.

72. Slevin C. How they sell trade deals: promises made, then broken. *Public Citizen News* 25(4) July/August 2005: p 1.

73. Moyers B. *Moyers on America: A Journalist and His Times.* New York: The New Press, 2004: 19-20.

Index

Q

About the Author

John Geyman, MD is Professor Emeritus of Family Medicine at the University of Washington School of Medicine in Seattle, where he served as Chairman of the Department of Family Medicine from 1976 to 1990. As a family physician with over 25 years in academic medicine, he has also practiced in rural communities for 13 years. He was the founding editor of *The Journal of Family Practice* (1973 to 1990) and the editor of *The Journal of the American Board of Family Practice* from 1990 to 2003. His most recent books are *Health Care in America: Can Our Ailing System Be Healed*? (Butterworth-Heinemann, 2002), *The Corporate Transformation of Health Care: Can the Public Interest Still Be Served*? (Springer Publishing Company, 2004) and *Falling Through the Safety Net: Americans Without Health Insurance* (Common Courage Press, 2005). Dr. Geyman is a member of the Institute of Medicine.

Also from Common Courage Press

Falling Through the Safety Net

Americans Without Health Insurance

John Geyman, M.D.

This is a most important book by one of America's leading experts. We are paying dearly in health system inefficiency and unnecessary pain and suffering because of the cracks in our safety net. Without attention to this issue as illustrated in this text, we will never eliminate disparities in health among different racial and ethnic groups in this nation.

—David Satcher, 16th U. S. Surgeon General,
Director, National Center for Primary Care at Morehouse School of Medicine

A compelling description of our dysfunctional health care system, a reasoned analysis of its problems, and a persuasive argument for a single-payer insurance plan as the best solution—written by someone with real understanding and first-hand experience. A much-needed lesson that ought to change a lot of minds. I recommend it strongly.

—Marcia Angell, M. D.,
Senior Lecturer in Social Medicine, Harvard Medical School,
Former Editor-in-Chief, *New England Journal of Medicine*

Once again, the legendary master of family medicine addresses with clinical compassion the widespread concerns about "unsurance" and uncovered medical costs. Geyman's well-researched recommendations should be read by everyone.

—Donald Light, Professor of Comparative
Health Care Systems, Princeton University

224 pages, $18.95, ISBN 1-56751-254-2
Publication date 2005

Common Courage Press
PO Box 702
Monroe, ME 04951
1-800-497-3207   fax 207-525-3068
www.commoncouragepress.com